ELMIRA

Death Camp of the North

Michael Horigan

STACKPOLE
BOOKS

0 11557 03276 5

Published in paperback in 2006 by
STACKPOLE BOOKS
5067 Ritter Road
Mechanicsburg, PA 17055

Printed in the United States of America

10 9 8 7 6 5 4 3 2 1

ISBN 0-8117-3276-2 (paperback)
ISBN 978-0-8117-3276-5 (paperback)

The Library of Congress has cataloged the hardcover edition as follows:

Horigan, Michael
    Elmira : death camp of the North / Micahel Horigan.— 1st ed.
        p. cm.
    Includes bibliographical references and index.
    ISBN 0-8117-1432-2
    1. Elmira Prison (Elmira, N.Y.) 2. New York (State)—History—Civil War,
1861–1865—Prisoners and prisons. 3. United States—History—Civil War,
1861–1865—Prisoners and prisons. 4. Prisoners of war—New York (State)—Elmira—
History—19th century. I. Title: Elmira Civil War prison camp. II. Title.

E616.E4 H75 2002
973.7'72—dc21

                                                                2001049744

The evil that men do lives after them,
The good is oft interred with their bones.
—Shakespeare, *Julius Caesar*

For Rose and Bus
and
Tom Byrne
and
Billy Hilfiger

CONTENTS

Acknowledgments

This book had its origins in an Elmira College graduate study workshop on the Elmira Civil War prison camp. Frank Brady, then the dean of continuing education, asked me, in the spring of 1974, to teach the workshop in the autumn of that year. He graciously asked me to return for the next several years to teach the workshop. As the years went by, my research on the prison camp grew, and, in 1987, I decided to explore the question further. This led to an enjoyable sabbatical leave in 1988 and ensuing summers of research.

The late Tom Byrne, for many years the venerable Chemung County historian, was my mentor and guide from the time this book was no more than an idea. On many occasions, while I was doing research at the local historical society, he would briefly stop at my table and provide words of encouragement. His profound knowledge of local history kept me on course whenever I began to veer away from the facts. His sage advice and critical scrutiny of the first five chapters benefited my manuscript in countless ways.

I am particularly grateful to three of my friends—Bob Callahan, Tom Daly, and Jerry Whalen—for their generous reading of the manuscript in various stages of completion and for their helpful suggestions and meaningful criticism. Their moral support sustained me in moments of doubt and disappointment. I am also indebted to Ray Fortier whose interest in my endeavor led me to Stackpole Books.

Another friend, Mal Marsden, went the extra mile in reading the manuscript four times. His brilliantly imaginative editorial advice proved to be invaluable. His meticulous discrimination, scholarly judgment, gentle criticism, and thoughtful proposals strengthened the manuscript.

Bill Hynes, my distinguished teaching colleague and cherished friend, was helpful in the manuscript's early stages. Margot Magnusen, another dear teaching friend, read the entire manuscript and, in doing so, provided many important suggestions and corrections. Two other close friends, Clare Reidy and Joe Caparulo, contributed advice that resulted in scholarly improvements in the early chapters. The late Albert "Chick" Hilbert, for many years the Chemung County Historical Society's staff historian, allowed me to go over his copious prison camp files in the privacy of my own study.

I am, of course, most grateful to Stackpole Books and for editor William C. Davis's decision to accept my manuscript for publication. His kind appraisal of my work served as an inspiration to improve the text. Leigh Ann Berry, my editor, proved to be a tower of patience, knowledge, kindness, wisdom, and good judgment. Often my entreaties amounted to no more than meaningless apprehensions, but Leigh Ann's sound and sensitive counsel prevailed. Whether it was a major problem or a superfluous concern, she always came up with a logical explanation.

The following individuals very graciously granted me interviews: Dorothy Lewis Grant, the Reverend Robert Lester, the Reverend Donald Hoff, and the Honorable Daniel Donahoe. Therese Sammartino and Dave Dimmick at the Department of Veteran's Affairs contributed essential information on the burial of the Confederate dead. George Farr, town of Elmira historian, provided me with important articles and letters that truly enhanced numerous passages in the manuscript. His valuable assistance also aided me at the time I was working with the Chemung County Historical Society's newspaper collection. In addition to this, Mr. Farr granted me an interview.

The staff at the Chemung County Historical Society provided me with voluminous files of prison camp material. I wish to particularly thank Constance B. Barone, director; Tina L. Hager, museum educator; Amy H. Wilson, curator; J. Arthur Kiefer, Chemung County historian; Martha M. Ritter, librarian/archive assistant; Melissa Hollister; and Tim Decker. Chairman Bryan Reddick and the members of the historical society's library/ research committee backed my efforts in many ways. Also, county legislators Theodore Bennett and Cornelius Milliken provided vital support.

The staff at Elmira's Steele Memorial Library saw to it that I had access to Elmira's newspapers during the days of the prison camp. Especially helpful were Rita Dery, Owen Frank, Stuart Finch, Elwin "Bim" Van Etten, and Cola Thayer. The library's Rose Woodard deserves a special thanks for her help in attaining materials through the interlibrary loan.

Staffers of the Elmira College's Gannett/Tripp Library—especially Katie Galvin, Cara Pucci, and David Hughes—were extremely helpful. Bill Jaker of WSKG Public Television (Binghamton, New York) shared with me some of his research materials that he used in his 1993 documentary on the Elmira prison camp. In the years after the WSKG documentary, he also kept me informed whenever he learned of new data on the camp.

In the course of my research, I visited a number of libraries, museums, and archives. I wish to thank Michael Musick at the National Archives for his efforts in locating essential prison camp documents. The staff in the National Archives' search room also was extremely helpful as was Janita Cliette in the still picture branch. The staff at the Library of Congress went to extraordinary efforts to assure that I found what I was looking for.

John White and his staff at the Wilson Library at the University of North Carolina, Chapel Hill, furnished me with an abundance of materials from the Southern Historical Collection. Also, Michelle Neill and the staff at the University of North Carolina's Davis Library were extremely helpful. The staff of the Linn-Henley Library for Historical Research in Birmingham, Alabama, saw to it that the complete collection of the *Confederate Veteran* was made available to me.

The staff at the Olin Library, Cornell University, made it possible for me to examine an abundance of prison camp material. Mimi Jones, senior reference archivist at the Alabama Department of Archives and History, Montgomery, introduced me to a treasure trove of prison camp material. Steve Seames of the Maine Historical Society, Portland, was helpful in finding biographical files on Seth Eastman. Kenneth E. Thompson, Jr., of Portland, Maine, graciously allowed me to work with his collection of materials on Eastman.

Sylvia Sherman of the Maine State Archives provided much of the material on Eugene F. Sanger. James B. Vickery also led me to useful data on Sanger. Harrie Washburn of Sharon Springs, New York, graciously allowed me to use material from the letters of Capt. John Kidder. Danny Wheeler, commander in chief of the Sons of Union Veterans of the Civil War, provided useful information on the schedule and operation of Elmira's prison guard detail. Mary-Jo Kline, a distinguished academic, played an essential role in locating a number of primary sources.

I also wish to thank Kathleen Davis and Tony Ferguson of the Butler Library, Columbia University; Daniel Lorello, lead archivist of the New York State Archives; Frances Barbieri and Steve Mitchell of the Seneca Falls (New York) Historical Society; William A. Hamann of the Civil War Library and Museum, Philadelphia; Randy Davis, curator of the Loudoun Museum, Leesburg, Virginia; Nikki See of Twin Cities (Minnesota) Public Television; Bonnie Wilson of the Minnesota Historical Society; William Lay, Jr., curator of the Tioga County (New York) Historical Society; Carol Zabadah, site supervisor at the Andersonville National Historic Site, and Eric Reinert, curator at Andersonville. Mr. Reinert also granted me an interview.

The staff of numerous other libraries filled in many gaps, especially the New York Public Library, the New York State Library at Albany, the Baker Library (Dartmouth College), the Glen G. Bartle Library (State University of New York at Binghamton), the Hendersonville Library (North Carolina), the Pack Memorial Library (Asheville, North Carolina), the David A. Howe Public Library (Wellsville, New York), the Rundel Library Building, Central Branch (Rochester, New York), the Corning (New York) Public Library, the Maine State Library at Augusta, and the Axinn Library (Hofstra University).

Finally, there are some special individuals close to me who, during my years of research and writing, deserve much credit for their patience and understanding. My daughter Liz Ann and her husband, Brent Moore; my son Mickey, my son Timo and his wife, Angela; my son Tommy and his wife, Mary; and my son Jim and his wife, Lynne, all came to understand that my strange behavior and quest for isolation went with the territory. At times they rightly referred to the manuscript as "Horigan's Folly." Brent's skill with a camera is illustrated in this book, and Angela adroitly guided me through the bewildering labyrinth of copyright release requests.

Elizabeth, my wife, introduced me to the technological wonder of the ages—the word processor. Realizing that I am a nineteenth-century man (and proud of it), she stayed with me at crucial moments when my word processor began to do things that were beyond my comprehension. My son Jim, a computer genius, made several trips home from New England in order to resuscitate my word processor and preserve my sanity.

A special mention of my granddaughter, Katie Horigan, concludes these comments. Katie has been a major source of inspiration for me during the writing phase of this project. She loves the world of books, and has assured me that she is going to write a book report on *Elmira: Death Camp of the North* for her class at York (Maine) Middle School. With this in mind, I knew I had to do the best job possible in order to meet Katie's discerning standards. I hope I succeeded.

Michael Horigan
Elmira, New York
October 2001

CHAPTER 1

"A Choice of
Sound Military Logic"

In all of New York State, no other community was so intimately touched
by the Civil War as was the town of Elmira. Indeed, the war between the
states would leave an indelible mark on this small upstate city. Through an
evolutionary process dictated by wartime decisions, the town became a state
military depot in 1861, a federal draft rendezvous in 1863, and a prison
camp for 12,122 Confederate prisoners of war from July 1864 through July
1865. Geography most certainly had much to do with Elmira's role in
America's bloodiest war.

Located just north of the Pennsylvania border in western New York
State, Elmira (a Chemung County village of about 8,800 in 1861) claimed
considerable significance in New York State's transportation grid. The
Chemung Canal, completed in 1833, was the bustling village's nexus to the
state's lucrative commercial conduit—the Erie Canal. Woolen goods, lumber, shoes, barrels manufactured on a grand scale, and agricultural products
were funneled from Elmira to markets in Buffalo, Rochester, Syracuse,
Utica, Albany, and New York City.

During the canal's glory days, boats 60 feet long and 18 feet wide with
a cabin which housed a galley and sleeping accommodations for six moved
over the waterway to the lugubrious sounds of the steersman's horn. In
1850 the Seneca Lake and Chemung Canal Line announced that it was

ready to operate "with first class boats for the transportation of merchandise from the city of New York to Elmira and Corning and intermediate places with promptness and dispatch."[1]

The village prospered through the 1830s and 1840s; and, with the coming of the railroads, more economic success followed. The New York and Erie Railroad reached Elmira in October 1849. With a jubilant flair, one local newspaper boasted: "We are now placed within about fourteen hours of the city of New York. It is a great era in the history of our country to be in connection with the great market of our union in so short a period."[2]

Canal traffic, now competing with the railroads for shipment of Elmira's commerce, began to decline in the 1850s. But there would be one final burst of prosperity for the Chemung Canal in 1864 when the Civil War demands of Elmira's draft rendezvous and the prison camp would boost tolls to a record one-year total of $24,445.[3] With the wartime demands a thing of the past, however, the final year of dwindling canal traffic would be 1878—the year New York State, over the protests of Elmira's citizenry, decided to close the waterway. Thus, like a cherished family heirloom, the era of the fabled Chemung Canal became one of Elmira's most treasured legends.

In May 1851 completion of the New York and Erie Railroad to Dunkirk, New York, made Elmira a railroad hub. *Harper's New York and Rail-Road Guide* proudly referred to Elmira as one of the more important stops "along the New York and Erie Rail-Road, and a good specimen of the towns that seem to exhale from the American soil."[4] The national railway network connected Elmira to New York City, 273 miles southeast, and to Chicago, 650 miles west. Rails from Elmira to other New York State destinations extended 100 miles north to Rochester, and 165 northwest to Buffalo. The Elmira and Williamsport Railroad (this would become the Northern Central in 1864) gave passengers and shippers of freight access to points south, including the cities of Philadelphia, Baltimore, and Washington, D.C.

By 1860 railroad construction included 22,300 miles through states that would not secede from the Union during the Civil War. Some 9,000 miles of multigauged railroad track were located in states that would secede. The nation's railroads—as with commerce, industrial production, population, and financial institutions—did indeed reveal that the raw mathematics of the impending war was against the South.

With excellent railroad connections in place, Elmira's economy—with lumber mills and abundant woolen goods leading the way—did well in the

1840s and 1850s. The lumber business was literally a visible success, for stacks of pine boards, shingles, and logs, ready for shipment, lined both sides of the canal and frequently extended in length to three city blocks. Lumber coming out of Chemung County was reputed to be the best in the state, and individuals who dealt in the processing and sale of that product across the state knew the meaning of the term "Chemung lumber."[5] Finished woolen products were second only to lumber during the early 1850s. By the end of that decade, however, the demand for coal as fuel in homes, factories, and steam locomotives would seriously challenge the status of "Chemung lumber." Elmira would serve as a point of departure for coal mined in nearby Pennsylvania. All this would lend to Elmira's significance as a Civil War military depot.

Construction of a large rolling mill, completed in May 1861, added to the village's economy. It produced a variety of metal products, with railroad rails leading the way. Several barrel factories did well and, during the Civil War, one of these factories would quarter Union soldiers on a temporary basis and another would serve through the duration of the war as a military hospital. The Pratt Woolen Mill, established in 1842, survived a fire in 1848 to become an integral part of Elmira's economy. During the war it fulfilled a government contract by producing 1,000 yards of army cloth per day. Two smaller woolen mills added to Elmira's economic success. Two shoe factories, two tanneries, and an umbrella company lent to the village's relatively vibrant industrial stature as well. And, by 1860, business also thrived for three local breweries.

The village's considerable manufacturing endeavors were enhanced by a significant local agricultural economy that abundantly produced wheat, corn, potatoes, barley, oats, milk, butter, cheese, eggs, poultry, livestock, peaches, apples, grapes, cherries, pears, and tobacco. In 1857 a journalist referred to Elmira as a village that had "surpassed all its competitors in the race for improvements," and was located in the midst of "an agricultural country that has no superior in the world. . . . [I]ts streets are handsomely laid out, churches and schools are numerous; it possesses enterprising business men, an energetic press, banks that pay specie on the strength of their promises, and hotels kept by clever landlords, and stocked with the substantial things of life."[6] By 1860 the Brainard House, with its upper-crust ambience, was recognized as Elmira's finest hotel. During the Civil War it would serve as the residence of Elmira's Union military post commander and remain "crowded daily with guests from all parts of the State and nation."[7]

And to lend to the village's positive image, numerous publications often presented Elmira as a community where the common folk were God-fearing men and women who, imbued with the Protestant work ethic, embraced as an article of faith the dictum that diligent toil purges the soul of sin. The village leaders in business and politics, often imperious in manner, were men of unchallenged integrity. The skilled cabinetmaker was revered; an enterprising local hardware store owner was the epitome of economic success; and all community wisdom emanated from the sage advice of the village smithy and the corner grocer.

The discerning filter of history, however, reveals a far more disconcerting view of those antebellum days in Elmira. Indeed, stark reality shows that the canal and the railroads brought ne'er-do-wells to the village's quaint setting. Boatmen, railroad section hands, carters, farmhands, and others who provided the brawn so essential to industrial and agricultural success proved at times to be a rough crowd. The influx of newcomers, Irish and German immigrants, inexorably brought with it a considerable potential for social tension: i.e., the new arrivals were thought to be individuals of contumacious behavior and alarming drinking habits. Also, these working-class people brought with them an institution that at the time was viewed by much of Protestant America as anathema—the Roman Catholic Church. With an ethnic mix that resembled America's growing pains of that era, Elmira was in many respects a microcosm of Boston, New York City, and Philadelphia. And, at times, it came to be referred to derisively as "a canal town."

Nevertheless, Elmira twice in the 1850s was selected as the site for the New York State Fair. Much of the fairgrounds, located a mile west of town, was "as level as the top of a billiard table" and on the north side of the grounds was "a natural terrace some forty feet high with a slope just adapted to the successive rise of seats over another." The site included a long lagoon known as Foster's Pond and a race track which was thought of as "one of the finest in the union, and could be made the best in the world."[8] The fairgrounds quite naturally provided much joy and pleasure for the citizens of Elmira and surrounding communities. All this would fade with the coming of the Civil War. The fairgrounds would first house Union recruits and then quarter over 12,000 Confederate prisoners of war. To many of the Confederate survivors of the prison camp, the site of the county fairgrounds would be bitterly referred to as "Helmira."[9]

During the politically turbulent 1850s, Elmira's newspapers took on the great issues of the day. Nativism, racism, temperance, religion, the Underground Railroad, and abolitionism were sources of social and political disagreement in the village. The rancor of debate left Elmira's citizens divided and uncertain, and, like the nation itself, the village nervously confronted the future. And now in November 1860 the American people moved closer to division with the election of Abraham Lincoln—the first Republican ever to be elected president of the United States. His candidacy was enthusiastically endorsed by the *Elmira Daily Advertiser.* The *Elmira Daily Gazette* threw its support to the Democrat, Sen. Stephen A. Douglas of Illinois. It is not known which candidate a third newspaper, the *Elmira Daily Press,* might have endorsed.

With Lincoln's election, South Carolina initiated an ominous drumbeat when it became the first state to secede from the Union on December 20, 1860. Six other states in the deep South would follow by February 1, 1861, and the flame of secession would eventually spread to Virginia, Tennessee, North Carolina, and Arkansas. As winter turned to spring in 1861, the apprehensive citizens of Elmira waited. The focus on politics, social issues, and religious differences that had frayed the nerves of Elmirans now gave way to fear of a war.

With tension mounting in the dreary late winter days of 1861, Abraham Lincoln assumed executive power. If and when war should come, Elmirans could take comfort in the fact that the village was safely out of harm's way. Little did the community's citizenry know that on the eve of the confrontation at Fort Sumter in April 1861 the town was about to become a significant part of the great sweep of history that had moved the nation toward its darkest and bloodiest hour.

Charles Fairman, the primary mover of the *Elmira Daily Advertiser* and a longtime journalistic figure in the community, was perhaps President Lincoln's most salient political ally in the village. Five days after Lincoln's inauguration Fairman (adding the moniker *Republican* to the masthead of his weekly edition) declared: "The only chance of war is the wantonness on their [the seceding states'] part which will lead them to commence hostilities on the government in the discharge of its ordinary duties, in the casual mode." In calling for absolute support for the new president, Fairman concluded: "Whoever fails in this, fails in a clear and unmistakable duty; whoever opposes him in this, is guilty of treason."[10]

A wantonness on the part of South Carolina "to commence hostilities on the government in the discharge of its ordinary duties" came at 4:30 A.M.

in Charleston Harbor on April 12, 1861. Word of the firing on Fort Sumter reached Elmira in the afternoon of April 13. Frantic telegraphers tapped out ominous accounts of what was happening in Charleston, and, amid the flames and rubble, the fort, one of three federal posts in the harbor, surrendered on April 14.

From the great cities of the Eastern seaboard to the fledgling urban areas of the West, and all towns, villages, and hamlets in between, there was a resonant call to duty. As if someone had waved a magic wand, partisan politics, social issues, and religious differences (for the moment) were set aside. The surrender of Fort Sumter ignited a feverish patriotic pitch in the North that led throngs of men to recruiting offices. People went into the streets and church bells rang and everywhere there was the stirring sound of bands playing the martial strains of the day. Energy that had long been pent up was now being released in a kind of desperate joy.

Elmirans were told of the fall of Fort Sumter on the afternoon of April 15, and that evening the village's Concert Hall, an impressive brick building of graceful pediment, served as a rallying point where a highly charged crowd overflowed the structure. Local clergymen offered prayers for the nation and its people. Elmira's most prominent citizens delivered uplifting and patriotic calls for unity, duty, and victory. Indeed, the flaming ardor of a determined people was in the air that evening. A chronicler of that momentous event, writing thirty years later, recalled: "[T]he hall was packed full and the blood of the people was up." In a matter of days the village was transformed into a military center where "the sounds of drum and fife, a bugle in the distance, now and then, the discharge of a gun, the rattle of artillery wagons, the clattering of a horse with the clink of saber and spur were as frequent almost as the minutes of the day."[11]

President Lincoln had issued a call for 75,000 volunteers, and the Concert Hall meeting was Elmira's emotional reaction to that request. The response was overwhelming. On that evening the "Southern Tier Rifles," a guard company that was founded in 1840, volunteered almost to a man. This unit would become Company K of the 23rd New York, the first of four "home regiments" to march off to war.

A fervent patriotism that is unique to the initial stages of a nation's entry into war carried the day in Elmira, and on April 17, 1861, New York's governor Edwin D. Morgan officially designated Albany, New York City, and Elmira as military depots.[12] Three days later the *Advertiser and Republican,* reflecting the village's visceral desire for triumph over traitors, sounded a cogent call: "At length the nation is aroused, the cold Northern blood is stirred, this insolent rebellion will be endured no longer. The traitors have provoked their doom, defeat and infamy await them. . . . The Union must be preserved *by force of arms*."[13]

Men volunteering in their nation's service now responded in overwhelming numbers. Rawboned young men from the surrounding counties of Steuben, Schuyler, Tompkins, and Tioga joined those of Chemung County. Within weeks recruits were filing into Elmira from distant parts of the state. Indeed, the spring of 1861 became a time when an unbounded desire to serve the Union was pervasive. Journalists from other cities quickly noted that Elmira had become a fizzing pinwheel of patriotic fervor. A Buffalo reporter, writing in early May, observed that the village "now wears the aspect of war. . . . Flags deck the public buildings and private residences of the people."[14]

Elmira's spirited and angry reaction to the attack on Fort Sumter reflected the volunteer ardor throughout the North. Where communities such as Buffalo, Rochester, Syracuse, and Utica had always been thought of as commercial markets linked to the village by a canal system and the railroads, they now were viewed as places that would dispatch the flower of their youth to an Elmira that quickly became what journalists and others now referred to as "a garrison town." The accoutrements and cadenced tread of military regiments were now a presence that would remain through the duration of the war.

Within a month of the Concert Hall meeting, a New York City newspaper proclaimed Elmira to be "a gateway to the South." The journal added that the village's east-west transportation route was the Erie Railroad "over which any army might role [*sic*] and not disturb a bar. . . . The designation of Elmira as one of the rallying places for the Army of New York, was admirable. It was a choice of sound military logic."[15]

Elmira may have been "a choice of sound military logic," but it was, like the rest of the nation, ill-prepared to handle large numbers of recruits. Mirroring the nation's desultory efforts of mustering men for battle, the early stage of Elmira's war effort was a slapdash endeavor that, like Peer Gynt's onion, had no kernel. It had hastily made ready to receive ten companies; instead, forty companies inundated the town. By mid-May the community of 8,800 housed more than 6,000 recruits. Eight regiments comprising seventy companies were fully organized, and an additional number of unorganized companies were enough to form two more regiments.

The town's vibrant patriotism was accompanied by din, confusion, and frustration. Drawn from the various ethnic strains of the day, the regiments mustered at Elmira extended from the middle class to white Protestant farmers to working-class Irish and German Catholics. With few exceptions, the ascendant class (Mayflower descendants or men with similar credentials) assumed military positions of command. Local and communal gentry, i.e., a leadership class that in civilian life had exercised political and economic power and cherished distinct social privileges, emerged in charge of regiment after regiment in Elmira. In many cases, the officers, "being gentlemen of manly and gallant bearing, were cordially received into the best society at Elmira."[16]

Finding places to quarter the troops proved to be a monumental logistical problem. A barrel factory was converted to a barracks. Churches, storehouses, public halls, and some private homes were designated as temporary living quarters for the seemingly endless number of raw recruits. Another barrel factory would be transformed into a military hospital. Carpenters and laborers were commandeered to build official army barracks. The fairgrounds along the northern shore of the Chemung River would become the site of the ill-fated Barracks No. 3. By the end of the summer in 1861, Barracks No. 3 (later, as the prison camp, it would be officially designated as "Camp Chemung") would house 2,000 troops. Despite the disarray created by the presence of recruits almost equal in number to the village's citizens, a local journal noted with great flourish: "Men and citizens! Unfurl your banners, and the patriotic yeomanry flock around you! There will be room for all. Strike while the iron is hot."[17]

This was a unique experience for the young men being mustered into regiments. Never in their lives had anything even vaguely resembling the demands of war been visited upon them. And, if they survived, the memory of battle, disease, and death would stay with them for the remainder of their years. These recruits, swarming into Elmira in the spring of 1861, were (for the most part) raw, sincere, patriotic, and semiliterate. F. W. Baker, a private in the 24th New York, related his Elmira experience in a letter (May 12, 1861) to his wife:

> I sit now down to write a few lines to you to let you know that we have arrived all at Elmira sound we got her frida night about nine o'clock it rained some but we did not get vary wet we wer took to the Baptist church you may think it a quere place for

soldiers to be put in but it is so there is three companies for us in the church we fare pretty well yet we have to march about half a mile to our meals we have to eat beef stake Bread and butter coffee potatoes no cake or pies but they all feel well and in fiting order after we get drilled there is nine thousand soldiers in the place I wish you could see them march through the city it is enough to animate any body we were cheered as we came on the cars by ever thing men women and children handkerchiefs and flags were fliing from evry house and window as we came along such a time I never see nor I ever expect to see.[18]

By early June, with six different barracks areas rimming the village, the Elmira military depot was completed. Officers in charge noted that things were in fine working order. Journalists reported that well-constructed barracks, cook houses, and mess houses made Elmira the finest wartime facility in New York State. Thomas E. Byrne, Chemung County's historian for many years, has described the village in those early days of the war as a place where "a brave new exercise in ruffles and flourishes, in swords and roses" dominated the scene.[19] Cornet bands and patriotic drum and fife corps renditions accompanied by precision drill teams stirred the souls of the local citizenry with strains of martial music by day and by night. One journalist cheerfully noted that the snappy military performances attracted "bevies of rustic maidens, laden with smiles for the junior officers, and wondering dames, whose reminiscences are ever of the war of 1812."[20]

Inevitably, even the tapestry of military drill and music could not long distract all attention from the dire fact that shortages of munitions and equipment were ever present at the Elmira army post. Antiquated firearms of doubtful utility, shipped to Elmira from the dusty storehouses of arsenals at Springfield, Massachusetts, and Washington, D.C., were passed out to infantry units. There was a critical shortage of cannons because almost all federal artillery was in service at forts that dotted the distant American frontier. "New York, with her *Fifty Thousand* impatient soldiery," a local newspaper reported in June, "had [*sic*] not been able to perfect their [*sic*] equipment as promptly as was desirable nor has she, in all reports, been fortunate in the character and quality of those equipments."[21]

As late as October 1861 the U.S. Sanitary Commission (a private organization that, among other things, supplied troops with food, clothing, blankets, hospital materials and medicine) reported to Governor Morgan that in New York State serious military shortages existed. "The Government," a Sanitary Commission spokesman declared, "is asked why it does not go into the home market & buy the blankets & clothes it needs." Governor Morgan was also told that "there are at this moment 50,000 enlisted men without uniforms."[22]

The young, inexperienced recruits at Elmira and other military depots were destined to march into battle poorly trained, and at best partially prepared. In July 1861 a caustic William Tecumseh Sherman (then a Union colonel) noted: "Our men are not good soldiers. They brag, but don't perform, complain sadly if they don't get everything they want, and a march of a few miles uses them up."[23] Theirs would literally be a baptism of fire. As in Stephen Crane's *The Red Badge of Courage,* the horrors of war would assure the survival only of the fortunate.

For the ordinary soldier the tedious schedule of drill, the grueling 15-mile marches, and the perfunctory daily regimental parades became an incentive to move on. Patriotic allegiance to the Union also was a motivator among Elmira's recruits. An idealistic 19-year-old, Charles Condit Mosher of Chapinville, New York, commenced his Civil War journal on October 8 (three days before he entrained for Elmira): "Father told me that he saw that the war was turning on the question of slavery. . . . He is a strong Anti-Slavery man. . . . His father was in the war of the Revolution, a 1st Lieut in the 8th Mass. Inf. and he was in the war of 1812. Now it's my turn. I am going soon."[24]

Once it was decided when a regiment was ready to go south, many of its units—under the watchful eye of guards on the lookout for deserters—left Elmira in open cattle cars for the trip through Williamsport, Harrisburg, and Baltimore. Only brief stops at these stations would offer any relief on this difficult journey. The echoes of cheering crowds and the brass bands must have faded quickly for such travelers. And, as winter approached, cattle car rides from Elmira became even more difficult. The 85th New York boarded a troop train on December 3, 1861, to the tune of "The Girl I Left Behind Me." One member of the unit scribbled in his diary that "we got on board box cars—cold! no fires in any of them. The whistle blows. We are off to Washington."[25]

Nevertheless, departures were emotional events that lived forever in the minds of those who witnessed them. In early June, for example, the 770-man 19th New York (known as the "Cayugas") boarded a special train on the Elmira and Williamsport line. At the final evening parade (the night before departure), the 19th's commanding officer warned that those who were thinking of desertion "would 'be stopped with a bayonet if possible, and if not with a ball.'" The next morning a large crowd gathered on rooftops and in the streets near the depot to see off the regiment, and to one reporter, "the assembly seemed composed one-fourth of men and boys, and three-fourths of young ladies—many of whom doubtless, 'ran guard' at the female seminary [Elmira College] near the Cayugas' late quarters." The young college women fluttered "their handkerchiefs at, and [beamed] their smiles upon, the handsome captains, lieutenants, and ensigns of the Nineteenth, as the train moved off."[26]

The 19th's officers did not leave Elmira without the luxury of ancillary assistance. Reflecting the racial attitudes of the day, the *New York World* reported: "A recruiting agent succeeded during the last day or two in enlisting from the Brainard House and other hotels a corps of body-servants (colored) for the officers. These fellows had a farewell celebration of their own . . . and were petted, caressed, gifted and bussed by a large and well-dressed delegation of ace-of-spade negroes, mulattoes, and quadroons."[27]

By mid-July all ten regiments mustered at Elmira had been sent south. This brought to a close Elmira's first ninety days in the war. It proved to be the village's most active involvement in Union military activity during the entire conflict. In terms of a military presence, only the year of the prison camp would match this 3-month period in 1861. Governor Morgan confidently responded in late June to President Lincoln's request for a report on the status of every regiment that had been mustered in New York State.[28] And, in a move that undoubtedly reflected a hope for a quick victory, the governor ordered the Elmira Military Depot closed on July 12.

Elmira's "Southern Tier Rifles," along with the rest of the 23rd New York and other regiments that mustered at Elmira, experienced its initial sting of battle at a small river just north of Manassas, Virginia, called Bull Run. "Just heard of a terrible battle in Virginia," Marilla Park entered in her diary on July 23, 1861. Writing her observations of the Civil War at her home in Erin (a wisp of a hamlet twelve miles northeast of Elmira), she expressed a fear that "between two and three thousand Northern people [were] killed and a great loss on both sides."[29] The losses at Bull Run on July 21, 1861, were far less than what Marilla Park feared, but the news of a Confederate victory devastated those who had hoped for a Union triumph within ninety days.

Details of the battle filtered north through the telegraph lines: for the Confederacy 625 dead, and 975 wounded; for the Union, 625 dead, 950 wounded, and more than 1,200 captured. Citizens of the North abruptly came to realize that a serious and determined war effort was essential. Editor Charles Fairman offered these sober words: "This temporary reverse, with the serious loss attending it, will teach the nation some valuable lessons. War is not an affair to be *extemporized* at a moment's notice. . . . We must learn not to expect everything to be accomplished in a day."[30] There was in this unsparing view the pervasive realization that another major military campaign could not be initiated without serious attention being given to the important matters of organization, training, and discipline. In short, military depots such as Elmira must make a concerted effort to construct a formidable army. It was in this context that Governor Morgan officially reopened the Elmira Military Depot on July 30, 1861.

The day following the Union's defeat at Bull Run, President Lincoln called for 500,000 volunteers to serve three-year terms in the military. Upon receiving Lincoln's request, Governor Morgan issued a call for 25,000 volunteers in New York State. With a Buffalo regiment arriving in Elmira the first week in August, the village returned to its role as a military post. By September Elmira was once again "a garrison town," and the community would continue to hum with military activity until well after the conclusion of the war. Between April 1861 and April 1865, twenty-four regiments of infantry, four companies of artillery, and six cavalry units consisting of 20,797 officers and men were mustered and trained in Elmira and transported south.[31]

The training and transporting of men did not take place without causing considerable tension between the village's citizens and the presence of the military in the town. As early as mid-May 1861 a village newspaper reported that "there is now in Elmira few if any short of 6000 troops, and among the number there are many rough fellows."[32] There were reports that one of the village's cemeteries was vandalized by soldiers who broke some tombstones and turned over others, and one of Elmira's three breweries was raided by a large number of recruits. The village court docket for June 1861 contained the following charges: forty-one drunk and disorderly; twenty-one assault and battery; twenty-one petit larceny; one grand larceny; three violation of an ordinance for a total of seventy-four infractions. "A large share of the offenders during June," a local newspaper lamented, "were disorderly volunteers."[33]

On a far more serious note, in July 1861 a Rochester newspaper reported that two soldiers were murdered on Elmira's Main Street bridge. "During the melee," the report claimed, "knives were freely used, and the two men received stabs which proved fatal to one of them instantly, and the other was in a dying state when our informants left. Elmira is getting to be a pretty rough place to live in, we should judge. Four soldiers have been murdered there within a week."[34]

Even though it was (in the eyes of some) "a pretty rough place to live in," Elmira functioned as an essential hub of wartime activity. The village served as a state military depot until July 1863 when it became a federal draft rendezvous. With the number of volunteers dwindling, Congress passed an ambiguous bill in July 1862 that empowered President Lincoln to call the militia of the respective states into federal service. Referring to the law as one "of dubious legality and confusing arithmetic," historian James M. McPherson has concluded: "The government did not hesitate to use this power to reach across the state boundaries and institute a quasi-draft."[35]

This was followed by Congress's passing, and Lincoln's signing, the Enrollment Act on March 3, 1863. This law established a draft that "commuted" those who could either send a substitute or pay $300 cash to the federal government. Obviously more wealthy Americans could take advantage of "commutation." In New York State this meant that lower-class, working-class Irish and Germans would form a significant percentage of drafted men.

A segment of the Enrollment Act germane to Elmira's military situation subdivided each state into sections that were, in some cases, labeled "provost marshal districts."[36] New York State, with 20 percent of the North's population, was to be divided into three draft rendezvous posts—Buffalo, New York City, and Elmira.[37] On July 18, 1863, in an abrupt War Department memo that offered nothing in the way of explanation, Brig. Gen. Edward D. Townsend, the War Department's assistant adjutant general, informed Capt. L. L. Livingston of the Elmira Draft Rendezvous that the draft rendezvous at Buffalo was closed and all officers, recruits, and stores were ordered to Elmira.[38] The following day the War Department instructed Brig. Gen. William A. Hammond, surgeon general of the U.S. Army, to staff the Elmira Draft Rendezvous with medical officers.

"Will this," queried Elmira's assistant adjutant provost marshal general, "be the General Rendezvous for this Division of the state?" The inquiry, addressed to the War Department, continued: "There is no place in this

Division of the state with Barracks to receive so many men as will be drafted. And no point so convenient for transmitting them South."[39] In responding to the inquiry, Washington notified Elmira's military authorities that the village was officially designated as the General Draft Rendezvous for Western New York State. Now the village would take on even greater importance as a military post. Also, for the duration of the war, Elmira would remain within the military jurisdiction of the federal government.

With the draft in place, coarser types of individuals now made up even greater numbers of the soldiery in Elmira—"rough fellows" (to use the Gazette's term). There was considerable concern on the part of those whose understanding of Elmira's identity was based on Anglo-Saxon culture. These draftees, most of them working-class Irish from New York City, exacerbated the fear that what remained of a coherent culture would now undergo further erosion. By 1864, with the draftees filling the regiments, the degree of hostility between the soldiers and citizens escalated. Predominantly Roman Catholic in religious faith, intemperate in drinking habits, lacking in education, and perceived as incorrigible in behavior, these "outsiders" proved to be a source of tension and fear.

Reports in the local newspapers in 1864 of conflicts were as shrill as they were frequent. Local editors constantly pointed to the shortcomings of the military and called for some semblance of order. "Who," the Gazette asked, "is to blame? Some person is or ought to be for the unsoldier-like manner of some of the troops now in Elmira. They appear perfectly loose in their behaviors, being allowed unrestrained to go about as they please. . . . [They are] lawless, reckless men, who under the disguise of a blue coat, profess themselves soldiers."[40] In August 1864 an angry Advertiser fired another editorial volley: "We understand that patrol guards are frequently seen drunk on the streets—that they have improperly interfered with citizens and strangers at the Depot, and been guilty of many other annoyances and outrages disgraceful to themselves and their regiments."[41]

More and more, conflicts between jittery citizens and raucous soldiers and between the local law enforcement agency and the military patrol at times resulted in physical confrontations. The most violent incident involving Union soldiers in Elmira occurred on February 25, 1864, and came to be known as the "Battle of the Chemung." Six companies of the 1st Michigan (a volunteer cavalry unit known as the "Woodchoppers") arrived at Elmira's railroad depot, and were scheduled to be transferred to a southbound train. While waiting for transfer, the Michigan officers and enlisted men scattered through the town. They swarmed into bars where they became intoxicated, physically attacked patrons, and destroyed property. Overwhelmed, saloonkeepers watched helplessly as the Woodchoppers drank their whiskey and wrecked their places of business.

Leaving in their wake a chain of smashed saloons and visibly shaken bartenders, the Michigan soldiers then ran into the streets and claimed they would burn the town to the ground. They wreaked havoc upon the stores of local merchants as terrified Elmirans ran for their lives. The drunken soldiers barged into a hotel known as the Franklin House and smashed furniture, mirrors, desks, and glasses. Even when a patrol guard under the command of a captain and a lieutenant confronted the rioting soldiers, the vastly outnumbered patrol was quickly overpowered.

Word was sent to Barracks No. 3 and several companies of infantry with fixed bayonets, accompanied by a battery of artillery, rushed to the scene. Officers drew their sabers and shots were fired. The rioting Woodchoppers were finally brought under control, and those suspected of instigating the riot were held for court-martial proceedings. "During the affray," an official report concluded, "one soldier of the 1st Mich. Cav. was killed, four wounded and one of the Provost Guard of the 1st Battalion Invalid Corps was badly wounded in the arm as to render amputation necessary."[42] Elmira was placed under martial law, and all places of business were ordered closed for the remainder of the day.

It was perhaps at this moment that Elmira's citizens came to painfully realize that the village's position as a vital military post exacted a heavy price on the community. Yet the turmoil that unfortunately came with the presence of the military did not deter one branch of the War Department from thinking of Elmira as something more than merely a rough town that served as a draft rendezvous. As far back as the late spring days in 1862, Col. William Hoffman, the U.S. commissary general of prisoners, began to ponder the potential of Elmira's accommodations for new use. He instructed Capt. Henry M. Lazelle to inspect the military depot at Elmira and determine its capacity for quartering troops. Captain Lazelle was further instructed to list the dimensions of the various barracks and the number of men they could accommodate. Finally, Lazelle was ordered to check all facilities for fuel and water and then report to Hoffman in person.[43]

Captain Lazelle's report included detailed assessments of the military facilities at Albany, Utica, Rochester, Buffalo, and Elmira. He emphasized Elmira's potential to quarter large numbers of soldiers. His report shows four barracks areas in the community that could, through crowding, house 11,000 soldiers. All four "camps" are described in great detail. Included in the report are descriptions of what eventually became Barracks No. 1 and Barracks No. 3—the only two military quarters that remained active during the years the War Department directed operations in Elmira.

Lazelle's report noted that the Arnot Barracks (Barracks No. 1) consisted of "a plot of ground quite level, not easily drained and considerably lower than the surrounding country." To complicate matters, well water "on the grounds and from the junction canal south of it is unfit and must be hauled."[44] During the days of the prison camp, Barracks No. 1 would remain quarters for Union soldiers.

Captain Lazelle observed that "Foster Barracks" (by 1862 known as "Camp Rathbun") "is admirably adapted to military purposes." Twenty buildings (18 feet by 88 feet by 8 feet) on the grounds could accommodate 2,000 men, and "a different arrangement of bunks would readily give accommodations" for 1,000 more soldiers. Two mess houses could seat 1,000 men each, and kitchen facilities were "sufficient to cook for 2,000 at once." The report was submitted to Colonel Hoffman on June 25, 1862.[45] The commissary general of prisoners would keep Lazelle's report in mind—especially in light of the fact that Camp Rathbun by 1864 would evolve into a 32-acre area, with the addition of ten new barracks (25 by 80 by 12), that could accommodate 4,000 men.

The following month (July 22, 1862), at a place called Haxall's Landing on the James River in Virginia, Maj. Gen. John A. Dix of the Union and Maj. Gen. Daniel H. Hill of the Confederacy, each designated by their respective sides, signed what came to be known as a cartel. This agreement to exchange prisoners of war was cobbled together between the armies, not the governments.[46] Before this agreement, some prisoners were often held for a period of time, and others were exchanged immediately after battle when opposing generals could reach an agreement.

In the North, Confederate prisoners of war were quartered in such places as old forts and temporary stockades, even (briefly in 1861) at Ellis Island—the sight that was destined to become the storied place of entry for millions of European immigrants. And less than a mile from Ellis Island, the fort on Bedloe's Island in New York Harbor would house Confederates in 1864 and 1865. Twenty-one years after the Civil War, in a clear illustration of irony being in abundant and tragic supply, the fort on Bedloe's Island would serve as the base for the Statue of Liberty.

The cartel now specified that once prisoners were released, they were not to rejoin the military. The Confederacy initially proposed a formal agreement, but President Lincoln refused to do this because it smacked of official recognition of the Confederacy. Lincoln finally agreed to a prisoner exchange between Union and Confederate armies and thus made possible the agreement between General Dix and General Hill. For a variety of reasons the Dix–Hill cartel was doomed to failure. An obvious weakness of the agreement is that it was at best a tenuous document that rested upon the fragile word (and nerves) of generals who were more and more tempered by the horrors of battle. Indeed, within the next year the rigors of war fostered practices well beyond the boundaries of a gentlemen's agreement.

Publicly, the U.S. government ended the cartel in April 1863 by arguing that the Confederacy had violated terms of the agreement between the armies. On April 17 Lt. Gen. Ulysses S. Grant, by that time a reasonably well-fixed star in the Union's military firmament, became the first field general to suspend prisoner exchanges. Grant said he suspected the Confederacy of allowing released prisoners to rejoin the military ranks, and there is strong evidence to support his suspicions.

Privately, General Grant concluded that holding Southern prisoners would deplete the manpower of the Confederacy. The North, with its overwhelming advantage in population, would not experience a shortage in manpower, and its military bureaucracy agreed with Grant that a war of attrition would work in favor of the Union. Many historians have argued that the decision to terminate the cartel quite possibly saved lives by shortening the war. From a humanitarian standpoint, however, the cold, brutal logic of a policy forbidding the exchanging of prisoners would culminate in the physical and psychological destruction of thousands of human beings—a destruction that was perpetuated by Americans against Americans.

Supporting General Grant's reasoning was Secretary of War Edwin McMasters Stanton—an intelligent, arrogant, ambitious Pittsburgh trial lawyer who became part of the Washington establishment in 1857. Regal in bearing, imperious in manner, versed in the ancient canons of Anglo-Saxon law, the Ohio-born Stanton desired wealth and public recognition. By the mid-1850s, his reputation as an attorney and a Jacksonian Democrat stretched throughout the Ohio Valley from Pittsburgh to Louisville, Kentucky, and to the Atlantic coast from Boston to Charleston, South Carolina.[47]

One of Stanton's great gifts was his canny ability to conceal his political beliefs when currying favor and position in the political arena. When

Edwin McMasters Stanton, President Lincoln's autocratic secretary of war.

seeking support in his quest for the post of secretary of war in 1862, he astutely moved through a formidable maze of political factions. Some saw this as nothing more than mysterious caprices of his character and thought. To his harsher critics, Stanton was thought of as being analogous to the Vicar of Bray, the sixteenth-century English priest notorious for changing his principles or opinions to suit the time or circumstances. Whatever his motives, Stanton had served as attorney general under President James Buchanan, a Democrat, and now, as the nation moved into the second year of the war, he was called upon again to assume a cabinet-level post—replacing Simon Cameron at the War Department.

Secretary Stanton confidentially agreed with Grant that holding Confederate prisoners of war would deplete Southern manpower and bring the war to an earlier conclusion. In an undated memo, Stanton wrote: "The general presented the same argument to me before I could advance it to him."[48] More importantly, President Lincoln agreed that an end to the prisoner exchange would curtail the South's ability to carry on the war. The cartel was now a dead letter.[49]

As for where to put Confederate prisoners, the secretary of war delegated this matter to his commissary general of prisoners—Colonel Hoffman. Hoffman's father, Col. William Hoffman, had served in the War of 1812, and the son carried on the family's military tradition by accepting an appointment to the U.S. Military Academy in 1825. An 1829 West Point graduate (eighteenth in his class of forty-six) and decorated combat officer of the Mexican War, Hoffman was a tall, erect, imposing figure with an unkempt beard.

Serving in Texas in 1861, he was taken prisoner at the outbreak of the war and held by the Confederacy until August 27, 1862. Shortly after his release, he moved on to Washington, D.C., where his grasp of the War Department's arcane Civil War bureaucracy was matched only by his parsimonious, budget-conscious edicts that resulted in withholding large sums of money that were earmarked for the purchase of prisoner-of-war rations, clothing, shelter, and medical supplies. Money withheld by Hoffman for the purchase of rations alone would result in the return of $1,845,126 to the government at the conclusion of the war.[50]

In addition to his propensity for tight-fisted fiscal thinking, Colonel Hoffman possessed a thorough understanding of all Union military posts. This knowledge was essential for the officer in charge of prisoner-of-war

*Col. William Hoffman,
the commissary general
of prisoners, poses for the
camera in front of his
office on F Street North
at the corner of 20th
Street West.*

LIBRARY OF CONGRESS

camps, for by the spring of 1864 the available prisons could no longer handle the large number of captured Confederate soldiers.

On the fateful day of May 14, 1864, Brig. Gen. Edward D. Townsend,
speaking for the adjutant general's office, informed Colonel Hoffman that
"there are quite a number of barracks at Elmira, N.Y., which are not occupied, and are fit to hold rebel prisoners. Quite a large number of those
lately captured could be accommodated at this place."[51] Hoffman then
pulled from his files the dimensions of Elmira's military facilities that the
meticulous Captain Lazelle had presented to him two years earlier. Five days
later the commissary general of prisoners informed Secretary Stanton that
Elmira could provide relief for the crowded prison conditions at Point
Lookout, Maryland, and proposed "that one set of the barracks at Elmira

may be appropriated to this purpose."[52] On the same day Colonel Hoffman informed Lt. Col. Seth Eastman, post commander at Elmira, that he would "receive instructions from the Adjutant-General to set apart the barracks on the Chemung [River] at Elmira as a depot for prisoners of war."[53]

With Hoffman's letter to Eastman, the die was cast. Elmira was about to become an integral part of an archipelago of prison camps that dotted the North from Fort Warren in Boston Harbor to Gratiot Street Prison in St. Louis. The town's history would now take a fateful twist. In the minds of Secretary Stanton and Colonel Hoffman, Elmira—with its superb transportation connections—must have seemed a wise selection. Perhaps they thought, in the words of a newspaperman writing in 1861, Elmira was "a choice of sound military logic."

CHAPTER 2

"I Judge the Number…
Will Be 8,000 to 10,000"

The formidable task of establishing a prisoner-of-war camp at Elmira was placed on the weary shoulders of Lt. Col. Seth Eastman, a West Pointer in his thirty-fifth year of military service. Now a bearded, craggy, rheumatoid figure, Eastman had been in poor health for several years. And, according to one of his officers, he had a drinking problem. It was claimed that during the day the Elmira post commander would stop at the living quarters of a member of his staff where he "never refused to take a little something for his 'stomach's sake' . . . and of course he always left in the best possible spirits."[1] Yet Eastman, his health problems notwithstanding, was thought of as a venerable commander by his officers and men and the citizens of Elmira.

Seth Eastman came from old New England stock. In 1729 his great-great-grandfather, Capt. Ebenezer Eastman, moved from Massachusetts to what eventually became Concord, New Hampshire. His father, Robert Eastman, left Concord to settle in Brunswick, Maine, where Seth was born on January 24, 1808—the first of thirteen children. Robert hoped that his son would attend Bowdoin College, but young Seth from his early boyhood thought of a military career. He entered West Point on July 1, 1824, where he did well in mathematics, natural philosophy, engineering, tactics, and artillery. He mastered a command of the French language and read (in original French) Voltaire's *Charles XII.* His near perfection in the subject of drawing was a harbinger of his significant achievement in art. A classmate of Col. William Hoffman, Eastman was graduated from the U.S. Military Academy (ranking twenty-second in a class of forty-six) on July 1, 1829. Since he evidently repeated his first year at West Point, it took him five years to graduate. He was commissioned a second lieutenant and assigned to the 1st Infantry.[2]

Eastman's long and distinguished military career included serving at a number of frontier forts—including Fort Crawford (Wisconsin Territory), Fort Snelling (Minnesota Territory), Forts Duncan and Chadbourne (the State of Texas), and Fort Crittenden (Utah Territory). He rose through the ranks—being promoted to the rank of first lieutenant (November 1836), captain (November 1839), major (October 1856), and lieutenant colonel (September 1861). Following a 7-year (January 1833–January 1840) tour as an assistant instructor of drawing at West Point, Eastman served in the Florida (Seminole) War from January 1840 through June 1841. On four different occasions during the 1840s, he filled the position as post commander at Fort Snelling. From February 1850 to May 1855 he served as an illustrator in the Bureau of the Commissioner of Indian Affairs. And, from August 1855 to October 1856, he was the commanding officer at Fort Chadbourne.

Eastman did two tours of duty with the War Department in Washington, D.C., between 1857 and 1861, and at the outbreak of the war he took the position of mustering and disbursing officer for Maine and New Hampshire. After all his years at distant frontier posts, a return to his native New England must have seemed extremely pleasant.[3]

He remained in New England until January 1863 when he was appointed military governor of Cincinnati. While in Cincinnati, Eastman became part of a national story when he presided over a military commission that convicted Clement L. Vallandigham for "disloyal sentiments and opinions, with the object and purpose of weakening the power of the Government" at the time of an unlawful rebellion.[4] Vallandigham, a former Democratic congressman who had lost his seat in 1862 as a result of Republican gerrymandering, was a nationally recognized opponent of the Union's military operations against the Confederacy. His case became a *cause célèbre* for copperheads throughout the North.

Eastman's personal life was happily marked by his marriage in 1835 to Mary Henderson, the 17-year-old daughter of Dr. and Mrs. Thomas Henderson. Mary Henderson Eastman, a faithful and admiring wife, bore four

Lt. Col. Seth Eastman, a West Point graduate and noted artist, served as Elmira's post commander at the time the prison camp was established. MINNESOTA HISTORICAL SOCIETY

sons and a daughter while enduring the hardships of army life. A remarkable woman in her own right, she wrote seven books. Her most controversial literary endeavor came in the form of a response to Harriet Beecher Stowe's *Uncle Tom's Cabin*. Within months of the publication of Stowe's book, Mary Henderson Eastman, a Virginian, wrote *Aunt Phillis's Cabin; Or, Southern Life as It Is*. It was a rebuke of *Uncle Tom's Cabin* as well as a defense of Southern life, and proved to be a best-seller in the American South.

The ironies of the Civil War lead one to wonder what Mary Henderson Eastman's thoughts were of Confederate prisoners of war being incarcerated at Elmira under the command of her husband. *Aunt Phillis's Cabin* may have been her most popular book, but perhaps her most important work was *Dahcotah; Life and Legends of the Sioux around Fort Snelling*—a study of the character and works of the Sioux Indians she came to know while her husband was stationed at Fort Snelling.[5] Her fine literary skills were complemented by her husband's great talent as an artist.

As early as 1836 art critics were taking notice of Seth Eastman. In April of that year one of his paintings was exhibited at the National Academy of Design in New York City. A New York City newspaper acknowledged that he now took "his stand among our landscape painters."[6] Landscapes, mostly of the American frontier, federal forts and, perhaps most importantly, the unfettered depiction of Indian life were captured on canvas by Eastman during his extensive military career.[7] In 1837 he published a scholarly treatise on topographical drawing and in 1838 he became a member of the National Academy of Design.

Preferring to pursue his military career, in 1839 he declined a position as professor of topographical drawing and painting at Jefferson College, Missouri. His reputation as an artist would grow over the years, and his paintings became a regular feature of exhibitions at the National Academy of Design. In 1848 a St. Louis newspaper proclaimed: "Since we have known something of Eastman's pictures, and of Indians, we have ranked him as out of sight the best painter of Indian life the country has produced."[8]

Two years after the Civil War, the U.S. Congress commissioned Eastman to paint Indians for the Committee on Indian Affairs and federal forts for the Military Affairs Committee. Today Eastman's paintings of military forts are displayed without fanfare in a remote section of the west corridor on the main floor of the Capitol in Washington, D.C.[9] One of his paintings hangs today in the Rockwell Museum in Corning, New York—just sixteen miles west of the prison camp that he commanded.

Disabilities and diseases that accrued in the line of duty over a 34-year military career resulted in Eastman's retirement from active service on December 3, 1863. Six weeks later he was reactivated and assumed command of the Elmira Draft Rendezvous on January 21, 1864. Upon arriving in Elmira, Eastman and his wife and their youngest child, a son, took up residence at the Brainard House. As post commander, his primary duty was to have the draft rendezvous at all times in a state of preparation for the reception of volunteers and drafted men. Mary Eastman was well received by the town's gentry and devoted much of her time to raising money for the war effort.

Settling in as post commander, Eastman went about the business of managing military matters in Elmira. The channel of communications between Elmira and Washington was routed from Lieutenant Colonel Eastman's desk through an amalgam of separate and often competing offices (adjutant general, quartermaster general, surgeon general, commissary general of prisoners, and others) and on for final approval to the office of Secretary of War Stanton. Eastman's opinion of Stanton is (not unexpectedly) unrecorded. Steeped in a wide ambit of military mores and efficacy, he clearly comprehended the rigid rules of the U.S. Army—among them that he must execute the orders of his military superiors. And those orders carried the imprimatur of Secretary Stanton.

In the early spring of 1864 the Elmira post commander's primary concerns related to the accommodation of troops and the construction of new post hospital facilities. After considering constructing hospitals in the immediate vicinity of each barracks, it was finally decided to build a 400-bed unit to be located about one mile from each barracks post. Completion of construction was projected for early July. This meant there would be no hospital facilities inside Barracks No. 3 at the time the prison camp was established.

On May 2 Eastman informed Brig. Gen. Lorenzo Thomas, adjutant general of the U.S. Department of War, that construction of twenty new barracks was completed and repairs on old barracks allowed the Elmira post (consisting of Barracks Nos. 1 and 3) to accommodate up to 6,000 troops. He also told General Thomas that construction of the new hospital was behind schedule.[10] Thus, on the eve of the proposal to make Elmira a prison camp, officials at the War Department understood that there was no hospital and the combined capacity of Barracks Nos. 1 and 3 was 6,000.

Such was the status of Elmira when on May 19 Lieutenant Colonel Eastman was directed by the War Department to "set aside the barracks on the Chemung river for the accomodation [*sic*] of rebel prisoners."[11] On the same day, in a separate message from Colonel Hoffman, Eastman was notified that Barracks No. 3 west of the village line would be "inclosed by a suitable fence . . . [constructed] after the style found to be most secure at other depots." Hoffman continued: "There should be ample room between the fence and the buildings, that prisoners may not approach it unseen." The commissary general of prisoners next called for a "report on the condition of the barracks, and any other additions which may be required, and the number of prisoners the place will accommodate." Eastman must have been surprised to read the next passage: "From what I have heard, I judge the number [of prisoners] will be 8,000 to 10,000."[12]

Crossing in the mail that day was another of Eastman's reports to General Thomas. Apparently an influx of recruits (a common occurrence at Elmira) had moved Eastman to lower his barracks accommodations estimate to "five-thousand additional men." And again Eastman noted that hospital construction had been delayed for the want of carpenters.[13]

The proposal that Elmira's Barracks No. 3 should serve as a prison camp with a capacity of 8,000 to 10,000 Confederate prisoners of war was now in motion. Significantly, that figure came from Washington—not from the post commander at Elmira. As to how Colonel Hoffman arrived at this estimate remains to this day the single most mysterious aspect of the Elmira prison camp story. Surely he was aware of the fact that Elmira's accommodation limit was 5,000 prisoners of war. Eastman had made it clear on May 2 that total capacity for Barracks Nos. 1 and 3 was 6,000 and then ten days later lowered that figure to 5,000. Yet the commissary general of prisoners persisted that Elmira will quarter upwards of 10,000 prisoners of war.

Colonel Hoffman's arbitrary prisoner-of-war figure is a sticking point that would lead to charges more than a century later that Elmira was deliberately established as a death camp. Indeed, author Lonnie R. Speer, in his extensive study of Civil War prison camps, has written: "The tragic period of Civil War concentration camps was inaugurated with Elmira prison in the North and Andersonville in the South."[14] Speer contends that from its inception the Elmira camp was a deadly place. Andersonville, established in February 1864, preceded the opening of the Elmira prison by five months. Both prisons are remembered today for their high death rates and questionable management.

In informing the adjutant general on May 22 that he had received the order to establish a prison camp, Lieutenant Colonel Eastman noted that the guard detail was woefully insufficient to secure a large detachment of prisoners of war.[15] On the following day the Elmira post commander, in acknowledging Colonel Hoffman's May 19 missive, declared that Barracks No. 3 could "comfortably accommodate three thousand troops without crowding." After calling attention to the excellent condition of the buildings, Eastman, in lucid terms, stated: "Four thousand prisoners of war could be quartered in them [with crowding] and there is plenty of ground room on which tents could be pitched to accommodate one thousand more." He also informed Hoffman that the mess house "is sufficiently large to seat twelve to fifteen hundred and the kitchens can cook daily for five thousand. There is an excellent Bakery that can bake daily six thousand rations."[16] If anything, the capacity of the kitchen facilities made it clear to the commissary general of prisoners that Barracks No. 3 could not reasonably accommodate 10,000 prisoners of war.

On May 29 Eastman recommended to General Thomas that, in lieu of hospital tents, temporary sheds be constructed at Barracks No. 3 for the care of sick prisoners of war.[17] And then, to obfuscate matters, on the following day Lieutenant Colonel Eastman received two telegraph messages from Washington stating that orders to establish Elmira as a prison camp had been rescinded.[18] Weary and in ill health, the puzzled post commander must have questioned, *sotto voce,* the judgment of his superiors in Washington. The unexplained revocation now unexpectedly surceased prison camp preparations and brought forth at once a moment of considerable confusion and a great sigh of relief within Elmira's chain of command.

Six days later, June 5, Eastman advised General Thomas that the fence enclosing Barracks No. 3 was near completion and it was best to complete it in order to prevent desertion.[19] Work on the fence was completed on June 12. Twelve feet high, the barrier enclosed the 32-acre area. Sentry boxes (forty in all) were placed every fifty yards and a platform four feet below the top of the fence on the outside would allow the guards to walk their respective posts. A large main gate on Water Street served as the camp's main entrance, and, on the south side of the prison, an auxiliary gate allowed access to the Chemung River where the prisoners bathed during the good weather.

On that day the fence enclosed thirty barracks. Twenty of the buildings, it will be recalled, were constructed in 1861 and measured 18 feet by 88 feet and 8 feet high. These twenty buildings could house 2,000 prisoners of war. The ten additional barracks—20 feet by 80 feet and 12 feet high—

A lone sentry walks his post at the northeast corner of the fence that encompassed the prison camp. CHEMUNG COUNTY HISTORICAL SOCIETY

were (as mentioned in chap. 1) built between the summer of 1863 and June 1864 and had a capacity of housing 1,500 men. It was on this basis that Lieutenant Colonel Eastman arrived at a figure of 4,000 prisoners of war (with crowding) in barracks.

Eastman, in completing construction of the fence, had made a wise decision, for Colonel Hoffman informed the Elmira post commander on June 22 that by "direction of the Secretary of War the barracks (No. 3) at Elmira will be prepared to receive prisoners of war according to the instructions in my letter of the 19th [May]." Hoffman then noted "it is advisable, if practicable, to inclose ground enough to accommodate in barracks and tents 10,000 prisoners."[20] It is abundantly clear that Secretary Stanton, a man whose infirmities of temper and contempt for the Confederacy were the subjects of newspaper editorials in both the North and South, officially reversed the May 30 telegrams of revocation. And equally as clear was Hoffman's determined insistence that 10,000 prisoners of war would be quartered in Elmira.

Eight days later Lieutenant Colonel Eastman lent his own hand to the questionable proposal when he informed the adjutant general's office that "Barracks No. 3 has been set aside for the accomodation [*sic*] of prisoners of war. . . . These barracks are now ready to receive prisoners." The post commander added that there was a dearth of Union officers to administer the "about fifty [Confederate] companies of 200 men each."[21] If anything, Eastman's response was that of a veteran officer who understood the order to house 8,000 to 10,000 prisoners of war in Elmira was within the realm of a military orthodoxy tantamount to dogma.

On the same day that Eastman notified Washington, a second opinion in support of the 10,000 figure came from Capt. John J. Elwell, Elmira's assistant quartermaster. Elwell informed Maj. Gen. Montgomery C. Meigs, the quartermaster general of the United States, "that Barracks No. 3 has been placed in complete condition for the accommodation of 10,000 prisoners and the necessary guard. . . . Wells have been sunk, and all the necessary arrangements made for the immediate occupation, should it be required."[22]

Thus, on the eve of the first Confederates' arrival in Elmira, Hoffman's 10,000-prisoner estimate was now an *idée fixe*. Both ends of the communications pipeline—Washington and Elmira—were about to make decisions that were based on an exchange of thoughts that ranged from 10,000 prisoners to the accurate number of 5,000 back to the unrealistic 10,000 figure. Through the course of this exchange, the commissary general of prisoners stood firm on the 10,000 figure. Officers in Elmira, adhering to the military's Spartan code of discipline and unquestioned obedience, within a 5-week period came around to the figure that was mandated by Colonel Hoffman.

Lending to this unmistakably bad decision is the word from Washington on May 30 that Elmira would no longer be considered for the purpose of housing Confederate prisoners of war. This held sway for the next three weeks and added to an already muddled situation. Indeed, the handling of the entire matter supports those critics who have argued that complete power was in the hands of incomplete men. And Elmira's prison survivors who lived into the twentieth century could, in moments of petulance, with some justification compare the War Department's thinking to that of the Mad Hatter's tea party.

With the approval of Elmira as a prison site, the rules and regulations for the camp were established by the commissary general of prisoners in a circular already in place and dated April 20, 1864, and by special orders issued by Lieutenant Colonel Eastman on July 2. Upon arrival, prisoners were divided into companies of 84 men (later this would be increased to 112) with their respective rank, regiment, and company listed on the camp rolls. Prisoners who were civilians were to be listed by town, county, and state. Each company was under the command of a commissioned Union officer and a Union sergeant was assigned as an orderly. As the camp census grew, officers would assume responsibility for several companies.

Private retailers and wholesalers in the Elmira area were contracted six months at a time for items such as meat, fruit, vegetables, flour, and other food items. Lumber, coal, and firewood also were contracted through the private sector. A bakery (24 feet by 108 feet by 12 feet) was located parallel to the mess house (41 feet by 396 feet by 8 feet). Clothing (other than socks, underwear, and shoes) was restricted to gray in color. The color restriction included pants, shirts, and overcoats.

The camp sutler (a retail shopkeeper inside the prison) was to be approved by and operate under the control of the post commander. In the beginning prisoners of war were allowed to purchase a large number of items that included dried or fresh fruit, cakes, pies, several kinds of dried or canned fish, cheese, crackers, nuts, lemonade, cigars, chewing tobacco, writing paper, pens, ink, postage stamps, and clothing of gray color. The camp sutler, a civilian, was taxed a small amount (based on his sales) by the post commander.

A prison fund was established from allotted money not spent on the needs of the camp. For example, both the sutler's tax and the money saved from any proposed purchase of something that was then rejected because it did not meet standards were placed in the prison fund. Money left by deceased prisoners also became part of the prison fund. Money from this special account could be used for purchasing articles not provided for by regulations such as table furniture, cooking utensils, laundry kettles, and the means of improving or enlarging barracks and hospitals within the prison structure. Guards, clerks, and other employees engaged in jobs connected with the maintenance of the camp were paid out of the prison fund. Prisoners who held positions such as waiters, clerks, hospital orderlies, cooks, bakers, kitchen workers, ward sergeants, and general laborers were also compensated through this fund. All prisoners of war who held jobs were allowed extra rations.

Letters, limited to a single page, could be written and received by the prisoners. No prisoner of war was allowed to write of discontent with conditions within the camp. Lieutenant Colonel Eastman appointed a staff of noncommissioned officers to examine and possibly censor all letters before they were forwarded or delivered to the prisoners. Prisoners who were seriously ill were allowed short visits from their nearest relatives—provided the visitors were deemed loyal to the United States. With few exceptions, only persons who had official business were allowed inside the camp, and they were not allowed to communicate with the prisoners.[23]

Regulations for guarding the camp were put in place by Eastman. A full guard detail consisted of 8 commissioned officers, 32 noncommissioned officers, and 260 privates. The guards secured specific areas inside the camp—e.g., the cookhouse and mess house, the receiving area for wholesale goods, the administrative headquarters, the hospital—and the walkway between the sentry boxes on the fence that encompassed the prison. The new guard detail relieved that of the previous day at ten o'clock each morning and remained on duty for twenty-four hours. The detail was divided into three units in order that each unit remained on duty for two hours at a time. This allowed each man four hours rest out of six. In the event of a critical situation, the entire detail would be called to duty.[24]

Only the secretary of war had the power to grant a parole or release for any prisoner of war, and this in almost all cases required an oath of allegiance. The question of prisoners taking the oath of allegiance was strictly regulated by the War Department with final approval at the discretion of the secretary of war. Those who took the oath and were released from prison and given train fare to a destination in the North where they were required to remain for the duration of the war. If the war continued for two years beyond the date of their release, the released prisoners were eligible to be drafted into the U.S. military forces.[25]

The theory of the oath of allegiance resulting in release from prison was quite different from stark reality—i.e., there were relatively few Confederates released from Elmira.[26] A number of Elmira prisoners, upon taking the oath, were granted jobs within the camp at five cents a day and a sufficient amount of rations. Although not released, these men held a distinct advantage when it came to survival. They were, however, derisively referred to by their fellow Confederates as "oathtakers"—a bitter term of dishonor. It was for this reason that many of Elmira's Confederate prisoners of war adamantly refused to take the oath of allegiance. Others, fearing intimidation and derision, also declined to take the oath.[27]

R. B. Ewan of the 10th Virginia, one of legions of prisoners who refused the oath, perhaps summed it up best when, over four decades later, he recalled: "This [the offer of taking the oath of allegiance and being released] was a severe blow to my loyalty. . . . But I told the Colonel [Col.

Union soldiers during one of the rest periods that was part of their 24-hour shift. Behind the soldiers is a guardhouse and to the right of the sentry standing on the fence (but not in the picture) is the main entrance to the prison.

CHEMUNG COUNTY HISTORICAL SOCIETY

Benjamin F. Tracy] I could not take the oath as he had prescribed. I was a Southern man, born and bred in the belief that our cause was just and good, and I had sworn to stand by it and my country, and would prefer to go back to the pen with the boys and die there if need be."[28]

With the Elmira post commander apprised of the rules that would govern the prison, the final detail in the opening of the prison camp was carried out by Colonel Hoffman when he contacted Col. Alonzo G. Draper, the Union commander of the prison camp at Point Lookout, Maryland. Draper was told on June 30 to prepare 2,000 Confederate prisoners of war for assignment to Elmira. The prisoners would be sent to Elmira in groups of 400 and transports would be furnished at intervals of two or three days.[29]

Thus, the stage was set. On Saturday, July 2, 400 prisoners of war departed from Point Lookout (located on the Maryland side of the Potomac River on Chesapeake Bay) by steamer. They were transported to New York City where they were taken across the Hudson River to Erie Railroad boxcars at Jersey City for the journey to Elmira. The 17- to 20-hour trip entailed stops for fuel and water and a prisoner head count that always meant that prisoner-of-war trains took longer to come from the New York City area.

Initiating a sad ritual that would be repeated frequently over the next several months, the first prisoner-of-war train arrived at Elmira's railroad depot on Wednesday, July 6, 1864, at 6 A.M. The 399 Confederates (one died during the train ride) were received by Maj. Henry V. Colt (104th New York), the prison camp commander and a man who would quickly become known to the prisoners for his evenhanded approach to prison matters.[30] Far removed from the great Southern physiocrats, these foot soldiers came from the ranks of Robert E. Lee's Army of Northern Virginia. They had experienced the grisly alchemy of war at Antietam, Fredericksburg, Chancellorsville, Gettysburg, and Spotsylvania. By the summer of 1864 many of them understood what William Tecumseh Sherman, arguably the finest field commander in the Civil War, would say more than a decade after Appomattox: "I have seen war in all of its horrible aspects. I have seen fields devastated, homes ruined, and cities laid waste; I have seen the carnage of battle, the blood of the wounded and the cold faces of the dead looking up at the stars. That is war." And then came his imperishable words: "War is hell."[31]

Now hundreds of Elmirans—some wary, others curious, and some compassionate—gathered in the early morning hours to observe the first prison arrivals. In columns of four, the weary, tattered Confederates seemed to take on an air of *dramatis personae* as they moved at a surprisingly spirited gait along Elmira's streets the two miles from the railroad station to the camp. The stately elms, the exquisite village green, the elegant buildings of the business district, the town's Victorian mansions of considerable style and dash—all were sharply defined beneath a magnificently flawless summer sky. In stark contrast, the prison's gates—great, cumbersome, thick, heavy structures—silently awaited their arrival.

In describing the march to prison of the first group of prisoners, Charles Fairman's firsthand observation in the *Advertiser* noted:

> The 'rebs,' who arrived yesterday, wore all sorts of nondescript uniforms; besides the regular dark, dirty grey. Some had nothing on but drawers and shirts. . . . They were a fine looking body of men physically, taller than average, for the most part, made up of two classes, the old and the young, the middle age having a small representation. They did not exhibit a high degree of intelligence,

but looked to be men that would go where they are told, let what might happen: although lean and lank, yet evidently possessing the vigor and litheness to go through thick and thin. Of course they were black, sunburnt and dirty; but they took their lot cheerily and laughed and joked among themselves. . . . They marched off lively towards Barracks No. 3 from the depot, seemingly gratified by their recent change of base.[32]

A. J. Madra of Tarboro, North Carolina—a member of the 30th North Carolina—would be the first of this "fine looking body of men" to pass through the camp's gated entrance and enter a world of marginal existence. Madra, a survivor of Elmira, years later would recall: "I was at the head of the column, walking by the side of a U.S. sergeant, and he remarked to me: 'You are the first "Reb" in the prison.'"[33]

On Monday, July 11, 250 more prisoners of war arrived—one of them being recognized as a former Elmiran. This would be the first of several instances where men who formerly lived in Elmira or the surrounding area would be noticed by local observers. The following morning 502 Confederates arrived, as one of them put it, "in the pretty little city of Elmira." Looking out from the prison camp grounds, a member of this third group of arrivals observed: "The whole site is a basin surrounded by hills which rise several hundred feet, and are covered richly and thickly with the luxurious foliage of the hemlock, ash, poplar, and pine."[34]

A sanguine editor Fairman would, at the very beginning of the prison camp's existence, set the tone for his newspaper. "We got a peep at the Johnny Rebs yesterday," he wrote the day following the arrival of the first group of prisoners, "by looking through a crack in the fence. They are a tough looking set. By way of offset to the disagreeable customers inside the fence, Jim Post, at the sutler's shop presented us a capital cigar, and we marched away full of fire and smoke, as large as life and twice as natural."[35]

Four days later Fairman noted that the "'Johnny Rebs' are quite the lions for the visitors of Barracks No. 3." He then cited that country folk "are hardly willing to go home after their shopping is done, without a peep at the varmints, and those of the town, during the cool evening dews, don't fail of securing a like privilege." Fairman next alluded to the prisoners' fear of a "scarcity of rations" based on "small compunctions at the way our poor fellows have been starved, and perhaps surmising some retaliation." Concluding with a claim that the camp's survivors would come to question

widely, the ebullient editor confidently assured his readers that a "continued supply of full rations will likely disabuse them [the Confederate prisoners of war] of the impression that the North is capable of practicing
inhuman fiendishness, after the manner of the detestable government under
whose flag they serve."[36]

The July 12 arrivals brought the camp's total to 1,151 prisoners—a
mere shadow of what was to come. This was the census when Lt. Col.
Charles T. Alexander, a U.S. Army surgeon and official medical inspector
of prisoners of war, submitted a report of his July 11 and 12 inspection of
Elmira to Colonel Hoffman on July 14. Stating that the camp "is at present
in good condition," Alexander called Hoffman's attention to sinks
(latrines)—some "being placed upon a slough, at present stagnant, others
over vaults [sewerlike structures], they may soon become offensive and a
source of disease." In doing so, Alexander described the problem created by
Foster's Pond, the body of water inside the camp that ran parallel to the
Chemung River and remained stagnant most of the time. Lieutenant
Colonel Alexander proposed "suitable drainage" of the pond to remedy a
potentially dangerous sanitary problem.

He next reported that he requested Lieutenant Colonel Eastman to
send Hoffman's office a full report of the situation and to submit "at the
same time a plan of the camp that all might be readily understood." Alexander then informed Hoffman that the camp's barracks facilities could accommodate 5,000 prisoners (this is 1,000 more than Eastman's original
estimate). His report next cited that possibly 5,000 more prisoners could be
quartered in tents. The possibility of 5,000 men in tents should have alerted
the War Department; alas, it did not. And, in recording a lack of medical
facilities, Alexander called for the construction of a 300-bed hospital inside
the camp. In conclusion, he emphasized the absence of a medical staff, an
unsuitable diet for the sick, a paucity of blankets and bedsacks, and the need
of a laundry.[37]

Enclosed with his letter, Alexander included an official inspection form
which in part said that the drinking water was "abundant, good, healthy."
Condition of the barracks, including "heating, cleansing, ventilation," was
good. Rations were good, but clothing was "fair, deficient in blouses, pants,
blankets, shirts, bootees [socks]." The condition of the sick was "bad" and
the principal cause of illness was diarrhea. And the lieutenant colonel concluded that the "morale, sanitary condition, personal cleanliness" of the
Confederates was "good, for prisoners."[38]

Alexander's report is at best a mixed review. He pointed to the unsanitary conditions created by the pond, and he called for an immediate remedy—suitable drainage. He alerted Colonel Hoffman to the lack of hospital facilities. An overworked doctor, William Wey, assigned to the care of Union soldiers in another part of town, was, in his one-a-day visits, being assisted by a medical cadet who was far from adequate. The failure to provide a chief surgeon and staff for the camp, along with the shortage of blankets, bedsacks, and certain items of clothing, directed attention to the prison camp's serious inadequacies.

Thus, on the ninth day of the camp's existence, Colonel Hoffman had been notified of the potential of Foster's Pond for posing a serious sanitation problem—and he had been told that proper drainage would correct the situation. With more prisoners on their way to Elmira, the pond loomed as a dangerous hazard to the health of the camp. Also, as of July 14, Hoffman was now on notice that the prison camp's medical facilities were all but nonexistent.

Significantly, Lieutenant Colonel Alexander's report did not question, and perhaps accepted, the idea that 10,000 prisoners of war could be quartered in Barracks No. 3. Although he did not explain his failure to recommend to the War Department that additional quarters be constructed, it is possible that Lieutenant Colonel Eastman may have assured Alexander that this would eventually be accomplished.

As we have seen, Alexander's report also affirmed that the drinking water was "abundant, good, healthy." The abundance of the water supply was never in question, but the belief that it was good and healthy would eventually prove to be mistaken. By October nine wells inside the camp would be drilled to depths that ranged from 15 to 22 feet. A high water table and a continued neglect of the pond's unsanitary condition would culminate in fatal results. Proper drainage of the pond was, unfortunately, not viewed as a priority at that time.

The request to remedy the problem that Foster's Pond presented in July 1864 would have to come from Elmira's commanding officer. For some reason Eastman did not address this problem until the middle of August. Approval of a plan to correct this condition would have to emanate from Secretary Stanton, and, even when the War Department was warned of the need for drainage, approval would not come soon enough. Indeed, the lethal result would be a contaminated body of water that poisoned the camp's drinking water. And to the survivors of Elmira, Foster's Pond would forever remain a symbol of death that at times took on metaphorical dimensions.

On the morning of July 15 the *Advertiser* undramatically noted: "Five hundred more rebel prisoners are expected to arrive this morning, or at least were announced on their way here this evening."[39] The train, carrying an actual number of 833 Confederate prisoners of war, was coming from Jersey City and was scheduled to eventually arrive at Elmira's railroad depot. This was to be the final leg of a journey that began at Point Lookout on July 12 when the prisoners of war boarded a steamer destined for New York City. The steamer arrived in New York at three o'clock in the afternoon on Thursday, July 14. The following morning at six o'clock the prisoner-of-war train, consisting of three boxcars and twelve coaches, began its long journey to Elmira.

At one o'clock in the afternoon, by now four hours behind schedule, the train reached Port Jervis, a town whose unique geographic location touches the states of New York, New Jersey, and Pennsylvania. At Port Jervis the train took on a supply of fuel and water, and shortly after two o'clock began a stretch of its journey through the rugged terrain of northeastern Pennsylvania. Averaging twenty miles per hour, the train was expected to arrive in Elmira ten to twelve hours behind schedule. The first twenty-three miles of the journey, running along the Delaware River west of Port Jervis, cut through the Pocono Mountains on a single track of the Erie Railroad. A series of sharp curves made this segment of the trip particularly treacherous, for often these curves limited the vision of the engineer.

About fifty minutes after the slow-moving train left Port Jervis it passed through Shohola, Pennsylvania, a town nineteen miles farther west. The Shohola stationmaster signaled that all was clear through to the end of the single-track segment of the run. But all was not clear. A coal train made up of fifty cars had been cleared at Lackawaxen Junction, Pennsylvania, the western end of the single-track section, to steam eastward to Port Jervis. It was now on a collision course with a train carrying a crew of four and a human cargo of 833 Confederates and 122 Union soldiers.

The system of running trains on a single track with the aid of telegraphed messages that constantly updated the status of traffic over that 23-mile stretch worked well—if accurately executed. But the telegrapher at Lackawaxen Junction, one Douglas "Duff" Kent, was suffering from the previous evening of excessive drinking. Kent slumped over his desk as the telegraph machine produced a steady drumbeat of clatter that filled the small, warm room. When asked if the track was clear to Shohola, Kent responded that all westbound trains had passed and the track was now clear for the eastbound coal train. Kent had been ordered to detain all trains at Lackawaxen Junction until the prisoner-of-war train had safely negotiated the single-track segment. "At 2:45," according to one account, "the telegraph operator at Shohola signaled Kent that the troop train was passing by, heading west, and in that instant disaster became inevitable."[40]

West of Shohola, a railroad section hand described the prisoner-of-war train as it passed him: "It was a fine summer day and we were working on the track about a mile or so above Shohola. I saw the prisoner train go by. It was filled with gray-coated men, while on the platforms of the cars stood the Union guards."[41] Just minutes later, at 2:50 P.M., at a place called King and Fuller's Cut, the two trains came together in a collision that was eerily muffled by the sharply rising mountains on both sides of the railroad track. The engineer and conductor of the coal train were the only survivors of either railroad crew. They jumped from the cab of the engine just before the crash.

Almost all loss of life on the Elmira-bound train occurred in the first three boxcars. Of the thirty-seven men in the first car, only one survived. Although there were many injuries in the cars at the rear of the prisoner-of-war train, no one was killed. In the confusion, five Confederates managed to scramble to safety and escape into the rugged recesses of the Pocono Mountains. They were never heard from again.

The macabre site led one newspaper to compare the scene to "tales of blood, scenes of slaughter, and the accumulated horrors of the battle-field . . . [brought] to us, face to face, amid the quiet of civil life." The reporter noted that "above all, the fearful groans and heart rending cries of the injured and expiring will never be forgotten. Some of the corpses were shockingly mutilated, heads completely crushed, bodies transfixed, impaled on timbers or iron rods, or smashed between the colliding beams, while one man was discovered dead, sitting on the top of the upturned tender, in grotesque and ghastly mockery of the scene around him."[42]

Relief crews dispatched from Port Jervis found some Confederate dead mangled beyond recognition and others placed in orderly rows alongside the railroad track. The bodies of Union guards were wrapped in blankets and placed at the edge of a nearby field. The rescue efforts, led by Capt. Morris H. Church of the 11th Regiment Veteran Reserve Corps, accounted for forty dead Confederate prisoners and fourteen dead Union guards. Captain Church, in charge of the 121-man guard detail that had brought the prisoners from Point Lookout, feverishly directed the grim operation. Within a matter of days, three more guards and eight more prisoners would die.

Railroaders and prisoners of war who survived the accident dug a trench (76 feet long, 8 feet wide, and 6 feet deep) alongside the railroad track. Crude pine coffins were cobbled together, and what amounted to a mass grave was filled in and marked as accurately as possible. The remains of Confederate prisoners of war were placed four to a single coffin, while each dead Union guard was buried in his own coffin. This grave, between the track and the Delaware River, would remain until 1911 when the bodies were exhumed and brought to Elmira, where a large single memorial stone (known as the "Shohola Monument") listing the names of the dead marks their present resting place in the Woodlawn National Cemetery at Elmira.

The chaos and shock that followed the collision made identification of the dead a task that ranged from difficult to virtually impossible. Captain Church, filing his official report a week after the accident, alluded to this in saying that a great number of the dead Confederates "were so disfigured that it was impossible to recognize them, and five escaping whose names are unknown, I am unable to give a correct list of killed."[43] One writer, relating to the five unidentified escapees, has concluded that "it is highly possible that some of the names of the Shohola Monument are those of the escapees; while some of the rebels who were killed were listed as having escaped."[44]

The track was opened the next morning and at eleven o'clock Captain Church ordered prisoners and guards, including most of the wounded, to board a replacement train. This train stopped for fuel and water at Deposit, New York, where a Binghamton, New York, newspaperman conversed with several of the prisoners. While in the Deposit depot, the reporter observed that "an old farmer gave to the inmates of one car a very appropriate harangue, advising them to take the oath of allegiance, and come and live among us." The farmer assured "them that there was plenty to do, and good wages to be had; and they would fare as well as the farmer's family did, and be respected, if they only behaved well—as that was all the qualification necessary to secure respect at the north."[45]

The reporter conversed with the prisoners during the ride from Deposit to Binghamton, and, in an account that most likely reflected the divided psyche of the Confederate Army at that stage of the war, he wrote: "Some of them, in conversation, exhibited considerable braggadocio, say they were very anxious to get back to fight again; others expressed them-

The Shohola monument in the Confederate section of Elmira's national cemetery marks the common grave of the Union soldiers and Confederate prisoners of war who were killed in a train accident on July 16, 1864, near Shohola, Pennsylvania. The remains of the Shohola dead were brought to Elmira in 1911.

BRENT MOORE

selves as tired of the war—said they went into it reluctantly, and because they had to, and would like to have leaders in front, and they stand behind them." The journalist went on to say that the Confederates "were very poorly clad," and "the average was not much inferior to our own men, except as to intelligence; in this they were deficient."[46]

The train, numbering twenty cars, rolled on to Binghamton and then to the stops between that city and Elmira. At the different stations along the way people gathered to converse with the prisoners and give them ice water, crackers, sandwiches, and tobacco. The arrival of the survivors in Elmira at 9:30 Saturday evening instantly turned the railroad depot into a grisly scene of critically injured human beings. A large crowd of citizens and soldiers, some who had gathered at the train station hours before arrival time, did what it could to comfort the injured.

There was some evidence of moral support for the prisoners that night, and the actions of one sympathizer clearly disturbed the editor of the *Adver-tiser,* who noted that "one of their [the arriving survivors of Shohola] sym-pathizers told them to cheer up, they had plenty of friends, and proceeded to console them in the most approved copperhead language at his com-mand. The officer in command of the guard, happening to hear him, ordered some of his men to arrest the traitor and put him where he belonged. We hope the order was obeyed."[47]

The Confederates able to walk were removed first and were ordered to form several lines, with guards on every side, in the street that ran parallel to train station. Some of them, with haunting visions of what had happened at King and Fuller's Cut, were visibly shaken. As they stood in shadowy clus-ters awaiting orders to march to the prison camp, the flickering street lamps seemed to lend a ghostly air to the grim scene. After several delays, they finally trudged off to Barracks No. 3 where they received a warm meal. Lieutenant Colonel Eastman and Surgeon William Wey, the Union surgeon assigned to Barracks No. 1, then saw to it that the injured, eighty-five in number, were placed on baggage wagons that contained litterings of hay.

A call went out for lint, bandages, and clothing. Through the night seven men with fractured thighs and five men with fractured legs were given special attention. One newspaper account stated that "seven or eight of them [were] cases requiring amputation, which could not be performed at Shohola."[48] This being the conventional medical procedure of the day, it is probable that more than seven or eight amputations were carried out that night.

At midnight, a Confederate prisoner and hospital clerk was among those called to work through the night with the Shohola wounded. "Many of them were in horrible condition," he jotted in his prison diary, "and when I went to the hospital the following Monday I found the wounds of many still undressed, even the blood not washed from their limbs." He went on to note that the *Advertiser,* "the administration paper in Elmira, of this morning [Monday, July 18], proclaims to the world that the poor fellows were humanely cared for!"[49]

Several newspapers angrily demanded that the Erie Railroad come forth with a satisfactory explanation of what happened. In going a step fur-ther, the *New York Tribune* claimed: "All the blame seems to be traced to the telegraph operator [Duff Kent]." Discordant residents of the Shohola area revealed to the *Tribune* that Duff Kent "was intoxicated the night before the accident, and it was nothing unusual for him to be in that condition when assuming his post of duty."[50]

A local judge conducted an inquest in Shohola the day following the accident, questioning Duff Kent and others. On the same day, in an inexplicable turn of events, everyone involved in the accident was exonerated. To the astonishment of Shohola's residents, exoneration was granted despite persistent newspaper reports that Kent was addicted to alcohol. That night Duff Kent attended a dance in the nearby village of Hawley, Pennsylvania. The following day, with an incensed public calling for justice, Kent left the area and was never heard from again. To the citizens of Shohola and surrounding communities, the judge's exoneration of Duff Kent would forever remain a mystery.

Captain Church submitted his report of the accident to Lieutenant Colonel Eastman who in turn forwarded it to Colonel Hoffman on July 26. The report was then sent on to the secretary of war with an endorsement from the commissary general of prisoners. In his endorsement, Hoffman related to Stanton that there was misconduct on the part of one of the telegraphic operators. He then informed Stanton that the guilty party had immediately left the area.[51] No official inquiry of the Shohola accident was ever made. Thus, in what was one of the worst train wrecks in the history of American railroads, no one would ever be brought to justice through the judicial system.

On Tuesday evening, July 19, in the wake of the Shohola disaster, Col. William Hoffman arrived by train in Elmira and registered at the Brainard House. That evening he dined with his old U.S. Military Academy classmate, Seth Eastman. In the course of their dinner conversation the two veteran officers perhaps discussed the wartime fortunes of another of their West Point classmates—Robert E. Lee. The following morning Hoffman wired his Washington office: "Send the officers at Old Capitol to Fort Delaware. Enlisted men to this Depot by via [*sic*] Harrisburg."[52]

Next, he and Eastman—reunited briefly on an extremely hot July day—set out to inspect the Confederates' accommodations at Barracks No. 3, where two of the prisoners injured at Shohola died on Monday, July 18. As Hoffman toured the prison camp, the *Advertiser* carried a short paragraph stating that 3,000 more prisoners from Point Lookout would arrive in Elmira shortly to join the 1,900 already incarcerated in Barracks No. 3.[53] The commissary general of prisoners now observed firsthand that which he had been told earlier by Lieutenant Colonel Eastman and Lieutenant

Colonel Alexander: that the prison camp lacked a hospital, a chief surgeon, and a staff of surgeons. Hoffman witnessed on that day the inability of those on hand to cope with the over eighty injured prisoners from Shohola. Indeed, four weeks and five days would pass before a chief surgeon would report for duty at the camp.

It also must be noted that on the day of Colonel Hoffman's visit there was no evidence that Lieutenant Colonel Alexander's observations of poor food for hospital patients and a shortage of clothing and blankets had been addressed. And, if anything, Foster's Pond was worse than it was nine days before when Alexander called for "suitable drainage." Also, the commissary general of prisoners saw barracks that could accommodate no more than 4,000 men—this on a site where he said 10,000 prisoners of war would be quartered. This refusal to acknowledge the camp's actual limitations did not augur well for the Confederates in the months ahead.

Nevertheless, Colonel Hoffman was extremely satisfied with his tour of the camp. He left Elmira on an evening train. "Col. Hoffman," the *Advertiser* reported the following morning, "spent the day yesterday in examining into the condition of those at Barracks No. 3. He professed himself highly pleased with the accommodations and arrangements which have been devised for their comfort."[54] There is no record showing that Hoffman ever returned to Elmira.

What Hoffman saw in Elmira was far more potentially explosive than what Lieutenant Colonel Alexander saw nine days earlier. The Shohola wounded, with seven more arriving on July 22, must have cast a sobering pall over the camp. Yet Colonel Hoffman remained "highly pleased with the accommodations and arrangements." This positive assessment was obviously put forth for public consumption. Indeed, his position was a response to the dictates of political reality. Even political reality, however, could not have prevented an experienced observer from seeing that conditions in this camp were potentially dangerous. A seasoned military officer such as Colonel Hoffman must clearly have recognized in this prison camp a situation where adequate care was nonexistent.

And, in a moment of sober reflection, editor Charles Fairman's July 22 observation served, perhaps unwittingly, as a harbinger of things to come. In citing that a detachment of Confederates was to be transferred from Washington, D.C., to Elmira, he informed his readers: "We understand that our authorities have so many prisoners on hand, it is quite a difficult matter to make a proper disposition of them."[55]

CHAPTER 3

"They Amount to No More than Dead Men"

"As we marched through the streets of Elmira," Sgt. Berry Benson of McGowan's South Carolina Brigade recollected many years later, "two by two, ragged, dirty faces pinched with hunger, the people came out on the sidewalks to see Lee's soldiers going to prison. Had I seen any of the men, I know I would have hated them, but I had eyes only for the pretty girls."[1] Benson was among the 662 prisoners who arrived in Elmira on July 24 from Washington's Old Capitol Prison. Their journey by train to Baltimore and then through Pennsylvania by way of Harrisburg and Williamsport to Elmira was far less arduous than the boat trip from Point Lookout to New York City and on to Elmira by way of the Erie Railroad.

Another July arrival, Anthony M. Keiley, a newspaper editor in Petersburg, Virginia, at the time of his capture in May and a former lieutenant with the 12th Virginia, was one of only a handful of Confederate officers received in the camp. Keiley was a short, erudite, engaging man who, like the vast majority of Elmira's prisoners of war, came by sea from Point Lookout to New York City—a trip that took well over fifty hours to complete. "The man who first invented going to sea," he recalled in his colorful memoirs of the war, "was an infidel and a fool." Keiley described the harrowing journey in a vessel that "was such a crazy and unseaworthy craft, that in the event of a storm there was little prospect of our ever seeing land

Sgt. Berry Benson of McGowan's South Carolina Brigade. Benson survived Elmira and went on to become a noted authority in the business accounting field. CHEMUNG COUNTY HISTORICAL SOCIETY

again." While on the boat, the Confederates' "only food was one ration of bread and a couple of ounces of adipose [fatty meat]."[2]

Another early arrival in Elmira was Walter D. Addison, an officer in Breathed's Battery of Stuart's Horse Artillery. In recalling his journey from Point Lookout, Addison (another of the few Confederate officers to be incarcerated in Elmira) claimed that the "men remained crowded together like sheep for many days . . . in the sweltering heat of July." And, with more than a touch of bitter irony, he concluded that the journey by sea "was on a par with the condition of the Yankee slave ships with a cargo of human souls purchased with a cargo of Boston rum."[3]

The long echo of the harrowing trip from Point Lookout to Elmira carried well into the twentieth century when in 1940 James Huffman, perhaps the last living survivor of the prison camp, published his wartime memoir. Huffman, a member of the 10th Virginia, saw action at the first and second battles of Bull Run, Chancellorsville, Gettysburg, and Fredericksburg before being captured in May 1864 at Spotsylvania. Late in his life, in a personal narrative of the Civil War years, he reflected on being "driven on a big vessel, like any other livestock." He spent two days and a night on a ship "so crowded we did not have room to stretch out to sleep, but sat upright and snoozed a little."[4]

Wilbur W. Grambling, captured on May 6, 1864, while serving with the 5th Florida during the Wilderness campaign, was sent to Elmira and marched through the streets of the town to the prison the same day as did Berry Benson. "About 600 more prisoners," Grambling recorded in his prison diary on July 28, "came in this morning from Point Lookout. . . . They are looking bad. Some so poor they look like it is hard for them to navigate."[5] That day Grambling had observed men who were suffering from dehydration.

On August 1 the camp census officially listed the transfer of 4,424 prisoners of war to Elmira. Eleven had died and two had escaped.[6] In a matter of three weeks and four days 4,411 Confederates were quartered in a 32-acre area that still lacked proper hospital facilities, a chief surgeon, and a medical staff. This overwhelming number of prisoners dictated the need for lighting at night, and that need was answered when forty-one kerosene lamps with large reflectors attached were put in place on July 26. A lamp was hung against the fence inside between every sentry box around the entire circumference of the grounds. The bright reflection from the lamps aided the guards in the detection of any movement inside the camp during the night watches.

As the number of prisoners increased through the hot, dry days of July, so did unsubstantiated accounts of unrest inside the camp. Stories of planned escapes circulated about town. On July 13 the *Advertiser* related to a rumor making its way through the community that a disturbance had occurred among the Confederates. The following day the newspaper informed its readers that all was quiet inside the prison camp. The following week Elmirans were assured that there "is no truth to the flying rumor about town yesterday [July 22] as to the shooting of a rebel at Barracks No. 3."[7]

On Saturday noon, July 30, 820 Confederate prisoners of war arrived in Elmira from Point Lookout, the largest contingent to date to be transported to Elmira. A column of Confederates four deep extended almost a quarter of a mile—the entire length of Railroad Street. The great number of captives, arriving on a single day, attracted a large number of Elmirans who lined the streets to observe the long, slow march to Barracks No. 3.

The following night a serious disturbance did take place inside the camp. According to a local newspaper, a number of prisoners (a precise figure is not mentioned) concocted a plot to raid the guardhouse and procure a number of shovels and picks. They then hoped to demolish the fence and liberate themselves from the camp.[8] The Confederates' plan, scheduled to be activated at eleven o'clock that evening, was discovered and put down by Union guard patrols inside the camp. In the aftermath, several prisoners prowled about the grounds, and one, A. P. Potts of the 38th Georgia, was shot. According to members of the Union guard detail, Potts was ordered to halt and, not heeding the order, was shot in the side. The bullet was removed and the prisoner lived.[9]

In reporting on the unrest in Elmira, the New York Evening Express claimed: "For some time past there has been a large number of Rebels imprisoned at the Federal Barracks in Elmira, and it is stated that they have recently become more defiant than usual, and that they would probably make an attempt at escape. The force at the Barracks was decreed insufficient to keep them in order."[10]

Stating that the 820 prisoners who had arrived July 30 were inciting the unrest, the New York Evening Post described the new arrivals "as [being in] almost desperate and turbulent spirits" and "difficult to control." The Post further claimed that Lieutenant Colonel Eastman was compelled to request two or three more regiments of militia from the Department of the East, New York City.[11] A day later the Post reported that "there was much excitement among the rebels and also among the inhabitants of Elmira . . . there will probably be no [further] difficulty, though the prisoners are numerous, and none of them are well disposed towards their keepers."[12]

Editor Charles Fairman angrily stood athwart the published reports of the Express and the Post when he heatedly stated that there "was no real disturbance, yet New York [newspapers] increased it to hideous proportions." And, in an earlier edition, Fairman emphatically informed his readers that the "'rebs' will not probably find our authorities 'napping.' If they see fit to try their hand again, it may be to their personal sorrow."[13]

There are no substantial newspaper accounts or official military reports as to the cause of the unrest on the night of July 31 inside Barracks No. 3. The New York Evening Post's view that the prisoners who arrived on July 30

A member of a contingent of black troops guards a Confederate prisoner of war. Some 200 members of the U.S. 20th Colored Troops were assigned to Elmira to serve as part of the prison's guard detail.
CHEMUNG COUNTY HISTORICAL SOCIETY

were in "desperate and turbulent spirits" and "difficult to control" may well account for it. Or the insufferable July heat may have played on the nerves of the crowded inhabitants of the 32-acre camp. On August 1, a local newspaper complained: "The brazen heat of summer seems to be upon us in all its fierceness."[14]

Perhaps a more plausible reason lies in the fact that 30 of the 200 drafted colored troops assigned to Elmira were detailed at that time as a patrol guard inside the prison camp.[15] In reporting the incident, one newspaper account stated: "A rebel was shot, as alleged, but was not mortally injured, and it seems that the negro guardsman warned the prisoner before he fired."[16] If this was the case, Confederate resentment of the presence of black guards could very well have been the source of the trouble.

It was, indeed, no secret that Southern prisoners adamantly opposed being guarded by black Union troops, as demonstrated in postwar memoirs, essays, magazine articles, and newspaper interviews. James Huffman was just one of thousands of Confederate prisoners who recounted his resentment of black Union troops serving as prison guards. At Point Lookout, prior to his being transferred to Elmira, he first had to cope with the "bitter pill . . . [of] the Negro guards." And Huffman heard for the first time a phrase that became a quasi-universal cry of victory through the final two years of the Civil War for black Union soldiers: "The bottom rail on top now."[17]

Lieutenant Colonel Eastman ordered a three-man board of officers to convene at Barracks No. 3 on August 4 to determine the facts of the incident of July 31. After hearing testimony from three Union soldiers, it was determined that Granville Garland (the sentinel who wounded A. P. Potts) "was justified in firing on the prisoner." Eastman, in his report to Colonel Hoffman, stated that Potts "was ordered three times to halt and did not obey the order. On that night the sentinels were very vigilant, and all the troops under arms in anticipation of a break-out by a portion of the prisoners." The investigation revealed that the same sentinel had fired a shot at a prisoner and missed before "wounding [Potts] slightly with a buckshot."[18]

In the aftermath of the incident, Eastman informed a local newspaper that he had at his command 1,300 soldiers—800 of them veterans of combat—who "are ready at a moment's notice to quell any disturbance that may take place at Barracks No. 3."[19] Three days later Eastman ordered that the only officers or enlisted men permitted within the enclosure of the camp are those who were at that specific time assigned to guard duty.[20] Twelve days later the Elmira post commander issued the following order: "No discharge of fire-arms except in performance of duty will be permitted within the limits of Camp Chemung [Barracks No. 3]."[21]

Tightened security notwithstanding, the U.S. Christian Commission was granted permission to enter the camp in order to distribute large numbers of Bibles, religious books, and newspapers to the prisoners. And, after some discussion, Eastman approved the admittance to the camp of local clergymen for the purpose of conducting Sunday services.

The Reverend Thomas K. Beecher of The Park Church, the first clergyman to be allowed inside the prison, conducted the initial religious service for the prisoners at five o'clock on Sunday afternoon July 24. "They [the prisoners] turned out in full force," reported the *Advertiser,* "and listened attentively and respectfully to all he [Beecher] had to say."[22] The Reverend Beecher and Father Martin Kavanaugh, pastor of Elmira's St. Peter and Paul's Roman Catholic Church, proved to be the two most popular men of the cloth among the prisoners. In those days of pronounced social tension between Protestants and Catholics, a warm bond of friendship existed between Beecher and Kavanaugh.

Beecher, who had already served as the chaplain for the 141st New York, remains to this day Elmira's most storied religious figure. He was one of thirteen children of the Reverend Lyman Beecher—the noted Presbyterian clergyman, founder of the *Connecticut Observer,* president of the Lane Theological Seminary in Cincinnati, and champion of liberal causes.

Thomas K. Beecher's half brother was the Reverend Henry Ward Beecher, the abolitionist who gained national fame in 1856 by shipping boxes of Sharps Rifles to free staters in the Kansas Territory during the days of "Bleeding Kansas." He argued that the rifles were a stronger force than the moral arguments of the Bible. Thus, the term "Beecher's Bibles." Catharine Beecher, Thomas's half sister and the oldest of Lyman Beecher's children, made her mark as a reformer who wrote, lectured, and promoted liberal education for women. In 1832 she founded the Western Female Institute. Another half sister was the most famous member of this remarkable family—Harriet Beecher Stowe, the author of *Uncle Tom's Cabin.*

A colorful, complex, controversial man, Thomas K. Beecher was (according to some local authorities) an abolitionist who did not preach about abolitionism, and a drinker who preached temperance. An examination of local history points to evidence of Beecher being active in Elmira's underground railroad. Yet, according to his biographer, Beecher denounced "abolitionists with particular venom."[23] Whatever his position was on social issues, Thomas K. Beecher was a man who viewed Elmira's Confederate prisoners of war with great compassion.

Father Kavanaugh, on the other hand, was a reserved, quiet, undemonstrative man of faith. He at first experienced some trouble in gaining access to the camp on weekdays in order to hear confessions. His perseverance prevailed and the relatively small group of Roman Catholics (one estimate places the number at 242) in the camp were allowed to attend mass and receive the sacraments of Penance and the Holy Eucharist. Writing on the 100th anniversary of the camp's existence, Father Robert F. McNamara—the official historian for the Roman Catholic Diocese of Rochester, New York—described Kavanaugh as "a person of strong fiber in an emergency . . . [who] did not flinch when duty called him to administer the sacraments to men in the contagious [smallpox] ward."[24] Prisoner Anthony

Keiley's memoirs describe Father Kavanaugh's sermon as "a Christian discourse" as opposed to that of a Reverend Bainbridge, "a freedom shrieker [whose] speech was one long insult to the prisoners."[25]

Roman Catholic bishop John Timon of Buffalo (at that time Elmira was part of the Buffalo Diocese), at the request of Father Kavanaugh, visited the prison camp on the first Sunday of September. "Visit rebel Prisoners. . . . Pray and preach" is part of the account the bishop entered in his diary. Bishop Timon was a strong Union man who nevertheless maintained a sympathetic view of Elmira's Confederate prisoners of war. His sympathy and compassion can be traced to his life as a missionary priest in Missouri and Texas.[26]

Prior to his visit to Elmira, Bishop Timon requested that Father Kavanaugh be granted permission to serve as the prison camp's chaplain. On August 23 Bishop Timon and Father Kavanaugh were notified that the War Department had rejected the request on the grounds "that Elmira was not a chaplain post, and a selection for the position of chaplain cannot therefore be made."[27] The Sunday of Timon's visit was unique in that he was one of two bishops to preach inside the camp on that day. Later in the day Bishop Matthew Simpson, the Methodist bishop of Syracuse, addressed the prisoners of war.

Other aspects of the prison camp's management would not proceed as well as did the religious services. Foster's Pond, the stagnant body of water that ran parallel to the Chemung River and extended from the eastern border of the camp to within five feet of the fence on the west side of the enclosure, would come to the attention of the *Advertiser* for the first time on July 26 when it informed its readers that conditions were "to be improved by letting in a running stream of water through a ditch dug to the river." This, the newspaper stated, would "relieve a deleterious miasma that might be otherwise unhealthful."[28]

Presumably, the *Advertiser* procured this information from Lieutenant Colonel Eastman. Yet the military had no specific plan of action at that time to remedy the situation. The only previous written reference to the pond was Lieutenant Colonel Alexander's report of July 14, which stated that Foster's Pond "may become offensive and a source of disease" and that "suitable drainage" was the solution. In his correspondence with Washington through the remainder of July, Eastman alluded neither to the report nor to the condition of the pond.

Colonel Hoffman, aware of Alexander's July 14 assessment, also remained silent in regard to this matter. Coupled with his physical presence in Elmira on July 20, Hoffman's silence only lends to the charge of neglect at a time when over 4,000 prisoners were confined at Elmira by late July. It was, indeed, at this crucial juncture when none of the decision makers (Secretary of War Stanton, Hoffman, and Eastman) took any action at a time when the pond was increasingly becoming a source of deadly disease. Their failure to address the issue during the early stages of the camp would prove to be a fateful and fatal mistake.

Only the Department of War had the authority to respond to this problem. Yet a means of lessening the danger of epidemics did exist, one that was not bound by the simple certitude and blind absoluteness of the military. Building materials were available and prison labor was abundant. The War Department, however, ignored the problem during the crucial month of July. Many Confederate survivors of the prison camp would later conclude that Secretary Stanton simply wished to exact retribution.

Still, on July 27 a local newspaper stated that the construction of a new prison hospital to be made up of six wards (35 feet by 136 feet by 12 feet) had begun. It would be larger than the 400-bed Union hospital in the west part of town. Prison labor would be used, with those Confederates working on the project earning extra rations and five cents a day.[29] Unfortunately, only four of the hospital wards were finished and in working order by September 1. Three more medical wards would eventually be completed, each the same size as the original four. Hospital construction commenced none too soon, for an outbreak of measles in the now crowded camp would mark the last days of July.

It was now August 1 and the prison camp still lacked a chief surgeon and medical staff. This matter is yet another in a series of questions that defenders of the camp's integrity have difficulty explaining. Army red tape and an overworked War Department's bureaucracy is an argument supported by those who say the camp was not a place of retaliation. Critics say it was by design; delay can be traced to the invisible hand of the secretary of war.

On July 29, 1864, three weeks and two days after the first Confederates arrived in Elmira, the Department of War ordered Maj. Eugene F. Sanger to assume the position of chief surgeon at Barracks No. 3. At that time Sanger had been awaiting orders for assignment in Baltimore. He reported by letter to Colonel Hoffman and in person to Surgeon Charles McDougall, U.S. Army, Medical Director, Department of the East (New York City).[30] On August 6, eight days after receiving his orders, Sanger reported for duty to Lieutenant Colonel Eastman. Thus, a full four weeks and three days after the prison camp's opening, a chief surgeon was assigned to administer Elmira's prisoners of war. There is no recorded explanation as to why it took a month to have a chief surgeon in place at Barracks No. 3.

Upon his arrival in Elmira, Sanger—like many other officers—had his wife and children join him at his new post. His journey to Elmira would initiate the tenure of the most controversial Union officer to serve during the time of the Elmira Civil War prison camp. Born on October 18, 1829, in Waterville, Maine, Eugene Francis Sanger was a spare, sardonic, dour New Englander of Dutch ancestry. The second of four children, he was the oldest son of Zebulon and Charlotte Wayne Sanger. His mother was a distant relative of Gen. Anthony Wayne of Revolutionary War fame. Zebulon Sanger's roots went back several generations to Framingham, Massachusetts. Extremely intelligent, Eugene F. Sanger completed preparation for college in Waterville schools. He went on to study three years at Waterville College (now Colby College) and then transferred to Dartmouth College, where he graduated in 1849.

During the winter of 1849–1850, Sanger served as a tutor in the family of Lawrence B. Washington on the Virginia estate where George Washington was born. He then returned to Maine where he pursued the study of medicine, a subject that was his first love. After taking courses at the medical department at Bowdoin College, he went on to take his degree in medicine in March 1853 at Jefferson Medical College in Philadelphia. Before practicing at the Charity Hospital in New York City in late 1853, Sanger served briefly as an assistant surgeon at the Marine Hospital in Chelsea, Massachusetts. In the autumn of 1854 he continued his study of medicine in Europe where he "walked the halls" in the renowned hospitals of Edinburgh, London, and Paris. Returning to Maine in May 1855, Sanger established a medical practice first in the town of Ellsworth before moving two years later to Bangor where he remained (with the exception of the Civil War years) for the rest of his life. Throughout his extensive medical career, he was viewed as an exceptional, progressive surgeon of considerable skill.

With the outbreak of the war, Sanger—perhaps moved by his Republican political faith—happily accepted a commission as surgeon of the 6th Maine in June 1861. He served with the regiment first in the Army of the Potomac and then in the Department of the Gulf. In April 1862 Sanger reported to Maj. Gen. Benjamin F. Butler at Ship Island, Mississippi, where he served as a brigade surgeon. Later that month, following the capture of

Maj. Eugene F. Sanger, the prison camp's controversial chief surgeon, went on to a successful postwar career in Bangor, Maine, as an innovative surgeon. MAINE STATE ARCHIVES

New Orleans, he became the medical purveyor of the Department of the Gulf and surgeon in charge of St. James Hospital in that city. He next became medical director of the defenses of New Orleans, and in the spring of 1863 he was appointed surgeon in chief of Maj. Gen. William Tecumseh Sherman's division.

It was during the siege of Port Hudson, Louisiana, on the Mississippi River in May and June 1863 that Sanger received a wound that resulted in the loss of part of a leg just below the knee. Despite the seriousness of his wound, he continued to serve as medical director of the hospitals in Natchez, Mississippi, and the hospital steamers on the Mississippi River. In July 1864 Major Sanger was briefly assigned to serve as the surgeon in charge of the Union military hospital at Annapolis Junction, Maryland, near Washington, D.C. During the last week of July he was relieved of that position and awaited further orders in Baltimore.[31]

Possessing none of the martial bearing that often characterizes military persona, Major Sanger was a small, wiry man with a receding hairline and a graying goatee. Often curt and inconsiderate of others, he was a man of icy demeanor who projected a rock-hard confidence in the rightness of his views. At times this would get him into trouble with his superior officers. In a series of revealing letters to Maine's governor Israel Washburn, the prickly Sanger frequently expressed dissatisfaction with his assigned duties, his fellow surgeons, and his superior officers. In an 1861 letter to Washburn, Sanger emphatically demanded the dismissal of a fellow regimental surgeon. In accusing the surgeon of drunkenness, Major Sanger angrily proclaimed: "I insist that you shall either make an effort to have him dismissed, or I shall resign and assign through the papers my reason in self-justification."[32]

On September 21 Sanger informed Governor Washburn that he (Sanger) had "never received an answer to but one of my letters since I first became connected with the military. I don't know why you should neglect the medical department of the 6th." And, in a matter that remained unexplained, Sanger concluded his letter by stating: "Maj. Pierce attempted one of his famous petitions against my department to the . . . Government & I whipped him so thoroughly that it completely crushed him & satisfied him to mind his own business."[33]

Sanger also displayed a propensity for self-promotion in an October 2 letter to Washburn that claimed: "I am temporarily detailed to act as brigade surgeon of Gen'l Hancock's brigade of which we are a part. If I could get permission from the Secretary [of War] to appear before the

Medical Board, I could possibly secure the position permanently."[34] Seven
weeks later, in yet another letter to Governor Washburn, a still ambitious
Sanger wrote: "Shall I weary your patience & be asking too much if I ask
you to write the Secretary of War stating that Maine has sent out 12 regiments . . . is entitled to three brigade surgeons & ask that I be included
among those to be appointed."[35]

Eleven months later, writing from Fort Jackson, Louisiana, Sanger
informed Governor Washburn that "I really ache to be with the fighting
army." "I want to cultivate my art," he continued, "I want to put in use that
knowledge and experience which I have studied & labored for since I left
college, & for which there seems to be a great demand in the Western &
Eastern Armies."[36]

Sanger's view of the war called for a complete victory for the Union.
"The South," he wrote from Louisiana, "is coming to a realizing sense of
the unity of the North and their determination to put down this rebellion
at all hazards." The Confederacy, Sanger thought, was "beyond the pale and
must submit to the dictates of the victors." And he took comfort in the
assumption that "when the war ceased, all will wheel into line. The Masses
respect power and tamely submit."[37]

Quite remarkably, and by his own hand, Surgeon Sanger presented a
self-portrait that showed a man who was extremely self-centered, self-righteous, vain, vindictive, judgmental, cantankerous, supremely confident in his
ability, condescending of others, lacking in magnanimity, and free of self-
doubt. And now this ill-tempered man, albeit a very good surgeon, would
assume responsibility for the medical care of Elmira's Confederate prisoners
of war.

Major Sanger would be viewed by many as a great source of evil. The
former Confederate officer and newspaper editor Anthony M. Keiley, a
clerk in the prison hospital, remembered Sanger as "a club-footed little
gentleman, with an abnormal head and a snaky look in his eyes." "Sanger
was simply a brute," Keiley wrote a year after the war, "as we found when
we learned the whole truth about him from his own people."[38] Keiley was
only one of many Confederates who condemned Sanger.

Criticism notwithstanding, Major Sanger brought with him to Elmira
an impressive list of medical credentials. He possessed a good, quick mind
with a scholarly bent. He had gained a considerable knowledge of medicine
through his observations in Europe. And, at a time in medical history when
the majority of doctors were not much more than "quacksalvers," Sanger

was a physician of the first order. By dint of hard work, he had compiled an excellent record while holding several important medical posts during his years of service with the Department of the Gulf. Valor was also part of Sanger's military tenure, for after losing part of a leg during the siege of Port Hudson he continued to serve the Union through the duration of the war. At the war's conclusion, he was commissioned to the rank of brevet lieutenant colonel.

This does not condone or excuse the dark side of this man. Like a hobgoblin, it would continue to exist, side by side with his surgical skill and superior knowledge of medicine, through the remainder of his life. When he died in July 1897 his last will and testament stated that his daughter, Mary Charlotte Sanger, and his son, Sabine Pond Sanger, "have both deeply wronged and disobeyed me, I give and bequeath to each of them the sum of one dollar and no more." His second wife, Mary Robena Treat Sanger, was bequeathed an annual income, provided "the amounts so paid shall not exceed one third part of the net income of said trust estate." His son, Eugene Boutelle Sanger, a doctor and the youngest of three children, was bequeathed the greatest share of money and property. Sanger excluded his first wife from his will "because my divorced wife, Emily Fay Sanger, deserted me and taught my children to dishonor me."[39] If his last will and testament is any indicator, forgiveness was not in Eugene F. Sanger's makeup.

With Major Sanger's arrival in Elmira, the staffing of assistant surgeons began immediately. Within a week five doctors joined Sanger, and by September 10 there were ten assistant surgeons on the camp's medical staff.[40] The quality of the medical staff is unknown, but the general reputation of doctors who served in the Civil War was not good. It is likely that Elmira, with Sanger being the obvious exception, was not an aberration. Medical treatment of sick and wounded soldiers during the Civil War had such a low priority that doctors often were required to serve as musical director of the regimental band. Although a common practice, there is no evidence that this happened in Elmira.

One prisoner would recall that a "copperhead" surgeon was "a competent and faithful officer." This was Surgeon Charles E. Rider of Rochester and a member of the 54th New York. Rider was one of two doctors ordered to report to Sanger on August 8. "The rest of the 'meds,'" according to a prisoner of war who served as a clerk in the prison hospital, "were, in truth, a motley crew in the main, most of them being selected from the impossibility, it would seem, of doing any thing else with them."[41]

Three Confederate doctors were added to the prison's staff by early autumn. This was a common practice in prison camps, both North and South, throughout the war.

In late July Barracks No. 3 was officially designated "Camp Chemung," and on weekends that area (outside the prison fence) was the site of baseball games played between competing Union regiments. Every Friday night a concert was performed by one of the various military bands stationed in Elmira. The cadence inside the prison in July and August was marked by those Confederates who honed their considerable woodworking skills by practicing their craft in the manufacture of chairs and other articles of furniture. Those with artistic skills drew pencil sketches of prison scenes. And, upon receiving permission to have drums and fifes, some of the prisoners took part in their own musical presentations. They were not allowed to play "Dixie" or other Confederate musical pieces.

By mid-August a mess house for Union officers assigned to duty inside the camp was completed outside the fenced area. "A delightful dance," the *Advertiser* proudly announced, "inaugurated the occupancy of the new mess house, on Tuesday evening [August 16] last. We presume similar pleasant entertainments will follow."[42] Other areas of Camp Chemung were also in a state of expansion. With five Union regiments and two companies of artillery assigned outside the fenced area of Barracks No. 3, the area took on the appearance of a tented field. Union regiments prepared their food with fires blazing beneath kettles here and there. The campfires, late on those summer nights, portended ironically a glow of contentment and serenity.

In what was perhaps Elmira's most distasteful moment of buccaneering capitalism, "a man of genius," as one newspaper put it, "who sought his opportunity and was equal to the occasion, suddenly appeared at the camp, and apparently determined that the rebels should make his fortune."[43] In late July he constructed an observatory across from the camp, and citizens were given an opportunity to view the prisoners. "Ten cents admittance is charged," the *Advertiser* proclaimed, "to all who wish to ascend the steps and take a view."[44] Soon a horse-drawn bus began to shuttle sightseers from a downtown hotel to Barracks No. 3.

According to James B. Stamp, a sergeant in the 3rd Alabama, often "the observatory would be crowded, and especially on Sundays."[45] Referring to an "enterprising Yankee at Elmira," a Binghamton newspaper reported that the "proprietor has taken as high as forty dollars per day, as a reward for his enterprise."[46] Anthony M. Keiley noted in his prison diary that "one of the proprietors, who was part of the management of our pen, assured me that the concern paid for itself in two weeks." Keiley wryly added: "Patriotism is spelled with a 'y' at the end of the first syllable up here."[47]

In contrast to Keiley's view, a local newspaper boasted that the observatory "commands a splendid view of the rebel camp with the exposure. We advise all our friends who have not been up there to go at once. It will amply repay the small expense of getting there."[48] Another newspaper stated that the proprietor of the observatory "intends to keep in this tower a powerful glass, by the aid of which visitors can see the vermin which are said to be so plenty [sic] upon the bodies of the prisoners."[49]

Soon construction of a second observatory began. When it was completed in late August, the proprietors placed the following advertisement in the *Advertiser*: "Mr. W. and W. Mears have at considerable expense, erected a new Observatory three stories above the ground, where a fine view of the Rebel Prisoners can be obtained. A clearer view across the different avenues of the enclosure can be seen from this Observatory than from any other position."[50]

The site of the two observatories now took on the rollicking atmosphere of celebration and spectacle. One prisoner wrote in his diary that with the completion of the second observatory "a grand 'sight-seeing-and-sprucebeer' warfare began, which shook Elmira to its uttermost depths."[51] Refreshment stands of all sorts sprang up between the observatories. They took on the look of a "long row of rude wooden booths like those at a fair," a writer would recall three decades later, "or more like those that spring up in a night along a street that is the route to the grounds where a circus tent is to be spread."[52] Ginger cakes, lemonade, peanuts, crackers, beer, and whiskey were among the refreshments offered to the public by eagerly acquisitive entrepreneurs. In addition to the observatories and the refreshment stands, the saloons that lined both sides of Water Street east of the prison camp did a brisk business.

The diary of an individual who visited the observatories would surface three decades later and reveal what was seen in those 1864 summer days:

It was like looking down into an immense bee-hive. There was a constant motion on all sides, but without noise or confusion that could be heard. Groups were standing here and there, formed one minute, broken up the next; some men had built a fire underneath a tree and were baking corn-meal cakes; some one was com-

Looking directly west, a view from the Mears brothers' observatory. To the right is the original observatory and beyond that are three buildings that served as officers' quarters. The white brick Georgian-style structure in the background was at that time the Foster home. Today it serves as a medical arts center. The flagpole (upper left) stands at the main entrance of the prison. Chemung County Historical Society

ing or going every instant to or from every building whose entrance was in sight, and many were seated in the shadow of the trees whittling or fashioning some object, the character of which the distance forbade making out. In the space between the buildings and the fence nearest sat a small circle of men, with one on his feet who seemed to be speaking and making the most violent gestures. When he finished he seated himself in his place in the ring and another rose to go through similar exercises in his turn. A few feet from these men were five men playing cards. In the corner close at hand was a large tent that had a lonesome look. Into it, during the half hour of the visit to the eyrie, came two men five times, bearing each time on a stretcher the dead body of a man covered over with a piece of canvas.[53]

For a brief period the observatories and the refreshment stands rewarded their rapacious owners with handsome profits. During the second week of September the *Advertiser* noted that both observatories were "doing a rushing business."[54] Indeed, to the *Elmira Daily Gazette,* the observatories were the city's finest attraction: the "Upper Observatory [the original observation tower] should be visited by all strangers and citizens. The pictures taken from there will always be remembered with delightful interest. Photograph views of the rebel camp, and surroundings . . . have been taken and can be obtained by the public in a few days."[55]

On September 19, however, the entire enterprise came to an abrupt end. To the dismay of those who had gleefully raked in profits from the observation towers and the refreshment stands, the commissary general of prisoners ordered Capt. John J. Elwell, Elmira's assistant quartermaster, to take possession of the ground occupied by the two observatories.[56] The refreshment stands were quickly dismantled, but it was decided to retain both observatories for military purposes. This did not come as a disappointment to the Confederates, whose resentment of the observatories festered through the duration of the crass enterprise. "I am surprised that Barnum has not taken the prisoners off the hands of Abe," Anthony M. Keiley caustically concluded, "divided them into companies, and carried them in caravans through the country, after the manner of Sesostris, and other antique heroes, turning an honest penny by the show."[57]

The observatories were not the only sources of excitement in Elmira. On August 18, just after a prisoner-of-war train rolled to a stop at the Erie station, two Confederates leaped from the first car in an attempt to escape. As they ran from the train, a guard on the roof of the second car fired several shots that resulted in the killing of one and the wounding of the other.[58] Four days later Lieutenant Colonel Eastman reported that four Union soldiers, all using aliases, had been caught and charged with posing as Confederate prisoners. "These men were captured," Eastman said in his report to the Office of the Department of the East in New York City, "and brought here as Rebel prisoners of war. . . . I do not think these men can be fully convicted unless one of them turns states evidence."[59] Three of the men had been forwarded to the front from Elmira in June with the 97th New York. It was decided to send the four men back to the front.

With the prison census rapidly approaching 6,000, Eastman informed Hoffman on August 7 that Elmira was out of tents for prisoners of war.[60] More tents were forwarded to Elmira on August 9, and three days later Hoffman, aware of the growing prison census in Elmira, informed Eastman that it "is not expected that there will be mess rooms sufficient for all the prisoners to take their meals at once, and unless additional [room] is

During the late summer days of 1864, tents housed over 5,000 Confederates. Some prisoners slept in tents until late December when the last of the winter barracks were completed. Chemung County Historical Society

absolutely necessary no more will be erected."[61] The camp's kitchens and bakeries could prepare food for 1,600 to 1,800 men at a time.

By the end of August, with the camp's enrollment well over 9,000, the lack of sanitation in the prison mess hall became a source of concern. In an undated statement (written in the second week of September), Capt. Bennett F. Munger, a prison camp inspector, concluded: "The causes of the filthy condition of the mess-house were: First, the building is in such constant use it is difficult to keep it tidy; and, second, there was a temporary neglect on the part of the officers in charge."[62] By September 15 over 9,000 prisoners of war were being fed daily in the camp's mess house. This left very little time to thoroughly police the area between meals. It was swept after every meal and hosed down as often as possible.

The Confederates were limited to two meals a day and ate in designated shifts that ran from 6 to 9 A.M. and from 3 to 6 P.M. The mess house, accommodating 700 men at a time, consisted of long chest-high tables, which required the prisoners to eat in a standing position and to complete their meal in a fifteen-minute period. "The men were marched in two ranks," Marcus Toney of the 1st Tennessee would recall, "and separated at the head of the table, making one rank face the other. Each man had a plate and spoon; in the plate was a small piece of light bread, and on the bread a thin ration of salt pork."[63]

Through the summer, fall, winter, and into the spring, the routine was the same. "We went in a trot [to the mess house]," prisoner John King of Virginia recollected more than a half a century later, "canteens, buckets, tin cans, coffee pots rattling, old rags and strings and long unkept hair, dirt and grey backs, cheek bones projecting for there was little of us except skin and bones. . . . Here we went . . . and in crossing ditches some poor fellow frequently fell. We were obliged to leave him struggling to gain his position as our [eating] time was limited."[64]

Although over 9,000 prisoners now occupied the enclosure, the critical stage had already been reached in the middle of August when only 7,700 Confederates were housed in the camp. Eastman had then reported to Washington that "thirty-five hundred [prisoners of war] are quartered in barracks and the remainder in tents." He also stated that "two hospital wards have been erected within the enclosure, each sufficiently large to hold about seventy patients. Another is being erected."[65] Work on the additional hospital ward was being done by the prisoners of war. The *Advertiser* reported on August 22 "that the flat formerly occupied by the old race course has been spread with tents, which are already occupied by a goodly number of the rebs."[66]

Confederates who held jobs within the camp would be considered among the fortunate few. "I have got a position in the kitchen as a waiter," Wilbur Grambling scribbled in his diary, "and have much work to do and get plenty to eat."[67] Describing his job, Grambling wrote: "The way I spend my time. 1st set the table and then clean up afterwards, then 2nd read and knock about until 3 o'clock and 3rd it is dinner, which I have to take an active part in, working after the rest."[68] Yet a job and abundant rations did not prevent Grambling from voicing a yearning for his home in Florida. "I am getting very tired of prison," Grambling noted in a diary entry a little more than a week after his arrival in Elmira, "and am growing more so every day. The thoughts of staying here all the winter and perhaps till the war ends makes the time a great deal longer."[69] The thought of spending the entire winter season incarcerated in Barracks No. 3 must have depressed thousands of Grambling's comrades.

Unbeknownst to Grambling and his fellow Confederates at Elmira, the fate of all Southern prisoners would be sealed in mid-August when Lt.

Gen. Ulysses S. Grant—general-in-chief of the Union armies—made it clear that there would be no prisoner exchange. In a letter to Maj. Gen. Benjamin F. Butler, the Union's commissioner of exchange, Grant would expunge any thought of an exchange when he said: "Every man we hold, when released on parole or otherwise, becomes an active soldier against us at once either directly or indirectly. If we commence a system of exchange which liberates all prisoners taken, we will have to fight on until the whole South is exterminated." And then, with unconscious irony, came Grant's prophetic words: "If we hold those caught they amount to no more than dead men."[70] Grant's chilling logic carried the day; the decision as to whether Wilbur Grambling and his fellow Confederates would spend the winter in prison at Elmira thus became a *fait accompli*. And General Grant's words would unwittingly foretell the high incidence of death in Elmira.

At the very moment Grant was making his thoughts known to Butler, the military command in Elmira for the first time addressed the condition of Foster's Pond. The first report on the status of the pond was received on August 13 by Lt. Thomas R. Lounsbury, acting assistant adjutant-general at Elmira. It must be noted that Lieutenant Lounsbury was an exceptional officer who, after being wounded at the siege and surrender of Harpers Ferry, had held a number of important administrative posts before being assigned to Elmira in August 1863.

Born in the Seneca County village of Ovid, New York, and an 1859 graduate of Yale College, Lounsbury would go on to a long postwar career as a prominent professor of literature at Yale. A true man of letters, he would publish several scholarly analyses of the works of Chaucer and Shakespeare. In 1906 Thomas Raynesford Lounsbury was chosen as Yale's representative at the celebration of the University of Aberdeen's (Scotland) 400th anniversary.[71] A sterling officer, Lounsbury proved to be a valuable addition to Elmira's military staff.

It is difficult to imagine that Lieutenant Lounsbury, a reflective individual of scholarly bent, was not a man of compassion. And it is equally difficult to conclude that Major Sanger, the author of the lengthy August 13 report submitted to Lounsbury, was not a man who was determined to correct the turgid squalor of Foster's Pond. The problem for both men was that their authority in the matter of the pond did not go beyond the power of suggestion.

In a thorough account, Sanger reported that the pond was nothing more than a pool of stagnant water, becoming more offensive by the day.

Human waste from sinks (latrines) located at the edge of the pond was a major "source of miasma." "Seven thousand men," Sanger calculated, "will pass 2,600 gallons of urine daily. . . . A portion of this is absorbed by the earth, still a large amount decomposes on the top of the earth or runs into the pond to purify." To remedy this condition, he proposed a drainage system that would flush the basin of the pond. In his conclusion, Sanger reminded Lounsbury: "Unless the laws of hygiene are carefully studied and observed in crowded camps, disease is the inevitable consequence."[72]

Major Sanger thus began a process, even if in his own interest, of documenting in significant detail the shortcomings of the camp. Four days later Lieutenant Colonel Eastman forwarded a copy of Sanger's report to Colonel Hoffman. In doing so, Eastman stated "the pond inside the prisoners' camp at Barracks, No. 3, has become very offensive and may occasion sickness unless the evil is remedied very shortly." The "remedy for this," he continued, "is to dig a ditch from the pond to the river so that the water will run freely to it." Eastman concluded: "I respectfully request that you give instructions in regard to this with as little delay as possible, for if this work is to be done, it should be done immediately."[73]

This was Eastman's initial effort to inform Washington of the rapidly deteriorating condition of Foster's Pond. Surgeon Alexander had urged an entire month earlier that a detailed report of the pond's impact on the overall health of the camp be filed by the Elmira post commander. There is no clear explanation as to why Lieutenant Colonel Eastman for a full month failed to inform Colonel Hoffman of the growing danger of Foster's Pond. For whatever reason, Eastman's reluctance to report anything about the pond until August 17 would result in impending tragedy.

In fairness to the Elmira post commander, others of considerable rank were aware of the polluted state of Foster's Pond. In his July 20 visit to Elmira, Colonel Hoffman certainly gained firsthand knowledge of the pond's miasmic condition. Yet the best that can be said for Eastman is that it was poor judgment on his part that he did not submit a report to Hoffman until five weeks after Surgeon Alexander's inspection. If the Elmira post commander was tired, overworked and in a state of declining health, he clearly ought to have delegated a senior officer to file a report on Foster's Pond to the War Department. A man of Lieutenant Lounsbury's caliber most likely could have submitted a thorough account.

To complicate matters, Eastman would be bedridden from September 6 through September 20 before being relieved of his command for reasons of health. The awesome responsibility of commanding the camp and the draft rendezvous had become a physical grind that wore down the aging veteran officer.

Overcrowding was yet another problem during the final weeks of Eastman's command in Elmira. Colonel Hoffman was not unaware that Elmira and other camps were reaching their potential limits. In mid-August Hoffman informed Secretary of War Stanton "that the military prisons in the East have now nearly as many prisoners in them as they can accommodate."[74] Hoffman full well realized that the growing population of the prison camp at Elmira was very likely to cause Foster's Pond to increase its life-threatening contamination of the air and water. And yet in response to Hoffman's request for a full report of the pond's status, Eastman filed merely an indecisive missive which pointed to problems with nearby property owners that potentially could delay work on a drainage project. Also, he cited a lack of agreement with Major Sanger on how to purge the pond of its impurities.

In spite of Eastman's vacillation, he did reiterate the necessity of a drainage system. The general tone of his report, however, indicated that a drainage project was not about to be put in motion for the next several weeks. His report, filed one month before he relinquished his position as post commander, would be the final detailed account from Eastman on the matter of Foster's Pond. In relation to the status of the pond, he would never hear from Colonel Hoffman again.[75] The failure of the commissary general of prisoners to launch a work project in the good weather of late summer is puzzling. It now appeared, in the eyes of some, that a tactic of deliberate delay was beginning to come into being. That tactic would become part of the Elmira prison camp's legacy.

On August 25 Eastman forwarded to Hoffman Capt. Bennett F. Munger's inspection report of the camp. Munger reported that 226 prisoners were "sick in hospital and a larger number in quarters." He noted that a number of prisoners "in quarters are unable to attend sick call, and in some cases had not been visited by a surgeon in four days." Captain Munger then concluded: "Some are destitute of blankets and proper underclothes, and all without hospital rations; clothing of prisoners deficient, especially in blankets and shirts. The stench arising from the stagnant water in the pond is still very offensive."[76] In sending Munger's report to Colonel Hoffman, Lieutenant Colonel Eastman merely stated: "I have written to you in relation to the stagnant water in pond."[77]

With the prison census over 9,000, on August 26 Chief Surgeon Sanger cited the presence of scurvy in the camp. Scurvy, a disease caused by an unvaried diet that is lacking in fruits and vegetables, is not fatal; it does, however, break down resistance to other diseases. Sanger indicated a clear understanding of this in an alarming report to Lieutenant Lounsbury. In listing 793 scurvy patients, the camp's chief surgeon called for an increase in antiscorbutics (fruits and vegetables). Specifically, he requested that more potatoes, cabbage, and onions be included in the hospital diet. Sanger also noted that an acute shortage of hospital beds resulted in 593 scurvy patients being quartered in regular barracks.[78]

Major Sanger's August 26 report brought a September 8 response from Hoffman that granted permission for "the sutler to sell fruits and vegetables to prisoners during the prevalence of the scurvy."[79] This certainly would benefit most of Elmira's prisoners of war, for it was not uncommon for Confederate soldiers in the field to suffer from scurvy. Their diet generally consisted of cornmeal and bacon and salt pork, coffee, and something the soldiers called "sloosh"—a mixture of bacon grease and cornmeal that was swirled around in a frying pan.

Although crops such as hay and wheat suffered from the extremely dry, hot weeks of June and July in 1864, the local newspapers in August and September reported that fruit from the Finger Lakes just north of Elmira was abundant. "The fruit market," the *Advertiser* stated in a mid-August report, "gives good indication of a good supply of all kinds and afforded at cheap rates." Apples were "of a fair quality, at $1.00 per bushel," and "the more delicate fruits are exhibited for sale, too, in advance of the season."[80] No one could say that the camp's sutler experienced a shortage of fruit. A wiser policy clearly would have included a government purchase of fruit for general distribution within the camp.

The response to Elmira's scurvy problem from the Department of War was clear. Eastman was told to refer to a "letter of August 1st, 1864, which authorizes the purchase with your [Eastman's] approval of antiscorbutics for the prisoners generally whenever in the judgment of the Surgeon they are necessary."[81] In short, the authority to combat scurvy was in the hands of the Elmira post commander. Yet scurvy would continue to impair the health of the camp, and neither Eastman nor his successor made any effort to procure large amounts of fruit for the prison. Had they done so, it is possible scurvy could have been eliminated.

If Colonel Hoffman needed conclusive evidence that potential disaster was in the offing in Elmira, he received it in late August in a surprisingly energetic report from the ailing Eastman. He stated that prison mess room and kitchen facilities were "too small to accommodate 10,000 men." He recommended additional cooking and dining facilities, and a "mess–room should also be made for the hospital." Eastman next informed Hoffman that three hospital wards were completed and three more were under construction. In conclusion, the post commander stated: "I would also request to be informed if any arrangement is to be made for winter quarters for prisoners of war, and the troops now guarding them, who are now in tents. If so, it should be commenced immediately, owing to the difficulty of obtaining lumber at this point."[82]

As August gave way to September, the deteriorating status of the Elmira prison camp was evident to the military leadership at the local level and to the Department of War in Washington, D.C. There was a lack of proper housing, a dangerously unsanitary pond, an unnecessary shortage of fruits and vegetables, and inadequate hospital accommodations. Death in the month of August claimed 115 prisoners of war in Barracks No. 3. This brought the total number of Confederate dead to 126. On September 1 the camp's census was 9,480 men.[83] All the elements for an impending tragedy were now in place. General Grant's pragmatic metaphor that Confederate prisoners of war "amount to no more than dead men" was about to become a reality in Elmira.

CHAPTER 4

"A Rendezvous with Death"

September 1, 1864—the shank of the summer. The War Department, realizing that the camp was at capacity, suspended for a month any transfer of prisoners of war to Elmira.[1] The camp's official register of 9,480 prisoners of war would stand as the high census mark for the prison's 1-year existence. With autumn in the offing, the physical appearance of the compound (as seen from the observatories) projected a positive image. The west side of the prison was bedizened with ornate flower beds and neat walking paths that led to the quarters of Union sergeants who were stationed inside the camp. And prisoners' barracks and tents were placed in orderly rows that clearly impressed those looking on from the observatories.

With the arrival of September, citizens of Elmira, fearing prison escapes, were assured that every "precaution has been and will be taken to detect the least attempt of the 'rebs' at any game of smartness or circumvention."[2] On September 3, just west of the enclosed stockade, the 54th New York defeated the 56th New York in the weekly Saturday afternoon baseball game. And it was during those golden September days that the daily dress parade at Camp Chemung smacked of order and efficiency.

And there were positive signs in other areas. Indeed, despite the severely hot, dry months of June and July, the local newspapers repeatedly reported bumper crops of apples, pears, peaches, and a variety of fresh vegetables—especially potatoes. The corn crop was good and the August rainfall produced a tobacco harvest that was "brought forward to perfection." Breadstuffs also were abundant. In mid-September the *Advertiser* reported: "There has been a great hue and cry about the crops, their scantiness and small production, but it turns out that the general yield is fully up to the average."[3]

The Confederate prison at Elmira truly was, as historian Bruce Catton has written, a "camp in the middle of a prosperous state, . . . situated in a country whose economy was booming, maintained by a government that was strong and rich and that was going to live for a long time."[4] An integral part of Elmira's prosperity was its abundant agricultural production and, the vicissitudes of war notwithstanding, food was plentiful. Indeed, for the next half century and beyond survivors of Northern prison camps pointedly reminded their fellow Americans that quinine, chloroform, and other medicines were virtually unavailable in the South. The Confederate survivors also contrasted the paucity of food in the South with an abundance of agricultural products in the North.[5]

At this time, on the brink of autumn, it was generally viewed by those outside the prison camp that all was well. It was during those late summer days that some local citizens tossed bundles of food over the prison fence. And, for a limited period of time, a local grocer delivered oysters and crackers to the prisoners on a daily basis. "The prisoners at present appear quiet and contented," the *Advertiser* confidently assured its readers, "and are well cared for whether in sickness or health."[6] A New York City newspaper also affirmed favorable conditions when it reported: "The rebels are in the best of temper. . . . [T]he camp . . . is upon a dry handsome meadow; a rich farming region furnishes the needed supplies; and altogether the situation, for health and convenience, is not surpassed anywhere."[7]

When Confederate prisoners petitioned Lieutenant Colonel Eastman for permission to establish a school, the post commander approved and a graduate of the University of Virginia was designated to preside over the endeavor. Ten prisoners who were qualified teachers were appointed to conduct classes. "I was appointed one of the teachers," recalled F. S. Wade of McNeill's Texas Scouts, "the pay . . . [was] an extra ration." In claiming that he regained twenty pounds, Wade would state that the additional food "was the best pay I ever got for a job in my life."[8] A group of local women

Aside from woodworking skills and carpentry, some prisoners resorted to their artistic talent. This pencil sketch, entitled "Group of Rebel Prisoners," was signed by W. Norman and completed on September 10, 1864. CHEMUNG COUNTY HISTORICAL SOCIETY

furnished the project with used textbooks. School books along with pencils and slates came from other sources in the community. Elmirans prided themselves in this project, and many viewed it as a magnanimous gesture that augured well for the enlightenment of the prisoners of war.

Some prisoners could be seen making woodwork products. Much of the office furniture in the various official Union military buildings in Elmira came from the skilled hands of the Confederates. Perhaps the largest industry inside the camp was the making of finger rings and trinkets. "Our manufactured articles," recalled prisoner James Huffman, "were purchased mostly by outside people. The guards [and officers] who came on the inside bought largely and sold again to others outside."[9] This was done with a cavalier dismissal of the fact that it was technically a violation of post rules. Everybody seemed to "look the other way" when it came to the sale of rings and trinkets.

One Union officer who became active in the ring trade was Capt. John S. Kidder of the 121st New York. Kidder, an English-born volunteer with a strong sense of duty, emigrated to the United States at age twelve. At the outbreak of the war, he recruited a company that became part of the 121st.

He served with valor at Gettysburg in July 1863, and was seriously wounded by a gunshot to the face at Spotsylvania on May 12, 1864. Still in the process of recovering from his wounds, Kidder reported to Elmira in July 1864 and was assigned to command 1,000 Confederates.

Captain Kidder was one of those officers who lived in buildings, thirteen in all, outside the prison walls. The officers' quarters consisted of structures that were of different sizes, the largest being a triplex unit. These structures were subsequently divided into three-room bungalows that consisted of a kitchen, a bedroom, and a living room. Each bungalow was fitted with a heating stove and a cookstove. Furniture and bedding for these houses were often provided by the carpentry skills of the prisoners of war.

In September Captain Kidder sent a ring and a letter to his wife. In the letter he said: "Send Charley Matteson here with his box immediately. He can make money like fun. I can put him in a way of selling rings as many want them and I can furnish him all that he can sell. He can make a pile of money if he comes."[10] Later in the month Kidder informed his wife: "This you can keep to yourself, I have made $200 since I came here in the ring trade."[11] In the spirit that all was well at Barracks No. 3, local newspapers cheerfully reported the thriving business in rings and trinkets.

With ring and trinket sales doing well, the single negative aspect that surfaced from time to time in the local newspapers during those late summer days was the question of local sympathy for the Confederate prisoners of war. The *Advertiser* sarcastically noted: "Some one of the copperhead women who have joined in disgusting exhibitions of slobbering sympathy for rebel prisoners on their arrival here, has taken the trouble to write a letter to the Rochester *Union* slobbering some more about our comments on their conduct. . . . What a pity they [the sympathizing women and the Confederates] couldn't all be put in the pen together. It is a pity that such loving friends should be kept apart."[12]

Fairman's position was predictable and, of course, had been preceded during the midsummer days by accounts that endorsed a hard-line approach to the prisoners of war. The employees of the *Advertiser* reacted similarly in late July when Thomas P. Holland, a prisoner of war, wrote a letter to the newspaper's foreman. Claiming that he was a printer by trade, Holland asked (perhaps unrealistically) his fellow printers at the *Advertiser* for financial help. The full text of Holland's letter was carried in the newspaper, and the following day the foreman's response, in the parlance of the printer's trade, appeared in the *Advertiser*: "Before we shove up a great many 'quoins' we want to know how you came to handling a 'shooting stick' in the C.S.A. service. Please explain this *little* 'matter' so that we may feel 'justified' in helping one, who, though now 'locked up' has undoubtedly worked by the 'piece' and 'pied' the 'forms' of many good Union men."[13]

A caustic war of words, initiated during the early days of the camp among a number of Western New York newspapers, would continue through the month of September. The *Rochester Daily Union and Advertiser,* late in the month, weighed in with a "plague-on-both-your-houses" editorial. "It will appear," a *Union and Advertiser* reporter observed from Elmira, "that our government is imitating the example of the Jeff Davis government in cruelty to prisoners. It is evidently the purpose of the fanatics who control the two governments to wreak their vengeance and hatred upon the sick and wounded prisoners who fall into their hands."[14]

The question of sympathy for the prisoners of war aside, the *Advertiser* continued to describe the treatment of Confederates at Barracks No. 3 in positive terms. The reality inside the confines of Camp Chemung, however, was quite different from the optimistic newspaper accounts of late summer. Death was now becoming a grim factor. Back in mid-July the U.S. government purchased a half acre of Elmira's Woodlawn Cemetery for the purpose of burying Confederate prisoners of war. A wooden headboard with the name, company, and regiment of the deceased, and with the date of death painted upon it marked each grave.

By mid-September some prisoners turned their carpentry skills to the making of coffins. Late in the month a carpenter shop was established in the center of the camp for the sole purpose of making coffins of white pine. As the camp's death rate climbed, some men very possibly made their own coffins. In mid-September another coffin shop was established outside Barracks No. 1. The production of coffins within the prison stockade apparently could not keep up with the death rate.

It was at this time that signs of depression began to appear in letters that came out of the camp. One prisoner, with a gift for punning passages, wrote to a woman friend in Dixie: "The quarters in camp are passable, but the quarters in my pocket are not. Last night I had a mud-puddle for a pillow and covered myself with a sheet of water. I long for more whiskey barrels and less gun barrels, more biscuits and less bullets. How I wish you were here."[15] Other signs of dissatisfaction came in the form of prisoner reaction to the Union home guard—units assigned to guard the camp. The home guard (state militia) for the most part did not experience combat. Viewed by the Confederates at Elmira as a feckless collection of amateurs, the home guard, in the final year of the war, became notorious for their mistreatment of prisoners of war. Forty years later prisoner Thomas C. Jones, a transfer from Point Lookout to Elmira in August 1864, would recollect: "When we were guarded by the regulars they treated us with some respect, but the home guards had no mercy on us."[16] Jones's view was endorsed by one Union officer in charge of the prison guards who bluntly referred to the home guard as a "miserable set of scoundrels."[17]

As summer gave way to autumn, local newspapers began to occasionally take note of the camp's death rate. The stockade's well water, by now contaminated by the diseased pond, was beginning to take a terrible toll. As the contamination of Foster's Pond continued to grow more lethal by the day through September, the death rate also increased. By now the ignored warnings and proposals of Surgeon Alexander (July 14), Major Sanger (August 13), and Lieutenant Colonel Eastman (August 17 and 21) turned out to be only too valid. Sanger had reminded the War Department that, if the laws of hygiene in crowded prison compounds are ignored, disease is the inevitable consequence. Seventy-five years later, prisoner James Huffman would recall that the "well water looked pure and good but was deadly poison to our men."[18] Various kinds of bowel and kidney disease resulted in death for hundreds of the camp's prisoners of war. Chemung County historian Thomas E. Byrne, writing at the time of the camp's centenary, would conclude that Elmira had "a rendezvous with death."[19]

"Chronic diarrhea" was often the official diagnosis of illness in Elmira. Today it is known that the Confederates suffered from dehydration, ulcerative colitis (often a fatal infection of the lower intestinal tract), amoebic dysentery, and electrolyte imbalance (acute disorientation of the body's chemistry). Men already weakened by scurvy were especially vulnerable to more serious illnesses. Headaches, dizziness, fever, coughing, nausea and vomiting, and chills—all were symptoms that today would be traced to the contaminated well water. Despite Major Sanger's warning that the camp should observe the laws of hygiene, evidently neither Sanger nor Surgeon Alexander nor any other medical authority identified the well water as a potential cause of illness in the summer of 1864.

With medicine still in the dark ages, the American Civil War would prove to be a medical nightmare. Because sanitation and the germ theory were ignored by the great majority of military doctors, primitive battlefield medicine would result in thousands upon thousands of deaths. Ironically, reformers, not physicians, were the first to speak out against unsanitary conditions. The novels of Charles Dickens, for example, hinted strongly at the connection between disease and filth among England's working classes.

During the Crimean War (1853–1856), Florence Nightingale headed a corps of more than thirty nurses who dramatically reduced the mortality rate among their patients (British soldiers) to 2 percent. Miss Nightingale had little knowledge of germs, but her use of soap, hot water, and clean linen in treating the wounded all but eliminated cholera and dysentery. Although these diseases were prevalent in other British medical units, the medical profession as a whole was slow to make the connection between cleanliness and the successful treatment of patients. Indeed, it was not until a decade after the Civil War that England's Dr. Joseph Lister argued that wound dressings must be antiseptically clean in order to exclude microorganisms that produce disease. And Dr. Robert Koch's subsequent scientific study of medical microbiology led to the acceptance of Lister's postulates.

The acceptance of Lister and Koch came too late to aid medicine during the Civil War, but Louis Pasteur's work in the 1850s had already discredited the theory of spontaneous generation by arguing that microorganisms, present in unboiled water, could cause disease in humans. Pasteur's findings, however, were not readily accepted during the Civil War, despite the fact that his assertion that microbes existed in water was nothing new. Anton van Leeuwenhoek (1632–1723), a wealthy Dutch merchant who devoted much of his time to his hobby of grinding lenses, wrote letters to the Royal Society of London about 1683 with the observation that microorganisms existed in rainwater.

Despite Major Sanger's warnings of a lack of hygiene, Elmira was on the most part guided by accepted codes of medicine that did not recognize the pathogenic signs present within the prison camp. Yet implementing the commonsense recommendations that Foster's Pond be provided with an outlet to the Chemung River would have alleviated the most dangerous of unsanitary conditions. Unfortunately, at this crucial juncture the War Department did not respond to requests for improvements in the camp. And Eastman, by now seriously ill, made no attempt in September to prod Washington to action on the matter of the pond.

Another acute question was housing. With winter in the offing and over 5,000 prisoners in tents, the serious shortage of sufficient living quarters now loomed as a major problem. On September 4, in one of his last official acts as post commander, Eastman informed Washington that additional barracks should be constructed "with as little delay as possible." Then, in a sentence that seemed to symbolize the camp's general malaise, the ailing post commander added: "Scurvy prevails to a considerable extent among the Prisoners of War."[20]

To complicate matters, it was at this point that Major Sanger made his first request to be relieved from duty at Elmira. In a letter to the surgeon general's office, Sanger stated that his health was impaired by asthma which "has returned with unusual violence since I have been stationed at Elmira, rendering me almost unfit to perform my duties. If retained here much longer I must give up." Sanger requested transfer to a medical post in the Shenandoah Valley or a city general hospital. In forwarding Sanger's letter through channels, a military official added: "Should Surgeon Sanger be relieved, I would respectfully request that a Surgeon of experience may be detailed to relieve him."[21] With the impending departure of Eastman, Major Sanger would become even more dissatisfied with his assignment in Elmira.

On September 20 a haggard and sallow Seth Eastman was relieved of his command at Elmira. Illness had forced the West Point military veteran of thirty-five years to relinquish the difficult task of administering a prisoner-of-war compound in addition to Barracks No. 1, which at times housed up to 8,000 Union soldiers. The *Advertiser,* in paying high tribute to the popular post commander, stated that Eastman "assumed command here when military matters were in a chaotic condition." The newspaper noted that Eastman brought about immediate reform and "then came the imposition of a new labor of preparation for the reception of 10,000 prisoners. The work has been . . . carried out . . . to the entire satisfaction of the War Department."[22]

Lieutenant Colonel Eastman's successor came from a markedly different background than did the veteran military career officer. Col. Benjamin Franklin Tracy, the new post commander, was one of thousands of Civil War volunteer officers who gained their rank through their position in the community. As with Eastman and Sanger, Tracy's roots were in New England. Following the Revolutionary War, Thomas Tracy (a veteran of the war) moved west to New York State and settled in the tiny village of Apalachin in Tioga County—fifteen miles west of Binghamton and eight miles east of the thriving village of Owego. Benjamin Tracy, one of Thomas's sons, would successfully establish himself as a farmer. Here, on April 26, 1830, in this rural setting, his son, Benjamin Franklin Tracy, was born, the third of four sons. In addition to his three brothers, he shared his home with four children from his mother's first marriage.

The father of this large family encouraged education, and young Tracy attended a district school for eight years. It was during this period, while at play, that he lost the sight of his left eye. Upon completing his formal education at a private academy in Owego, Tracy (at age sixteen) took a job as a teacher at a district school in Tioga County. His interest in law most likely derived from his father's appointment as a justice of the peace when young Benjamin was eight years old. At age nineteen he began the study of law in an Owego law office, and at age twenty-one he was admitted to the New York State bar.

In 1851 the young lawyer married Delinda E. Catlin of Nichols, a tiny New York hamlet seven miles west of Owego. Tracy, a man whose distinguished appearance was marked by a handsome face and a dark brown beard that retained its jiblike trim, was considered "quite a catch" by the fair maidens of Owego and its vicinity. Standing almost six feet tall and weighing 170 pounds, his physique remained finely honed through his participation in physical activities such as baseball and other sporting endeavors. A devoted husband, he became the dedicated father of two daughters and a son.

Tracy began his practice of law in Owego in 1851 where in the court room he "combined a sharp mind and an engaging personality with a handsome physical appearance."[23] Soon he became interested in the politics of Tioga County. A staunch Whig who opposed both abolitionism and the expansion of slavery, Tracy was elected district attorney of Tioga County in 1853. With the demise of the Whig Party, he became a key figure in the organization of the Republican Party in 1854 in Tioga County, and emerged as the first county chairman of that fledgling political organization in 1856. He actively supported Republican John C. Frémont during the 1856 presidential campaign. As a rising Republican leader in Tioga County, Tracy worked closely with his good friend Thomas Collier Platt—a future Republican powerhouse in New York State.

With the outbreak of the war in April 1861, Tracy entered state politics. Campaigning as a strong Unionist and a supporter of President Lincoln, he was elected to the New York State Assembly in November 1861. It was in the Assembly that Tracy quickly allied himself with a rapidly rising star in the Republican Party—Henry Jarvis Raymond. Raymond at this time was on the verge of emerging as a member of a redoubtable Republican political triumvirate in New York State that included William H. Seward (Lincoln's secretary of state) of Auburn, and the state's domineering practitioner of political power—Thurlow Weed, a man who made his mark

Col. Benjamin F. Tracy became the Elmira post commander on September 20, 1864. Tracy would be in charge at Elmira during the prison camp's most difficult months. His postwar career would bring him national fame as President Benjamin Harrison's secretary of the navy. LIBRARY OF CONGRESS

in journalism in both Albany and New York City. With Tracy's influential support, Raymond was elected speaker of the Assembly. This would not be the last time that there would be collaboration between Tracy and Raymond. A supporter of Raymond on the most part, Tracy quickly gained a reputation as a notable political figure in the state Assembly.[24]

Unlike Lieutenant Colonel Eastman, Tracy, when he assumed command at Elmira, was at the beginning of a career that would take him to national heights. After moving his family from Apalachin to a pleasant residential section of Brooklyn, New York, his postwar career would be launched when President Andrew Johnson appointed him to the position of federal district attorney for the eastern district of New York State. Returning to private practice, Tracy would defend the Reverend Henry Ward Beecher in a famous 1875 adultery trial, which lasted six months and ended in a hung jury. Tracy's distinguished legal career would include a brief term as a judge on the New York State Court of Appeals (the state's highest court) in 1881–82.

In 1889 President Benjamin Harrison would appoint Tracy to the post of secretary of the navy. The new secretary would enthusiastically embrace the idea of a two-ocean navy, and immediately embark upon the construction of a powerful American fleet. Secretary Tracy's initial steps were significant and would come to fruition under President Theodore Roosevelt who sent America's "great white fleet" around the world in 1907.

Following Harrison's presidency, Tracy chaired a commission that drew up the charter for the incorporation of Greater New York City in 1896. In 1897 Tracy ran as the unsuccessful Republican mayoral candidate in New York City, and he remained active in veterans' affairs and (behind the scenes) in politics until his death in August 1915.[25] In 1920 the destroyer USS *Benjamin F. Tracy* was commissioned in memory of the former secretary of the navy. The *Tracy*, remaining on active duty through the Second World War, was retired in 1946.[26]

All this was ahead of Tracy, whose primary concern in 1862 was the fate of the Union. That summer he abandoned his political position and, in response to Lincoln's July 1 call for 300,000 volunteers, volunteered to serve his country. Since one's socioeconomic status determined one's general prestige, Tracy emerged as commander (with the rank of colonel) of the 109th New York—a regiment that was made up of recruits from Tioga, Broome, and Tompkins Counties. On August 30, 1862, Colonel Tracy and the 109th left Binghamton by train for Elmira and then on to points south. For the next year and a half Tracy's regiment performed the perfunctory task of guarding railroads in the Baltimore and Washington areas.

In the spring of 1864 General Grant moved to mount an all-out offensive against Lee's Army of Northern Virginia. In doing so, Grant ordered the majority of units (including Tracy's 109th) in the Baltimore and Washington sectors to the front. In early May Tracy and his inexperienced regiment were thrown into battle against tough, seasoned Confederate troops at the battle of the Wilderness. When the 109th faltered, Colonel Tracy took the regimental colors and charged the enemy. His unit quickly followed him into battle.

From May 5 through May 12 the 109th engaged the enemy in a series of fierce encounters that eventually took its toll on the courageous Tracy. Suffering from heat prostration and heart problems, he was diagnosed by military doctors on May 14 as no longer capable of enduring the rigors of combat. Responding with courage and valor to the shot and shell of combat, the patriotic Tracy had exhibited exemplary leadership. His brief but harrowing moment of battle over, he now reluctantly returned to his home to regain his health.[27] In June 1895 Tracy would finally be awarded the Medal of Honor "for gallant and distinguished conduct in action at Wilderness, Va., May 6, 1864."[28]

Through the summer months Tracy regained his strength to the point where he was able to rejoin the military in some capacity. On September 7, his health completely restored, he accepted another military assignment—this time as the commanding officer of the 127th U.S. Colored Troops. At about the same time his political ally from his New York Assembly days, the formidable Henry J. Raymond, journeyed to Owego to personally suggest to Tracy that he assume the position of military post commander at Elmira. There is great significance in this, for Raymond now possessed enormous political influence that is worthy of comment.

Looking as if he had just stepped off the pages of a Charles Dickens novel, Henry Jarvis Raymond, a man of imperturbable self-possession, was at the apex of political power in 1864. Short, bookish, dapper, monocled, replete with sideburns and gold-handled walking stick, he was one of the founders of the *New York Times* in 1851. Born in 1820 in Lima, New York, and a graduate (with honors) of the University of Vermont, Raymond was a stout Whig who, in 1856, became a key figure in the founding of the

Republican Party in New York State. For Raymond, this political sea change was characteristically a smooth transition. At the 1860 Republican convention in Chicago he supported fellow New Yorker William H. Seward's bid for the presidential nomination, but, when Abraham Lincoln won, the urbane and unflappable Raymond (and the *Times*) enthusiastically supported the party's nominee.

When the armies of the North and South gathered for their first pitched clash of the Civil War in July 1861, Raymond rushed to Manassas, Virginia, to personally cover the battle for his newspaper. Undaunted, he fearlessly moved from one point to another in the line of fire. One soldier wrote in his diary: "The first time I was under fire—the real article. Mr. Raymond (N.Y. Times) seemed as indifferent to it as Gen. Tyler."[29]

By 1864 the *Times,* with Raymond clearly in charge of editorial policy, had become one of the most powerful pro-Lincoln newspapers in the land. It was at this time that he and Thurlow Weed and William H. Seward had gained control of a fragmented Republican party in New York State. That same year Raymond, the author of several biographies, skillfully put together a political biography of President Lincoln. As a mover and shaker of the National Union Party (that is what Lincoln's Republican Party called itself in 1864), Raymond pushed for an early June convention. He molded the party's platform and dominated the various political spheres of the conference. He also successfully maneuvered convention delegates into nominating Andrew Johnson, a Union Democrat from Tennessee, for vice president.

Raymond's man—Abraham Lincoln—was nominated on the first ballot. Following the convention, the canny Raymond was chosen by Lincoln to serve as the national committee chairman of the National Union party. By the summer of 1864, President Lincoln was affectionately and rightly referring to Raymond as "my *Lieutenant-General* in politics."[30] In Lincoln's mind, Henry J. Raymond was a masterful practitioner of the sorcerer's arts of politics.

On September 10, 1864, Raymond personally called on Tracy, his old political ally, in Owego and handed him a brief letter of introduction that was addressed to Secretary of War Stanton. Raymond suggested that Tracy travel to Washington and personally hand the note to the secretary. The missive, written in Raymond's hand on National Union Party Executive Committee stationery, stated:

My dear Sir:

Col. B.F. Tracey [*sic*], who will hand you this note, is the officer whom you want for special duty at Elmira. You will find him
reliable and *efficient* in any good . . . work you may assign him.

Your ob't serv't
H.J. Raymond[31]

Indeed, Raymond's considerable political influence clearly had much to
do with Tracy's appointment to Elmira. In a curious sequence of events,
Tracy was commissioned on September 7 with the rank of colonel as commander of the 127th U.S. Colored Troops. Three days later he notified
Washington that he was reporting to duty.[32] This notification was one of
two letters written by Tracy on that day to Brig. Gen. Lorenzo Thomas,
adjutant general of the United States. Both missives and a signed oath of
office confirmed Tracy's acceptance of the appointment as commander of
the 127th; and, coincidentally, this was the very day that Raymond called
on Tracy in Owego to persuade him to take the position in Elmira.

Tracy, apparently after a lengthy discussion with Raymond, then wrote
(on September 10) Secretary of War Stanton: "Mr. Raymond supposed it
would be necessary for me to visit Washington in person and handed me
the inclosed note to you. Finding upon an examination of the papers that I
was ordered to report in writing, I have done so, and only inclose the note
[Raymond's letter to Stanton] to you that you may then more vividly recall
the circumstances of my appointment and the special duty to which as I
understand you intend to assign me."[33]

On September 19 the War Department stated that Tracy's order (dated
September 17) "to repair to Elmira, New York, and relieve Lieutenant-
Colonel S. Eastman, U.S Army, in command of the Draft Rendezvous and
the Prisoner's Camp, at that place, is hereby confirmed."[34] The following
day Eastman affixed his signature to a post order that officially turned the
Elmira command over to Colonel Tracy.

What remains intriguing about Tracy's official detachment from the
127th U.S. Colored Troops Regiment is the manner in which it was
accomplished. And equally engaging is the man who saw that it was done—
Henry J. Raymond. Also, Stanton's hasty approval of Tracy is a tantalizing

factor. It is clear that Stanton and Raymond wanted Tracy to succeed Eastman in Elmira.

What is also clear is that Raymond's *New York Times* spoke with considerable authority and was meticulously monitored by President Lincoln's
closest political advisers. The *Times* followed the prisoner-of-war situation
with diligence and conviction. Convinced that Union prisoners of war
were being mistreated by men plagued with distinctive moral infirmities,
Raymond and his editors in the early spring of 1864 called for retaliation.

"A chapter will be written by some future historian," the *Times* declared
in an editorial that went well beyond the patriotic injunctions and prim
moralisms of other Northern newspapers, "on the horrors of the 'Libby
Prison,' which will almost equal in fearful interest the records of the
Bastille." Castigating what it claimed to be the deliberate deprivation of food
and fuel and a premeditated policy of torture, the editorial referred to treatment of Union prisoners of war as "brutally and savagely cruel." "Retaliation is a terrible thing," the *Times* concluded, "but the miseries and pains,
and slow-wasting life of our brethren and friends in those horrible prisons,
under brutal officers, is a worse thing."[35]

Tracy's position on retaliation is unknown, but that he knew of Raymond's views is a safe assumption. And it is conceivable that Raymond's
view on this matter played an integral part in the Owego meeting between
the two men. They were, after all, staunch political allies who knew the
meaning of sharing each other's thoughts. And Secretary Stanton, the man
who approved Tracy's appointment to Elmira, was an enthusiastic advocate
of retaliation. As far back as five months before Tracy came to Elmira, the
secretary of war received a copy of a Union prisoner's April letter to the
New York Times. The letter described poor treatment at Libby Prison and
Belle Isle. "Not one-fourth of the rations sent by the United States in
November ever reached the prisoners," the prisoner of war stated, "and no
sanitary stores were ever delivered on Belle Isle."[36] Accounts of this nature
weighed heavily on Stanton's mind.

Stanton also heard from his commissary general of prisoners. "I respectfully suggest," wrote Colonel Hoffman on April 29, "as a means of compelling the rebels to adopt a less barbarous policy toward the prisoners in
their hands that the rebel officers at Johnson's Island be allowed only half
rations."[37] On May 3 Hoffman filed a lengthy report of his observation of
Union prisoners of war who had been returned from Richmond to
Annapolis, Maryland. Colonel Hoffman found the enlisted men among the

returning prisoners mentally and physically depleted. Again the commissary general of prisoners, convinced that Union prisoners of war were being deliberately starved to death, urged that retaliatory measures be put in place.[38]

Secretary Stanton, long suspicious of ill-treatment of Union prisoners of war and with the support of Colonel Hoffman and the *New York Times,* was now able to play a stronger hand. On May 5, in an initial move toward a policy of retaliation, he informed President Lincoln that Union prisoners of war "are undergoing ferocious barbarity or the more horrible death of starvation." The secretary of war then suggested that "precisely the same rations and treatment be from henceforth practiced to the whole number of rebel officers remaining in our hands that are practiced against either soldiers or officers in our service held by the rebels."[39]

It was at this time that Stanton, ever the wily administrator, decided to touch all the bases. "The enormity of the crime committed by the rebels towards our prisoners for the last several months," he wrote on May 4 to Sen. Benjamin F. Wade of Ohio, "is not known or realized by our own people, and cannot but fill with horror the civilized world when the facts are revealed. There appears to have been a deliberate system of savage and barbarous treatment and starvation."[40]

"Bluff Ben" Wade, one of those powerful master politicians who led the radical Republicans in the U.S. Senate, was a formidable ally. The most potent single political bloc in Congress during the war, the radical Republicans (known as "Jacobins" by those who disliked and feared them) would call for a Carthaginian peace in 1865. Historian T. Harry Williams sees Wade as a man "endowed with a brutal wit," who initially gained national recognition "by offering to meet the Southern hotspurs upon the field of honor with squirrel rifles at thirty paces as the weapons."[41] The redoubtable Senator Wade would render puissant political support for the secretary of war.

And what was President Lincoln's position? The shrewd, astute Lincoln was well aware of Stanton's volatile disposition. In citing the president's allowing his secretary of war to accept or reject executive orders, historian Richard N. Current has duly noted: "Such apparently was the division of labor between Lincoln and Stanton, between lenity and the law. If a life was spared, Lincoln could get the credit. If not, Stanton, with grim satisfaction might take the blame."[42] Lincoln privately explained his relationship with his secretary of war in this revealing comment: "I want to oblige every body when I can; and Stanton and I have an understanding that if I send an order to him which cannot be consistently granted, he is to refuse it. This he sometimes does."[43] One thing is certain: Stanton was a major decision maker in Lincoln's scheme of things.[44]

There is little doubt that the president allowed Stanton to wield extraordinary power that often appeared to be autonomous. The sagacious Lincoln had, however, when he deemed it necessary, the final word and his secretary of war knew it. The stark reality is this: Stanton and Hoffman wished to put forward a policy of retaliation; there is no documented objection to this idea from President Abraham Lincoln. Therefore, in the matter of retaliation, the virtually unbridled use of power on the part of the secretary of war would have no trouble quashing any opposition to his order that demanded a reduction in rations.

The War Department came a step closer to retaliation on May 19 when Colonel Hoffman notified the secretary of war that rations for prisoners of war could be considerably reduced. On the same day Secretary Stanton submitted Hoffman's recommendation for endorsement to the top echelon of the War Department—Maj. Gen. Henry W. Halleck, chief of staff; Col. Joseph P. Taylor, commissary general of subsistence and son of the late President Zachary Taylor; and Col. Joseph K. Barnes, acting surgeon general. There was some initial disagreement on certain reductions, but in the end all agreed on curtailed rations with one exception—those prisoners officially listed as sick. On May 27 the round of endorsements went back to General Halleck who informed Stanton of the proposed cut back in rations.[45] On the question of retaliation, it was clear by late May that Stanton and his ranking War Department officers now sailed by a fixed star.

Therefore, with the full backing of the War Department's upper echelon, the secretary of war ordered a general 20 percent reduction in rations. Signed by Colonel Hoffman, the circular order stated that rations for all prisoners of war held by the Union would be reduced as of June 1, 1864.[46] Savings on food purchases would be placed in a prison fund. General and special orders relating to prison camps made it clear that money from this fund would be used to purchase materials for prison camps that were not specified by the War Department. During the year of its existence, the Elmira prison camp's prison fund totaled $239,857.01; money not spent from the fund amounted to $58,151.54. The unspent funds were returned to the federal government at the conclusion of the war.[47] Well into the next century survivors of Elmira would relate to a paucity of rations. Little did they know that at the time of their captivity that less than 44 percent of appropriated funds would be spent for food and other essential needs.

And what did the reduction in rations portend? Historian James I. Robertson, Jr., has charged that the prisoner rations at Elmira were "restricted to bread and water."[48] Many of the camp's survivors would claim that the record almost invites such a charge. Historians Benjamin P. Thomas and Harold M. Hyman, in not quite as harsh a conclusion, have stated: "When properly distributed the reduced ration was sufficient to maintain health. But when mismanagement or vengefulness on the part of prison keepers entered into the picture, hunger and disease ensued."[49] It is difficult to argue that Stanton, Hoffman, Halleck, Taylor, and Barnes did not realize to a moral certainty that a reduction in rations would be devastating.

To exacerbate matters, on August 10 Circular No. 4 was issued by the commissary general of prisoners to all prison camp commanders. In ordering the prohibition of the purchase of food, (much of it consisting of fresh fruit) from the sutler's shop, the circular advised that all articles (clothing, food, and other items) sent to prisoners of war by relatives or friends be restricted to Confederates officially listed as sick. Camp sutlers were limited to selling the following items: writing materials, postage stamps, tobacco, cigars, pipes, matches, combs, soap, toothbrushes, clothes brushes, scissors, thread, needles, handkerchiefs, towels, and pocket looking glasses.[50]

This order, when in effect, would prove to be life threatening to the prisoners of war at Elmira. In 1908, in recalling the restrictions on food being sent to the camp, prisoner R. B. Ewan would note: "Many hundreds of boxes of provisions were brot [*sic*] in camp, but unless we were in the hospital, or could furnish a certificate of sickness, the ham, cheese, bread and pie were put back in the wagon and hauled out to fill other stomachs."[51]

From time to time the War Department would temporarily rescind the order, and allow prisoners of war to purchase food from the sutler. In the initial stages of Elmira as a prison camp, however, Stanton already had in place reduced rations that consisted of two meals a day, and the elimination of an auxiliary source of food, i.e., the sutler's shop. "The regulations of the pen are growing more strict," prisoner Anthony Keiley recorded in his diary on August 28. "No food," he observed, "is permitted to be sold to us by the sutler." And on September 11 Keiley's diary entry proclaimed: "The restricting of the prisoners to a uniform diet of bread and meat, and denying them the privilege of purchasing other food, are showing their effects in an epidemic, almost, of scurvy."[52]

Collective Department of War decisions most certainly had much to do with the reduction of rations. Three days before the June reduction order was issued, Maj. Gen. Benjamin F. Butler informed the secretary of war that in Richmond, Union prisoners of war *and* Confederate soldiers were on half rations.[53] If Butler's position is correct, this was a clear indication that the Confederacy was facing severe shortages of food. Yet those who support Stanton have argued that he had good reason to suspect the Confederacy of mistreatment of Union prisoners. They point to Capt. Henry Wirz, the notorious Confederate officer at Andersonville. Wirz became the very symbol of cruelty, and, when at the conclusion of the war he would be hanged by the neck until dead as a war criminal, a great number of Union veterans argued that justice had been done.

Also, Stanton may have heard of a letter attributed to Judge Robert Ould, the Confederacy's agent of exchange. In 1863 Ould allegedly stated in a letter to Col. A. C. Myers: "If the exigencies of our army require the use of trains for transportation of corn, pay no regard to the Yankee prisoners. I would rather they should starve than our people suffer. I suppose I can safely put it in writing, 'Let them suffer.'"[54] Although Judge Ould would vehemently deny writing the letter, its contents appeared in several newspapers during the postwar period. If Ould did not think this way, certainly others in the Confederacy did.

With a reduction of rations in place, Colonel Tracy was about to take his part in the tragic story of the prison camp at Elmira. Perhaps unwittingly, Tracy had agreed to an assignment where a policy of retaliation was already a fixed fact. A piece of the puzzle that will remain missing is Tracy's view on the question of retaliation. Whatever that view was, it would not be documented, nor would the new post commander ever allude to Raymond's role in his appointment to Elmira.

What is clear is that Tracy was willing to serve at Elmira under the domineering Stanton. And his appointment, initiated by Raymond, was quickly moved along and hastily approved by the secretary of war. This has left the matter open to critics who claim that Tracy's assignment to the Elmira post had less to do with his qualifications for such an appointment than with his willingness to adhere to Raymond's views and abide by Stanton's policies. Tracy was an astute observer of the politics of the day; therefore, his political acumen lends credence to his critics' charges.

When Colonel Tracy stepped off the train at Elmira's railroad depot on September 19, he moved into a volatile situation. By mid-September the post was indeed attended by certain dangers. The welcoming committee with its kind words, martial music, and patriotic gestures only served to distract attention from the state of the prison camp. At Elmira's Concert Hall, a dramatization of Harriet Beecher Stowe's *Uncle Tom's Cabin* played that evening before a packed house that included many of the town's most prominent citizens. There is no record that Colonel Tracy, his firm opposition to abolitionism in place, was in attendance. Also on the day of Tracy's arrival, the Union military began dismantling the refreshment stands (between the two observatories) that had hummed with profits in recent weeks. On the streets of Elmira Union soldiers frequented saloons and houses of prostitution. And at Camp Chemung on that day twenty-seven Confederate prisoners of war died.[55]

Citizens of Elmira were not yet fully aware of what was happening inside the prison camp. Neither was Colonel Tracy. Nine days after his arrival, the *Advertiser* informed its readers that "the new commandant of this rendezvous is inaugurating many changes and improvements in the manifold details of his command. Col. Tracy seems to be the right man in the right place."[56] The stiff-principled Tracy, a man whose thought processes were guided by legal dogma and a decade in local and state politics, would prove to be a starchy post commander. On the most part, his acceptance of orders from Washington reflected an understanding of the military's rigid margin of reason. He would, at times to his misfortune, view almost all questions and problems through the narrow prism of army regulations.

A willingness, however, to carry out the army's rules would not be enough. Elmira's new post commander inherited a situation that had essentially been ignored for months. Initially unaware of the camp's soaring death rate, he was soon confronted with the prison's lack of sanitation, the prevalence of disease, a shortage of proper housing, marginal rations, a paucity of clothing, and inadequate hospital facilities—all the result of inaction on the part of those in command in Elmira and (to a much greater extent) Washington.

Colonel Tracy's considerable intelligence and splendid leadership qualities would be seriously challenged. Four months after his arrival in Elmira, the frustrated post commander would recollect that illness had incapacitated Lieutenant Colonel Eastman in such a manner that he was barely able to sign over the duties to the new post commander. "I was compelled therefore," Tracy wrote, "to grope my way in the dark, learning the details and needs of a most intricate and difficult command as rapidly as I could."[57]

Just five days after his arrival at his new post, Tracy was confronted with Capt. Bennett F. Munger's ominous inspection report of the prison camp. Munger wrote of clothing being received on a daily basis, "but there is still great destitution." He reported the weather being unseasonably cold, "and those in tents especially suffer." The report told of a lack of stoves in hospital and barracks, and overcrowded hospital conditions that deprived about a hundred sick prisoners of war of a hospital bed. He reported that the sick in quarters "are fed on the ordinary prison ration, notwithstanding an order has been issued to treat them as in hospital." Captain Munger concluded: "During the past week there have been 112 deaths, reaching one day 29. There seems little doubt numbers have died both in quarters and hospital for want of proper food."[58] Munger's concise, final sentence would forever epitomize the haunting charge that is still with us today—that prisoners of war were intentionally starved at Elmira.

In submitting Captain Munger's report to the office of the commissary general of prisoners, Tracy cited a number of the prison camp's shortcomings—poor drainage, a lack of winter barracks, insufficient hospital accommodations, and the need for another mess house. In this report, the post commander specifically recommended a drainage system to correct the unhealthy condition of Foster's Pond.[59]

On the day that Colonel Tracy submitted his comments along with Captain Munger's report to Washington (the final day of September), death claimed Robert Wallace (35th North Carolina) and seven of his Confederate comrades, raising Elmira's total number of dead for September to 385. The September death toll for all prisoner-of-war camps administered by the Union military was 879. Forty-four percent of those deaths took place in Elmira.[60] The half acre of land that the government had purchased in July for burial of the Confederate dead was now full—this necessitated the purchase by the government of two acres of land contiguous to the original plot.

Burial of the dead was managed by John W. Jones, a runaway slave from the Elzy plantation near Leesburg in Loudoun County, Virginia. Jones, with his brother, George, and several others, walked all but eight miles from Virginia to Elmira in 1844. John taught himself to read and write, and served as sexton of the First Baptist Church until 1890. George Jones served for many years as the sexton of The Park Church. During Elmira's antebellum period, John Jones played a major role in aiding slaves to escape to Canada through the Underground Railroad. His very presence in Elmira made the village an important part of an intricate system that aided runaway slaves in

John W. Jones, a runaway slave from Loudoun County, Virginia, dug the graves and recorded the markers of the Confederate dead with meticulous care. After the war he served as sexton at Elmira's First Baptist Church for many years. CHEMUNG COUNTY HISTORICAL SOCIETY

the quest for freedom. More than a thousand escaped slaves passed through Elmira during the 1850s. The great majority of them, during their brief stay in the village, were housed and fed in Jones's home.

In 1912 author Clay Holmes described Jones as a man who "was positive in character, quick in his perceptions, just in all his dealings, courageous in what he thought to be right." In recalling the significance of Jones's part in the burial of the Confederate dead, Holmes would write: "The coincidence is that the last rites of so many who had been engaged in the rebellion, for no purpose but to preserve the institution of slavery, should be performed by one who had escaped from that slavery, and was one of the best examples of what freedom could and would do, even for a slave."[61]

The story of the Civil War is laced with tragic irony and John W. Jones's role is no exception. In the course of his duties at the cemetery, Jones came across the body of John R. Rollins, a Confederate soldier from Virginia. The former slave recalled the name of the overseer of the Elzy plantation—William Rollins. Jones recalled that John R. Rollins was a pleasant little boy in the 1840s, and, upon contacting sources in Leesburg, he received confirmation that this fallen Confederate prisoner of war was from the Elzy farm. John R. Rollins's name does not appear on the roll of the Confederate dead at Elmira; his remains, through the efforts of John W. Jones, were taken back to Virginia.

Jones was paid $2.50 per burial and was aided by Confederates who served as a graveyard detail. In a section between the Chemung River and Foster's Pond (an area the prisoners referred to as the "trans-Mississippi department"), something called the dead house, about 40 feet by 15 feet in size, was constructed in the far southwest corner of the camp. It was here that Confederates placed the remains of their fallen comrades in coffins, nine to a wagon, for the mile-and-one-half journey to the cemetery. The name, company, regiment, and date of death were written on a sheet of paper and placed in a small bottle that was tightly corked and placed under the dead prisoner's right armpit. A wooden headboard marked in large letters with the same information also contained in the corked bottle was then nailed to the coffin. Years later Jones reflected on the burial process:

> Each body was put into a pine box, and nine were brought to me at a time from the camp. I dug a trench large enough to contain a number of them, laid side by side or feet to feet, and so laid them. There were no devices of any kind or character at the graves. The boxes were unloaded from the ambulance in which they were brought from the camp, lowered into the grave and covered with earth. That was all.[62]

Prisoner James Marion Howard of the 12th Alabama recalled over forty years later how he became part of the graveyard detail. "There were eight of us," he would recollect, "and we were given three meals each day, and five cents per day as wages. . . . We buried our men on what was called 'Free Ground.' The place was low and marshy and the water often rose to a depth of three feet in the ditches. Where we buried our dead we had to take a pick and make a hole in the coffin on each side near the shoulders so as to sink the dead." Howard also remembered: "When we got the dead buried we were permitted to talk to the citizens as they came in great numbers every day. To them we could sell finger rings and watch chains."[63]

During the first week of October eighty-six prisoners of war died at Elmira.[64] On October 8 came the initial significant snowfall. "Winter set in rather unexpectedly," the *Advertiser* noted, "and held its fingers unreleased during yesterday. . . . [T]he strong searching, northern breeze, sending everywhere a pervading chill, gave warrant, last evening, of the first hard freeze to the fall."[65] The early autumn storm not only was the portent of a severe winter, but it also symbolized a virulent state of despair and desperation that now gripped the camp. With the October snow came reports from inside the camp that the stronger prisoners had begun to steal clothing and blankets from the weak.[66]

Indeed, if in the cold, bleak October dusk, one climbed to the top of either of the observatories that the military allowed to remain standing, one could look down on a pervasive lethal darkness where shadowy groups of men were barely clinging to a flickering semblance of hope. The prison camp was now a place of resignation, fear, and torpor. A scent of death lingered in the air.

"Most of These Causes May Be Removed, and that It Be Done Seems the Plainest Duty of Humanity"

Talk of retaliation was in the autumn air in 1864. The *New York Times* once again spoke of how the inhumane treatment of Union prisoners of war had "stained and sullied the vesture of Southern chivalry." Projecting a sense of moral outrage that was shared by the majority of newspapers in the North, the *Times* continued by reassuring its readers: "No such disgrace, thank God, touches the North! Everything that our own soldiers are allowed by law is cheerfully given to our prisoners. Such clothing, such food as the poor Southron never enjoyed at home, is heaped before him when in our hands. . . . None suffer from want." The *Times* then renewed its call for retaliation when it proclaimed: "[W]e believe that the most active measures should be undertaken to insure corresponding treatment of our own brave soldiers. We urge that rebel prisoners should no longer live in luxury while ours are dying of starvation and neglect."[1]

The *Times,* embracing the idea that avenging wrong deeds is a natural human emotion, was, not surprisingly, well received by many citizens in Elmira. And it should come as no surprise that the *Advertiser* viewed the *Times* as one of the finest newspapers in the nation.[2] More importantly, the *Times*'s position is a prime example of what historian William B. Hesseltine has referred to as "war psychosis." Hesseltine, in his classic analysis of Civil War prisons, stated that "an inevitable concomitant of armed warfare is the

hatred engendered in the minds of the contestants by the conflict." He further stated: "Seemingly, it becomes necessary for the supporters of one cause
to identify their entire personality with that cause, to identify their opponents with the opposing cause, and to hate the supporters of the enemy
cause with a venom which counterbalances their devotion to their own."[3]

A great number of people in the North felt that the South was guilty of
willful and malicious behavior in its treatment of Union prisoners of war.
And, as seen in the *Times's* October 2 editorial, it was accepted as a fixed
fact that Confederate prisoners of war were provided with abundant food,
clothing, shelter, and medical care. Small town editors such as Elmira's
Charles Fairman shared the belief that the only evil was that provided by
the Confederacy.

In September that view reached the desk of President Lincoln in the
form of a letter from Samuel White, a citizen of Rushford, New York.
White, concerned for his son's incarceration at Andersonville, proposed that
a Union force be sent to liberate those held captive in that Georgia prison.
He then stated what many in the North accepted as an unquestioned fact:
"The rebel prisoners at Elmira in this State live better than many poor people. They have wholesome food and enough of it, and are well provided for
in sickness. The contrast is great between these prisoners and ours."[4]

Charles Fairman and others who viewed the captivity of Union soldiers
as cruel bondage had little reason to know that the Confederacy was now
hard-pressed to provide food, medicine, and other necessities that sustained
life. The devastating impact of three years of war had seriously depleted the
South's agricultural production. Although many rural areas of the Confederacy by 1862 had shifted from growing cotton, tobacco, and hemp to subsistence crops such as corn, sweet potatoes, peas, wheat, and barley, food
shortages plagued the South. In April 1863 a bread riot had taken place in
the streets of Richmond. By July 1863 the Mississippi Valley was in the
hands of the Union army. This deprived the Confederacy of much of its
rice and sugar production. Wherever the opposing armies fought, the stern
exigencies of war rendered the land virtually useless. This was especially
true in Virginia and Tennessee.

And when in the spring of 1864 General Grant launched his unremit-
ting strategy of offensive warfare against General Lee's Army of Northern
Virginia, the result was an increased contraction of Confederate farmlands.
This was followed by General Sherman's march to the sea from Atlanta to
Savannah in the autumn of 1864. That campaign devastated cropland that

until that time had produced significant amounts of food. Sherman's powerful 62,000-man army, carrying out a scorched-earth strategy, destroyed all crops and centers of transportation. This seriously impaired any attempt to properly feed Union prisoners of war at places such as Andersonville. Charles Fairman and other Northern editors were clearly mistaken in thinking that the South could adequately supply food for Union prisoners of war. Slowly, the Confederacy saw its agrarian strength sapped by the invaders from the North. "Contrary to the sacred truism," historian Emory M. Thomas has concluded, "a nation of farmers could indeed go hungry."[5]

In the Confederacy, of course, the prisoner-of-war issue was seen as something where all evil was on the side of the Union. In his analysis of this phenomenon, William B. Hesseltine has noted that "information of the cruel treatment of prisoners in the North conformed with the psychosis which had developed among the Confederate authorities." The people of the Confederacy, he concluded, "believed as firmly as did the citizens of the United States that their soldiers in prison were the victims of barbarous treatment."[6] There were charges of conspiracy on both sides.

History has taught us that the elements of conspiracy often lurk ominously in the murky corners of political power, and individuals who possess power can often balance just deeds and cruel acts as they wish. The potential to plot mischief is ever present, and no two men understood this better than Stanton and Raymond. If the secretary of war, with his thoughts of retaliation, needed a reminder, it came from newspapers such as Raymond's *New York Times*. Another powerful national figure, General Grant, was also beginning to talk of retaliation. "When acknowledged soldiers of the Government are captured," Grant said in an exchange of letters with Gen. Robert E. Lee, "they must be treated as prisoners of war, or such treatment as they receive will be inflicted upon an equal number of prisoners held by us." Grant concluded his October 29, 1864, letter, by voicing his hope "that it may never become my duty to order retaliation upon any men held as prisoners of war."[7]

In the dank shadows of Elmira's bleak and chilly October weather, the consideration of Union retaliation was something the Confederate prisoners did not focus on. Their thoughts turned to the impending winter season that had given notice in the form of the early October snowstorm. On October 1 Wilbur Grambling entered in his prison diary: "Weather is cloudy and very unpleasant and cold. Don't expect to sleep much tonight as I only have one blanket to cover with and it is quite thin. Don't see how

I am to live this winter without more cover."[8] Hundreds of those incarcerated at Elmira possessed the wisdom to write home for the necessities of life. "Do not have me any fine or costly clothes made," wrote prisoner D. W. Bruin to his sister on October 6, "but something *heavy* & comfortable, suitable for this climate."[9] Blankets, overcoats, tobacco, smoking pipes, and darning needles were common requests in letters coming out of the camp.

Prisoners' thoughts of the coming winter months were offset by the *Advertiser's* emphasis on the late summer's good local growing conditions. "On the whole," the newspaper related in a biblical vein, "the blessings of the year have been imparted in no stinted measure, and the time is still distant when the gaunt form of famine or want can stalk through the land." And, in reporting "the choicest kind of fall growing weather," the newspaper told of grazing areas "ample enough to supply the browsing herds of cattle and sheep, and by so much lengthening out the short crop of hay, which must last from cold weather to spring again."[10] In short, there was no shortage of meat and fruits and vegetables in the Elmira area.

Charges by newspapers such as the *New York Evening Express* that prison conditions were extremely poor in Elmira were countered by claims that the quality of life in the camp was very good. One exasperated Union prison guard, in a lengthy letter to the *New York Times,* asked: "Shall we furnish them [the prisoners of war at Elmira] with brown-stone houses, ice cream, and feather beds?"[11] And, ignoring the grim death rate that gripped the camp, the *Advertiser,* by now officially authorized to publish legal notices for the War Department, cheerfully informed its readers that the Confederates at Elmira willingly spoke favorably of camp conditions and the good quality of food.

The journal also made it clear that the prisoners were contented, healthy and in good condition, "and they so express themselves to those who come in contact with them." And the newspaper concluded that scurvy and dysentery were diseases contracted by the Confederates before they came to Elmira and these particular maladies were rapidly declining inside the camp. The mortality rate, the newspaper confidently claimed, "will soon be materially lessened."[12]

Unfortunately, the claims of the *Advertiser* differed from Union authorities stationed inside the prison camp. A ranking Union officer at Barracks No. 3, in an October 1 letter to his wife, stated: "The rebs are dying quite fast from 8 to 30 per day."[13] As scurvy and dysentery continued to plague the camp, the death rate soared unrelentingly through the month of October.

With the grim prevalence of death and illness, a strange twist emerged at this juncture in the administrative thinking of the military. On October 3 Colonel Tracy issued what in retrospect became a most controversial edict—Special Orders No. 336. In stilted military prose, the order stated:

> Whereas the fresh Beef now being furnished at this Post is in the opinion of the Col Comdg unfit for issue, and inferior in quality to that required by contract. Therefore: Col. S. Moore, 16th Regt. Vet. Reserve Corps and Major Henry V. Colt, 104th N.Y. Vols. [the officers in charge of the prison camp] are hereby designated to hold a survey upon said Beef and to reject such parts or the whole of the said Beef as to them appears to be unfit for issue, or of a quality inferior to that contracted for.[14]

This order came at a time when the camp's rations had already been reduced by 20 percent and the sutler's shop had been forbidden to sell food to the prisoners. Now the stark reality was that limitations on rations became more acute, for cutting back ever so slightly on the supply of beef would escalate the probability of malnutrition. And a most intriguing ramification of Special Orders No. 336 is the fate of the rejected beef. The daily meat inspection frequently resulted in large amounts of beef being rejected for failing to meet the standards of the contract. The rejected beef was then sold to local meat markets and purchased by Elmira's citizens.[15]

All this rightly calls Colonel Tracy's judgment into question, for the order was something that emanated within Elmira's military chain of command. The post commander's beef order most certainly pleased those enthusiastic advocates of retaliation who functioned at the War Department's magnetic center. In increasing the potential for malnutrition, Special Orders No. 336 immediately became a factor in the camp's excessive death rate. If it was put in place with the hope that retaliation would compel the Confederacy to reform its own prisons, it failed. No possible "good" came from this order.

Those who support Colonel Tracy's order have argued that large amounts of meat were rejected in order that the unspent money be used to create an essential and substantive prison fund. A prison fund, however, emanating directly from the federal treasury would have met the prison's needs without endangering the prisoners' health. It is apparent, and unfortunate, that the War Department lacked the moral stature to establish such a fund. In short, the need to build up the prison fund at the expense of the Confederates' food allotment did not justify Special Orders No. 336. The prison fund at Elmira (eventually, it will be recalled, reaching $239,857.01) financed camp purchases that ranged from laundry kettles to the eventual construction of a sluice that greatly alleviated the unsanitary condition of Foster's Pond. This was accomplished at a terrible cost in lives.

In 1878 the shortcomings of Special Orders No. 336 were exposed, perhaps unwittingly, in the form of a letter to a local newspaper. In responding to an article written by a Confederate survivor of Elmira, Brig. Gen. Alexander S. Diven noted that on several occasions he accompanied Colonel Tracy to the slaughter yard where the beef was inspected. Diven was for a considerable time during the prison camp's existence the provost marshal of the Federal Draft Rendezvous of Western New York at Elmira. Control of the prison camp was distinct from his command. He recalled Tracy rejecting "beef, which, though it was such as I would often have been glad to have had for myself and my command, was not all of the quality contracted for, and such part was returned."[16] General Diven's observation that the rejected beef was good enough "for myself and my command" is a poignant revelation that goes well beyond the emotional memories of the camp's survivors.

If Diven is correct, evidence then points to Special Orders No. 336 as being an act that by any standard bordered on retaliation. And the order had tacit approval in the thinking of Stanton, Grant, Raymond, and the court of public opinion that was so cogently expressed in newspapers such as the *New York Times.* Clearly, Tracy erred in his blind allegiance (whether real or imagined) to a power structure in Washington that was bent on revenge. In addition, the hardened enmity on both sides, soldiers and civilians alike, made it easy to assume that purposeful mistreatment of prisoners was occurring on the other side. The evil actions of the enemy government were to be avenged. Thus it was relatively easy to carry out Special Orders No. 336. Finally, if Tracy did not issue the order in the spirit of retaliation, the best that can be said for him is that his sin in this matter was rigidity to the point of callousness.

Starvation, manifested in stages, would become visibly evident inside the prison camp. Weight loss, headache, fatigue, irritability, insomnia, and depression were the prevailing signs that became apparent to anyone who had access to the stockade. "I have seen groups of battle-worn, home-sick Confederates," Union lieutenant Frank Wilkeson, an officer in charge of a guard detail inside Barracks No. 3, would recollect nearly a quarter century later, "their thin blankets drawn tightly around their shoulders, stand in the lee of a barrack for an hour without speaking to one another. They stood motionless and gazed into one another's eyes. There was no need to talk, as all topics of conversation had long since been exhausted."[17] Over forty years after the camp closed, a survivor of Elmira would remember seeing "men go hungry a day and save their rations and trade them for tobacco," and "a prisoner discharge a quid of tobacco from his mouth and another pick it up, dry and smoke it."[18]

With great emotion (and in some cases exaggeration), the consequences of Special Orders No. 336 were sadly and bitterly chronicled in the postwar recollections of those prisoners of war who survived Elmira. "The meat ration," prisoner Anthony Keiley wrote in 1866, "was invariably scanty; and I learned, on inquiry, that the fresh beef sent to the prison usually fell short from one thousand to twelve hundred pounds in each consignment." Keiley's observation, in the final analysis, sees Special Orders No. 336 resulting in an escalation of malnutrition, starvation, and death. Keiley added that "when this happened, many had to lose a large portion of their allowance; and sometimes it happened that the same man got bones only for several successive days. The expedients resorted to by the men to supply this want for animal food were disgusting. Many found an acceptable substitute in rats, with which the place abounded."[19] Keiley bitterly observed that "in a nation, whose boast it is that they [the people of the United States] do not feel the war, with the world open to them, and supplies of all sorts wonderfully abundant, it is simply infamous to starve the sick as they did there [Elmira]."[20]

In clearly supporting those who argued that malnutrition was prevalent at Elmira, Union lieutenant Wilkeson, in his recollection of the camp, spoke of images of "Confederate prisoners, thinly clad, enfeebled by campaigning, and further weakened by insufficient supplies of food." Wilkeson remembered Barracks No. 3 as "a place to be avoided by men of good taste. The prisoners, it was alleged, were allowed the same rations, excepting coffee and sugar, that their guards received. They did not get it. I repeatedly saw the Confederate prisoners draw their provisions, and they never got more than two thirds rations."[21]

Many who survived Elmira were in agreement with prisoner Anthony Keiley and Lieutenant Wilkeson. Prisoner Walter D. Addison recalled: "No coffee, no tea, no vegetables, but a few beans to make tasteless watery soup consisting of the liquid in which the pork had been boiled."[22] Years later, prison camp survivor James Marion Howard claimed: "Our soup would usually be made of onions, rotten hulls, roots and dirt. None of these things were washed hence the dirt. I said this was soup. They CALLED it soup, but of all soups, this rotten onion soup has the worst odor. . . . It was brought to a boil and then taken up in tin plates and put on the table. This, with a piece of bread, was our ration at 3 P.M. And this was our ration every day."[23] Prisoner James B. Stamp remembered in the winter months the "insufficiency of food increased, and in many instances, prisoners were reduced to absolute suffering. All the rats that could be captured were eaten, and on one occasion a small dog that had followed a wood hauler into the camp was caught and prepared as food."[24]

"Our rations," prisoner T. C. Davis of the 40th North Carolina recalled, "consisted of loaves of stale bread an inch thick, tough pieces of steak, and occasionally broth."[25] G. T. Taylor of the 1st Alabama Battalion of Heavy Artillery would write forty-eight years later that "rations were very scant. About eight or nine in the morning we were furnished a small piece of loaf bread and a small piece of salt pork or pickled beef each, and in the afternoon a small piece of bread and a tin plate of soup." Taylor acidly concluded: "Elmira was nearer Hades than I thought any place could be made by human cruelty."[26]

Prisoner Marcus B. Toney had charge of a ward—a duty that entailed calling the roll once a day, making out a daily ration report, and submitting a report of the sick sent to the hospital and the convalescents returning to his ward from the hospital. "In the cook house," Toney stated in his Civil War memoir, "were a large number of iron kettles or caldrons in which the meat and beans were boiled. I suppose these caldrons would hold fifty gallons. The salt pork was shipped in barrels and rolled up to the caldrons, and with a pitchfork tossed in, then the beans—I have heard the boys say four beans to a gallon of water. Now when this is boiled down it gets very salty, and after three weeks of a diet of this kind a prisoner will commence to get sick."[27]

Bearing in mind that sole reliance on prisoners' recollections frequently results in facts becoming more enigmatic, other views must be given consideration. Thus, if a counter to the charges of a lack of rations at Elmira was needed, it came from prisoner Berry Benson's extensive postwar memoirs: "I don't give credit to one-tenth part of the ill stories that are told of either Southern or Norther[n] prisons. As to ill treatment, it would be a wonder if there were not some."[28] Yet the common thread that runs through the overwhelming majority of recollections of Elmira is a lack of food. Collectively, the charges of meager rations at Elmira set Benson's opinion off as a minority report. Stale pieces of bread, sparse amounts of vegetables, and a shortage of meat are sadly recalled by great numbers of Confederates who spent time at Camp Chemung.

In an intriguing twist, the most controversial account of a shortage of rations was written during the camp's existence. On December 30, 1864, prisoner John Brusnan, writing a one-page missive (the maximum allowed) on regulation 8-by-10 blue rag paper, somehow got a letter to his sister in Maryland past the military mail censors at Elmira. "I will give you," Brusnan wrote, "some idea of my situation. I would never have written to you for money, but I am almost starved to death." Next came the two sentences that, after the contents of the letter apparently appeared in newspapers, caused a great stir in the War Department: "I only get two meals a day, breakfast and supper. For breakfast I get one-third a pound of bread and a small piece of meat; for supper the same quantity of bread and not any meat, but a small plate of warm water called soup."[29]

Reaction to Brusnan's letter was swift and angry. Lt. P. E. O'Connor of the 10th Veteran Reserve Corps (Union) and a relative of Brusnan's recommended that Brusnan be limited to bread and water through the duration of his confinement at Elmira.[30] "It is almost unnecessary," Colonel Tracy angrily informed the Office of the Commissary General of Prisoners on January 15, 1865, "for me to say that the statements made by the prisoner Brusnan are outrageously false. The daily ration for each prisoner is uniformly as follows: For breakfast, eight ounces bread, eight ounces meat; for dinner, eight ounces bread, one pint and a half soup of excellent quality, made from meat, potatoes, onions, and beans."[31]

Two days prior to Tracy's sending this letter to Washington, Lt. Col. Stephen Moore, the commanding officer at Camp Chemung at that time, informed Elmira's acting assistant adjutant general that the prisoners of war receive on a daily basis the exact itemized rations that Tracy had listed. Moore added that the "great majority get a piece of meat in the soup."[32] Indeed, it was with great emphasis that the military command at Elmira, clearly in sync on the rations issue, testily denied Brusnan's charge of insufficient rations.

Public opinion in Elmira, influenced by the *Advertiser*'s editorials, supported the military's claim of abundant rations. The Confederates confined at Elmira were, according to the *Advertiser*, "treated with all the care and consideration that such persons are entitled to receive by Christian nations in any part of the world." Claiming that the prisoners' "rations are of a good quality and abundant in quantity," the reporter (apparently after a tour of the prison camp's facilities) related that the "bread which we have examined is as good as can be found in any bakery in our city." With a certainty that all was well inside the camp, the newspaper added: "Their soups, with which they are provided daily, looked rich and savory, and as it was about our dinner hour, we felt inclined like Oliver Twist, too [*sic*] ask for more soup."[33]

This newspaper report was filed on December 2, 1864; to that point 994 Confederate prisoners of war had died in Elmira. Critics who claimed that the *Advertiser* was motivated by a biased view that ignored the death rate and presented a falsely favorable account of the camp's status were quickly supplied with verbal ammunition. On the very next day Charles Fairman, apparently judging himself ennobled in recompense for services, came forth with a rather revealing account. "For our favorable notice of the meat and Butcher Department [of the prison camp]," the *Advertiser* boasted, "we have received a choice roasting piece which we shall enjoy with our dinner to-day and for which we return our kind and sincere thanks to Messrs. PAGET & ROGERS who seem to know what is fit and proper for loyal editors [*sic*] table as well as for a Government Inspector's examination."[34]

If nothing else, it is clear that Charles Fairman's *Advertiser* stood as a partisan drum major in support of Colonel Tracy and the chain of command that administered the prison camp. Yet, in spite of the *Advertiser's* staunch allegiance, what stands out as a most damning indictment of Tracy's claim of sufficient rations for the Confederates is General Diven's observation that the rejected beef was acceptable. Alas, the rejection of large amounts of beef that clearly were suitable for consumption contributed substantially to malnutrition and death.

Clearly, this was Tracy's greatest failure in his tenure as Elmira's post commander. Indeed, it was his most significant shortcoming because he either ignored or failed to grasp the fact that within the structure of the North's nine major prison camps there were webs of local discretion—i.e., much of the decision-making on the acceptance or rejection of rations, money for prisoners, clothing, etc., was inevitably left in the hands of the respective post commanders. Therefore, even if he had been bound by the War Department to reject substandard beef, he clearly failed to warn Washington that his rejection of the slightly inferior meat substantially lessened the food available to prisoners of war in Elmira. "A rule-book administrator,"

Tracy's biographer has written, "he may have been too prone to await Washington's final approval at a time when greater imagination combined with his evident capacity to hard work and a strong personality might have saved many lives at Elmira."[35]

To his credit, however, Tracy quickly recognized the danger posed by Foster's Pond and the urgent need for additional winter barracks, but the tragic repercussions of Special Orders No. 336 would haunt him well beyond the postwar era. His defense of the order restricting the beef supply would be viewed by legions of Elmira's survivors as an egregious variant of Marie Antoinette's alleged remark—"let them eat a small plate of warm water called soup."

Historians have correctly reminded us that the recorded experiences of Civil War prisoners are emotional, vituperative, recriminating, and often inaccurate. Volumes of harrowing accounts of prison life were published *ad nauseam* by the survivors of the camps, and when these works stand solely on their own, no accurate picture of prison life emerges. This rightly gives pause to the person who is seeking answers in the matter of prison camps. Therefore, in order to gain a proper perspective of what happened inside these camps, one must go beyond an examination of prisoners' recollections. This should be kept in mind, indeed, when one considers the recollections (cited above) of prisoners Anthony M. Keiley, Marcus B. Toney, G. T. Taylor, Walter D. Addison, James B. Stamp, T. C. Davis, James Marion Howard, and John Brusnan.

Nevertheless, those in authority did have official notification of Elmira's ration deficiencies in the form of an October 16 inspection report filed by Capt. Bennett F. Munger. Far removed from the emotional memories of Elmira's prisoners of war, Munger reported forty-four deaths between October 11 and 15. "The cause of this amount of sickness and death," he added, "is a matter of deep interest. That the existence of a large body of filthy, stagnant water within the camp had much to do with it can admit of no doubt." Turning to other causes of death such as insufficient amounts of food, he compassionately concluded: "Most of these causes may be removed, and that it be done seems the plainest duty of humanity."[36] The concern reflected in Captain Munger's final sentence is, unfortunately, an aberration in the collective military correspondence that relates to the Elmira prison camp.

Munger was viewed as a decent human being by many of the prisoners who survived the camp. One survivor of Elmira recalled: "I will say in jus-

Melvin Mott Conklin, a 20-year-old Union soldier from Owasco, New York, posed as a Confederate prisoner of war inside the camp. His success as a spy resulted in a marginal number (seventeen) of escapes from Elmira. CHEMUNG COUNTY HISTORICAL SOCIETY

tice to the officers, Captains Whiton and Munger, that they did what they could to alleviate the sufferings of the prisoners, but were almost powerless to render the aid they desired."[37] And, in 1866, prisoner Anthony M. Keiley would write: "Wherever he is, and whatever he does, however, Captain Ben. Munger has the good-will of every prisoner who ever drew rations at Barracks No. 3, on the bank of the Chemung."[38] Sadly, "the plainest duty of humanity" is a scarce commodity in a time of war. Instead, military administrators (some in Elmira and some in Washington) tolerated the reduction of the quantity of rations, and delayed action on improving sanitary conditions (Foster's Pond) and constructing additional barracks in preparation for the winter season.

Conditions in Elmira motivated great numbers of Confederate prisoners of war to consider the possibility of escape. Attempts at escape, sometimes on the verge of being hatched, were almost always aborted by a spy system that had successfully infiltrated the prisoners' ranks. A network of so-called Confederate "oathtakers" and a chief informant—Melvin Mott Conklin, a Union soldier from Owasco, New York—served the prison administrators well in detecting various escape schemes. Conklin, a young man who would marry and settle in Elmira and serve for many years as the city's postmaster, posed as a prisoner of war inside the camp. He and the "oathtakers" (in conjunction with the Union sergeants) would discover all attempted tunnel escapes—except one.

In mid-August two members of the Alabama Jeff Davis Artillery, John Fox Maull and John P. Putegnat, agreed to a tunnel escape plan with Frank E. Saurine of the 3rd Alabama. They were almost immediately joined by a fourth man, Washington Brown Traweek, who was also a member of the Alabama Jeff Davis Artillery. These four men concluded their carefully made plans of escape and began digging a tunnel on August 24 from a tent (occupied by Maull and Putegnat) located sixty-eight feet from the camp's northern wall.

According to a family descendant, Traweek "was a sixteen-year-old Overseer of a Plantation at Selma, in Wilcox County, Alabama, when he volunteered for duty in the Jeff Davis Artillery."[39] He came through the war unscathed. Maull enlisted at age eighteen and fired the signal gun which initiated the Confederate attack at Seven Pines, Virginia, on May 31, 1862. At Seven Pines, the Confederates were repelled by Maj. Gen. George B. McClellan, at that time the Union's imperious commander of the Army of the Potomac.

Putegnat was a 19-year-old boy when he entered the Elmira prison camp. Traweek and Maull had participated in the battles of Second Bull Run, Antietam, Chancellorsville, Fredericksburg, Gettysburg, and the Wilderness. All three were captured at Spotsylvania, Virginia, in May 1864 and sent from Point Lookout to Elmira in mid-August. Saurine, a native of Philadelphia, had married a Southern woman and was living in the South at the outbreak of the war. He was also among those captured at Spotsylvania.

The four Confederates began digging with a stolen spade, but, in abandoning it, concluded that it made too much noise. They immediately turned to tunneling with pocketknives, and, in doing so, discovered that this method would require a larger labor force. "We were all young and ambitious," Maull would write years later, "and we thought we could dig our way out in four or five days, but soon discovered it was no easy task."[40] S. Cecrops Malone of the 9th Alabama was quickly admitted to the surreptitious circle of tunnelers.

With their right hand on a Bible, the five men took an oath not to reveal any aspect of their escape project to any individual. Six more men were eventually allowed to become part of the endeavor; they were Gilmer

G. "Hickory" Jackson and William H. Templin of the Jeff Davis Artillery, J. P. "Parson" Scruggs of the South Carolina Holcomb Legion, Glenn Shelton of Mississippi (military unit not known), James W. Crawford of the 6th Virginia, and Berry Benson, the young man who had marched through the streets of Elmira on July 24 and "had eyes only for the pretty girls." All six of these men readily swore a solemn oath of secrecy.

Benson was the last to be admitted to the group. He had noticed Traweek taking stones from his pocket and dropping them in Foster's Pond. Benson, suspecting that the stones came from a tunnel excavation in progress, approached Traweek and warned him that "oathtakers" were about and they would report his actions. Traweek initially denied digging a tunnel, but Benson persisted. According to Benson's recollection years later, Traweek finally admitted "we're all bound by an oath not to tell it nor hint of it to the dearest friend, but you've found it out without my telling it, and now if you want to join us, I've no doubt the boys will all be willing enough to take you in. We want another good hand."[41]

The men removed the sod on the floor of the tent occupied by Maull and Putegnat and carefully preserved it for cover to deceive Union inspectors. They went down six feet and then began to dig their way toward the fence. They dug by day, one man gouging out what he could with a knife and another man directly behind him to haul out the dirt. The dirt was brought out in pint-sized bags that were made from an extra shirt owned by Putegnat. The men waiting in the tent filled their pockets with dirt and stones and then, as inconspicuously as possible, emptied their pockets in the pond and the drinking wells. Often they rid themselves of dirt and stones at dusk. Uniforms were turned inside out in order to conceal the red dirt of the tunnel.

Union sergeants frequently conducted inspections that required the prisoners to stack their tents while the ground was inspected for tunnels. Since prisoners worked as clerks and cooks and hospital aides, it was relatively easy to be tipped off as to when the next inspection was to take place. In order to conceal their efforts, the men would place boards three feet below the surface of the tent's floor and fill the area in with dirt. The sod was then carefully placed over the entrance to the tunnel. This proved to be a successful maneuver.

Although the ages of the men ranged from nineteen to twenty-one, digging the tunnel proved to be a formidable physical challenge. Benson

One of the pint-sized bags made from the shirt of prisoner John P. Putegnat. It was used to haul dirt out of the escape tunnel under Putegnat's tent. The box and two boulders were used to cover the tunnel's entrance. Plank boards were then placed at the surface of the entrance and sod was used to cover the boards. The inserted pictures of Putegnat show him as a Confederate soldier and years later as a bearded citizen of Alabama. CHEMUNG COUNTY HISTORICAL SOCIETY

would remember that "the tunnel was only large enough to admit the body and in some places it was a squeeze at that."[42] A limited amount of oxygen in a tunnel twenty to twenty-four inches in diameter proved to be a serious matter. The men complained of dizziness and headaches, and this problem required frequent relief for those doing the digging and the hauling of dirt.

To complicate matters, the dedicated excavators also suffered from a lack of nourishment. The standard fare of the camp's reduced rations simply was not enough to sustain them. "Parson" Scruggs attempted to counter the effects of the insufficient supply of food. Being a ward sergeant, Scruggs routinely ordered and delivered rations on a daily basis to the men of his ward who were too ill to walk to the mess house. Scruggs also saw to it that his fellow tunnelers were given abundant amounts of food.

At some point in mid–September the attention of the men turned to the possibility of digging another tunnel under a newly constructed hospital ward in another section of the camp. Traweek and Putegnat procured a spade and completed a tunnel in two nights. They decided to inform those working on the original tunnel project and go out the next night. The tunnel under the hospital was discovered, however, and the men returned to digging from the tent to the north fence.

The next day Traweek was taken from his quarters, charged with digging the tunnel under the hospital, and placed in a jail cell. During his stay in jail, Traweek was informed by Captain Munger that a surprise inspection would take place the next morning in an attempt to discover additional tunnels. Why Munger informed Traweek of the proposed inspection remains a mystery. One explanation might be that Munger was a school teacher who taught Traweek at Summerfield, Alabama, before the war.[43] Whatever the reason, that night Traweek, from his jail cell, got a message to Maull that a surprise inspection would take place the following morning. Maull made sure the tunnel was secured. The inspection uncovered an astounding total of twenty-eight tunnels. This amazing number of excavations pointed strongly to an amorphous system of escape activity within the camp. With its determined burrowers sworn to secrecy, the tunnel under the tent of Maull and Putegnat remained undetected.

Traweek spent close to three weeks in a jail cell before he was allowed to plead his case before Maj. Henry Colt, the officer in charge of Camp Chemung at that time. Colt, a short, portly man with a distinguished gray beard and jolly disposition, was known by the prisoners for his affinity for cigars and his fair-minded judgment in discipline cases. He was one of those officers who was well liked by the Confederates in part, perhaps, because he had experienced significant combat with the 104th New York. Traweek submitted his request for release, and in granting it, the avuncular Major Colt, his rumpled charm augmented by a wreath of cigar smoke, said that the young prisoner "had been too hasty in trying to tunnel out, and that if . . . [you] had taken . . . [your] time . . . [you] probably would have escaped."[44]

Traweek returned to his stealthy circle of excavators on the forty-first day of the tunnel's existence. By this time Frank Saurine had been cast out of the group. Saurine had stopped taking his turn at digging because he became interested in other tunnel projects. To his dismay, all tunnels except the one started under the tent of Maull and Putegnat had been shut down. On October 4 it was discovered that the tunnel excavation had veered to the right. This was corrected and the area of misdirection was used for depositing dirt. On the night of October 6 Washington Traweek, digging what he knew were the final few feet, hit a fence post. He and Berry Benson took turns digging under the fence. Finally, in the early hours of October 7, they reached the surface on the street side of the prison fence. Traweek, Crawford, and Maull (in that order) were the first men out. As Traweek crawled out, he heard the sentry on the platform above him cry: "Half past three o'clock and all is well."[45]

John Fox Maull's recollection of his first moments outside the prison was similar to most of the others. He heard two sentries above him and there were six Union soldiers gathered around a campfire directly across the street. "I stepped out as leisurely as my 'grit' would allow me," he recollected years later, "expecting every second to hear the word Halt, ready to spring as close to the Yanks as I could on hearing the command. But none came. I walked up within a few feet of the soldiers and turned to my right, like I was going down to the city."[46] Maull finally ran across Gilmer "Hickory" Jackson and William Templin. The three men made their way in broad daylight across the river west of the prison camp where they rested on the south side of the Chemung River close to the top of a heavily wooded, craggy hill known as Mount Zoar. Maull would remember: "We lay on the side of the mountain watching and talking and planning all day. We could see the prisoners gathered around our old tent, and there seemed to be a big stir among them all day."[47]

Maj. Henry V. Colt of the 104th New York served as the prison camp commander from its inception through December 1, 1864. He answered directly to the Elmira post commander. CHEMUNG COUNTY HISTORICAL SOCIETY

Ten men made their way to freedom by 4:30 that October morning. "I think I was the tenth man," Berry Benson recalled decades later, "and as it was a law of the society that, to avoid disputes as to precedence in going out of the tunnel [should] it succeed, the men should go out in the order of their admittance into the society, I felt my own chance of escape to be not large in any event, for nine men [could] hardly get away without discovery."[48] Benson succeeded and, after gathering some ears of corn and apples from a nearby farm, headed west through the village of Big Flats and the town of Corning. He then turned south and, with the help of a small compass and a crude map, made his way home by himself.

Cecrops Malone and John Putegnat took a northeasterly route that the morning after their escape brought them to a small farmhouse about six miles south of Ithaca, New York, a town thirty miles northeast of Elmira. There, they were taken in and fed breakfast. They walked through Ithaca and on to the tiny village of Varna where they took a hotel room and slept. They managed to remain undetected because Malone had somehow been able to hold on to two suits of civilian clothes while in prison. He and Putegnat forsook their Confederate garb and were able to get by undetected in their new clothes. They moved on to Auburn, New York (thirty-five miles north of Ithaca), where Malone took a job as a machinist and Putegnat as a helper. They eventually saved enough money to purchase train fare to New York City and on to Baltimore where they set out for points south. Undoubtedly, the odyssey of Malone and Putegnat was the most bizarre of all the escapees.

Traweek and Crawford swam across the Chemung River and made their way to near the top of Mount Zoar. They rested through the day at a vantage point that allowed them to look down on the confusion that consumed the prison camp. Unbeknownst to them, they shared the same vision of Camp Chemung with Maull, Jackson, and Templin. Also, "Parson" Scruggs made it across the river to Mount Zoar and peered down during the day on the whirring beehive that was Barracks No. 3. (On that day those escapees occupying three separate areas on Mount Zoar never met up with each other.) Using a small telescope, Traweek and Crawford saw "the confusion which was created when they missed us. We could also see the cavalry rushing around through the valley in search of us."[49]

Crawford and Traweek slept part of the day, and then started out that night for the long trek south. It took Crawford twenty-three days to make his way through enemy lines to his home in southern Virginia. In mid-November he bitterly informed the *Richmond Examiner:* "I succeeded in getting out from the clutches of the meanest people that have ever lived. It matters not where you put them, they are the same damned people. Our prisoners sicken and die twenty-five to thirty per day; but that seems to please them more than anything else." His fighting spirit apparently unbroken, Crawford concluded by stating that the South "should fight for ever before being subdued by such a nation; though I cannot see where old Abe is to get his next call from. They are scarcer from here to Elmira than they are in the Confederacy. I think they have played out, and not us of the South. Please take extracts and give the Yanks hell."[50]

The confusion that was seen from Mount Zoar on the morning of the escape existed inside and outside the camp. When Major Colt and his staff inspected the tent of Maull and Putegnat, all they saw were a pile of dirt and the entrance to the tunnel—silent remnants that attested to the Spartan diligence of the ten escapees. "I was surprised to see how crooked the tunnel was," a survivor of Elmira would recall many years later.[51] Prisoner Wilbur Grambling, obviously citing one of the many rumors that swept through the compound, jotted in his diary that "25 army men made their escape last night by tunneling. They got 25 horses. Commenced Aug. 19th. They dug 64 ft."[52] The confusion observed from Mount Zoar was in part traced to the fact that the Confederate ward sergeants did not report anyone absent on the morning of October 7. The following day the *Advertiser* assured a concerned community that, although none of the escapees had been recaptured, "there was a suspicion of their whereabouts."[53]

Nine of the ten men made their way back to the South. Glenn Shelton of Mississippi escaped but was never heard from again. For decades after the war they were celebrated in their respective communities as heroes. There was good reason to celebrate, for their remarkable achievement is considered to be the most spectacular escape in the annals of prison camps administered by the Union during the Civil War. What makes this escape even more meaningful is that only seventeen prisoners of war escaped from Elmira during the year of the camp's existence. Also, Elmira was the most secure prisoner-of-war camp managed by the North. Prisoner Marcus Toney would write: "The tunneling ceased after that successful attempt."[54] Toney was not correct; there would be more tunnel attempts. None would succeed.

Of equal importance is that they had escaped from a stockade where their Confederate comrades would continue to suffer horrendous mortal indignities. On the day of their escape, the death toll in Elmira had reached 667.[55] One of the escapees, making his way south through northern Pennsylvania, would recall an elderly woman in a farmhouse telling him that she thought 200 prisoners had escaped from Elmira on October 7. She then added: "Poor things, they are starving 'em to death, and I hope they'll all get out."[56] Lt. Frank Wilkeson, the Union officer who possessed a firsthand understanding of the prison camp in the autumn of 1864, would look back on the breakout and admit to being "exceedingly glad that these men had escaped."[57]

The October tunnel escape stands as perhaps the single most remarkable story of the Elmira prison camp. Other escapes of note from Elmira included one prisoner who was placed in a swill barrel by his Confederate comrades. With only his nose above the barrel's contents, he managed to pass through the main gate on the "swill wagon" unnoticed and emerge from his hiding place before the wagon reached its destination. Another prisoner stole a Union sergeant's ankle-length winter overcoat and walked through the main gate without being questioned. Still another Confederate successfully made it out of the camp with a forged pass.

The most bizarre escape was that of a Georgia prisoner of war (known only to his fellow Confederates as "Buttons"). Buttons had somehow managed to conceal fifteen dollars from prison authorities and, with this money, successfully bribed the Confederate keepers of the dead house. He was placed in a coffin and a cover was nailed lightly in order that it could be removed easily. The keepers then made sure that Buttons's coffin was stacked on top of the wagon that was destined for the cemetery one and one-half miles away. When the wagon reached a relatively safe distance from the prison camp, Buttons made his move. He popped open the lid of the coffin, jumped off the wagon, and began running at full speed toward the nearest wooded area. The horrified driver, in a state of disbelief, sat as motionless as a petrified piece of stone. Buttons was never heard from again.

The tunnel escape of October 7 came at a time when Colonel Tracy and his staff were engaged in processing between 1,200 and 1,400 Confederates for transfer in an exchange for Union prisoners of war. In an order dated September 29, Colonel Hoffman informed Tracy to make preparations for the transfer of prisoners of war who were not fit for service within sixty days. They were to be sent by train to Baltimore for delivery to Confederate authorities. No one who wished to remain in Elmira and take the oath of allegiance and no one who was too feeble to endure the journey would be transferred. Hoffman specified that those to be exchanged were to be accompanied by at least one medical officer and several able Confederates who had served in the camp hospital as attendants and nurses. A sufficient guard detail under the command of seven officers was ordered, as were cooked rations for two days.[58]

Colonel Tracy immediately appointed a committee of five officers—including Maj. Henry Colt, Lt. Col. Stephen Moore, and Major Sanger—to inspect and process the prisoners for exchange. Within a day of Hoffman's order, word of the exchange swept through the camp. Prisoner Anthony M. Keiley, in his capacity as a clerk in the camp hospital, noted in his diary that "the knowing ones are rubbing up their old complaints, getting their asthmas, rheumatisms, lame legs, etc., in working order for the examination about to take place."[59] Keiley requested permission to travel south as a nurse with those who would be exchanged. On October 9, two days before the scheduled departure of those being exchanged, his request was honored.

When several prisoners of those selected for exchange died between the time of the selection and the group's actual departure, other Confederates successfully bribed the camp doctors to include them on the journey south. Early on the morning of October 11 the prisoners for exchange made the two-mile trip from the prison camp to the town's railroad depot. They were described by a witness to the proceeding as "a ghastly tide, with skeleton bodies and lusterless eyes, and brains bereft of but one thought, and hearts purged of all feelings but one—the thought of freedom, the love of home."[60]

The caravan of 1,264 ill and wounded slowly made its way to the railroad station. All but about 300 were able to walk to the depot. The process took most of the day, and this time there was not the morbid curiosity that greeted the prisoners when they had arrived in Elmira three months earlier. Occasionally a compassionate citizen would step forward and hand a prisoner some wrapped sandwiches. "Great rejoicing and gladness prevailed among the number at the prospect of going home," the *Advertiser* reported, "perhaps to die or at least be among their friends once more."[61]

As Anthony M. Keiley left Barracks No. 3, he turned to Major Colt. "His eyes filled as he bade me good-by at parting," Keiley would recall, "and I fear my own were not altogether dry, as for the last time I wrung the hand of the true man, and humane, courteous official, Major Colt."[62] The prisoners entered the railroad station where three trains consisting of a total of sixty boxcars were quietly waiting for the long trip south. Shortly before dusk the three trains pulled out of the station and quickly made connections with a spur that set them on a course south on the Northern Central line.

The caravan's destination was Baltimore, where the prisoners would be transferred to three steamers that were scheduled to take them down the Chesapeake Bay to Point Lookout and finally on to City Point, Virginia, where the exchange was to take place. "It is hardly probable," the *Advertiser* stated with a degree of grim prescience, "that some will reach Point Lookout alive."[63] Perhaps the newspaper's premonition was based on the knowledge that, in spite of Colonel Hoffman's clear order, no medical doctor was on board any of the three trains.

Nevertheless, the *Advertiser* claimed that each of the "sick cars was well provided with attendants and pails of water and every care taken to make the invalids comfortable as possible."[64] One of the train's passengers, however, would recall: "The condition of a long train of box-cars, filled with such a number of helpless sick, confined in the same spot, and crowded unnecessarily during a ride of some two hundred and sixty miles, at the rate of less than seven miles an hour, can easily be imagined."[65] The journey by train from Elmira to Baltimore normally took fourteen to fifteen hours; the first of the three trains arrived in Baltimore forty hours after its departure from Elmira. During the slow, agonizing trip, death claimed five of the Confederates. Another prisoner of war succumbed shortly after he arrived in Baltimore. Military medical officials in Baltimore were shocked to learn that not a single doctor was on board any of the trains.

Surgeon Josiah Simpson, medical director of the Middle Department, VIII Army Corps, angrily reported to Colonel Hoffman that many of the prisoners arriving from Elmira were gravely ill. "I made a personal inspection of the men," Simpson stated, "and found a number unable to bear the journey. . . . [M]any should never have been permitted to leave Elmira."[66] At the same time Surgeon Simpson ordered the military surgeon in charge of West's Buildings Hospital to receive sick and wounded from the Elmira trains. Simpson stated in his instructions to admit as many "as humanity requires should be taken care of."[67]

The day after the three trains from Elmira arrived in Baltimore, a military surgeon boarded the steamer loaded with prisoners and bound for Point Lookout. Finding no medical officer, hospital steward, or nurse on board, he reported to Surgeon Simpson that someone "is greatly censurable for sending such cases away from camp even for exchange."[68] Surgeon C. F. H. Campbell, a medical inspector, then filed a devastatingly scathing report with Surgeon Simpson stating that sixty of the men were suffering from extended illnesses and too debilitated to make the trip. "Such men," Campbell wrote, "should not have been sent from Elmira. If they were inspected before leaving the place in accordance with orders it was most carelessly done, reflecting severely on the medical officers engaged in that duty and is alike disgraceful to all concerned. The effect produced on the public by such marked displays of inefficiency or neglect of duty cannot fail to be most injurious to our cause both at home and abroad."[69]

In a cover letter that forwarded all reports of the Elmira exchange to the commissary general of prisoners through the Office of the Surgeon General, an irate Surgeon Simpson suggested "criminal neglect and inhumanity on the part of the medical officers in making the selection of men to be transferred."[70] On October 24 Colonel Hoffman sent all reports dealing with the matter to the secretary of war. In doing so, he informed Stanton that Colonel Tracy was issued specific orders to guard against the transfer of prisoners of war who were too ill to travel. The incensed Hoffman, keenly aware that the transfer and its ramifications were a reflection on his office, then noted that "it appears that both the commanding officer and the medical officers not only failed to be governed by these orders, but neglected the ordinary promptings of humanity in the performance of their duties toward sick men, thus showing themselves to be wholly unfit for the positions they occupied, and it is respectfully recommended that they be immediately ordered to some other service."[71]

The blistering criticism that came from Colonel Hoffman and the military medical staff in Baltimore amounted to convincing evidence. Someone "is greatly censurable"; "many should never have been permitted to leave Elmira"; "disgraceful to all concerned"; "criminal neglect and inhumanity on the part of the medical officers"; and "both the commanding officer and the medical officers . . . neglected the ordinary promptings of humanity in the performance of their duties toward sick men"—all of these accusations, along with a call that the ranking officers in Elmira be replaced, reached Secretary Stanton's desk.

It can be argued that the testimony of the medical officers in Baltimore presented a compelling case for court-martial proceedings against Tracy, Sanger, and Colt. Yet the secretary of war remained silent. Nothing came of the incident, and all three officers carried on in their respective positions of authority at Elmira. If nothing else, Stanton's inaction gave his postwar critics another reason to charge the War Department with carrying out or at least of tolerating retaliatory policies.

Sanger's role was to determine which prisoners were fit to travel. Three weeks after the exchange, he claimed: "When the sick were sent from here for exchange I received no official information, nor was advised in reference to the matter."[72] In a letter to the surgeon general, Major Sanger would declare that the "train started without reporting to the medical officer, and before the nurses were assigned, blankets distributed, and many had been fed after a fast of more than twelve hours. I was ordered to appoint a given number of nurses and doctors, and my application for an increased number received no attention."[73]

This does not, however, satisfactorily explain why no doctors were assigned to any of the three trains. Sanger's explanation, if accurate, only illustrates the confusion that existed in Elmira at the time of the exchange. It also leaves for speculation the possibility that Tracy obfuscated matters deliberately. One thing is certain: the failure to provide doctors for the exchange became a major source of contention between Colonel Tracy and

Major Sanger. Each officer now saw the other as being responsible for this terrible blunder.

In the aftermath of the transfer of the prisoners from Elmira to Baltimore, a letter written by one Mary W. Rhodes (a resident of New England) appeared in the *Daily National Intelligencer,* a Washington, D.C., journal that backed Lincoln in 1860, but threw its support to the Democratic presidential candidate, Maj. Gen. George B. McClellan, in 1864. The editors of the *National Intelligencer* explained that the "letter was not written for the public eye," but "some to whom it was shown urged its publication as a public duty."[74]

Writing from Baltimore, Mrs. Rhodes described what she had recently witnessed in Elmira. "Though not permitted to go inside the prison enclosure," she stated, "I saw the condition of the fifteen hundred [*sic*] who were taken away for exchange, many of them in a dying condition." Obliquely indicting Stanton, Mrs. Rhodes continued: "It is useless to appeal to the Secretary of War. It rests with the men of the North to remove this foul stain from our country. The officers in charge of the prison at Elmira are kind and humane, but the condition of things is beyond their power to remedy." Citing the need for clothing, blankets, and food, she concluded: "I cannot, *will not,* believe that my countrymen of the North will permit this state of things to continue. . . . Those fifteen hundred [*sic*] pale faces are before me as I saw them pass me at the depot. . . . I saw in a city whose church steeples tower toward Heaven gentle women who would have given [food] . . . driven by brutal police and detectives from the mission bequeathed to them by the pitying Son of Mary. . . . I would plead for all the prisons, though I have only seen the horrors of Elmira."[75]

Although there was no specific response to Mary W. Rhodes's letter, Charles Fairman's *Advertiser* saw Mrs. Rhodes as one of those misty, besotted citizens whose sentiments oscillated between polarities of personal sympathy for the prisoners and political support for the Confederacy. Her letter was published in mid-October—a time in Elmira when the days were growing shorter and the nights colder. At this point nothing had yet been done about Foster's Pond. Construction of additional winter quarters was in its initial stages. A lack of meat in the daily rations was taking its toll. These matters weighed heavily on the fate of the men inside the walls of Barracks No. 3.

Outside the walls, just a few yards from the prison's main gate, a mid-October reunion dinner party and dance took place at the officer's mess house at Barracks No. 3. Friends and invited guests of the 54th New York shared laughter and fine food. "The room was tastefully decorated," the *Advertiser* reported, "and the music was par-excellence. Brave men and fair women mingled in the mazy dance with great spirit and delight. The entertainers spared no pains in making the occasion full of pleasure and memorable."[76] Thus, in an almost surrealistic setting, death and despair were separated by a few yards from the niceties of the good life. During the week of the 54th's reunion party, fifty-five prisoners of war died in Elmira. In October death claimed 276 Confederates inside Barracks No. 3. This figure brought the camp's death toll to 857. October was a month where once again Elmira's death rate was the highest of any camp in the North.[77] The *Advertiser* failed to note this fact.

CHAPTER 6

"There Has Been an Outrageous Negligence on the Part of Officials"

At the beginning of the Civil War nobody foresaw the horrendous consequences that the prison camps would wreak upon the nation. And when the disastrous transfer of 1,264 prisoners of war from Elmira to points south took place, there was no great hue and cry within the country for an investigation. Secretary Stanton's silence on the matter was not greeted with editorial indignation in a decidedly large percentage of Union newspapers. Perhaps this is because after three years and seven months of bloody conflict, the great majority of Northerners had now taken on a hardened and bitter view of the Confederacy.

Yet a curious ambivalence in the thinking of the commissary general of prisoners remains, defined by the polarities between Hoffman's enthusiasm for retaliation in the form of reduced rations for prisoners and his angry proposal to cashier Elmira's ranking officers for their part in the October transfer of Confederates. Indeed, Hoffman's divided thinking sheds some light on the Byzantine policy values of the Office of the Commissary General of Prisoners; i.e., it reveals an overall moral weakness that was endemic to the kind of military pragmatism that the War Department had come to embody.

If anything, moral courage was at a low ebb. In Elmira, the *Advertiser* failed to report the transfer in any way other than to state that it was a completed transaction. Editors such as Charles Fairman took their cue from a resolution passed by the U.S. House of Representatives on December 16, 1863, praising the Union's administration of prisoner-of-war facilities and denouncing the Confederacy's treatment of Union captives. The following May, a House committee that inspected prisoner exchange terminals at Baltimore and Annapolis, Maryland, released a thirty-page document known as *Report No. 67.* "The testimony," historian William B. Hesseltine has written, "taken by the committee and embodied in the report was sufficient evidence to the Congressmen that there was a fixed determination on the part of the rebels to kill the Union soldiers who fell into their hands."[1]

Report No. 67 was enthusiastically endorsed by the War Department—an office where insolently proud men conveyed an air of certainty that the Union's treatment of Southern prisoners of war was far too kind. In February 1864 Maj. Gen. Montgomery C. Meigs, the quartermaster general of the United States, told a New York City newspaper: "We are killing them [Confederate prisoners] by treating them as southern gentlemen until they die of gout."[2] This, of course, was hardly the case. General Meigs went on to suggest a work program (something that certainly would have benefited prisoners of war in Elmira) for all captured Confederates.

On the heels of *Report No. 67* came a request from the U.S. Sanitary Commission to conduct its own inspection and report. This was flatly rejected by the secretary of war. The U.S. Sanitary Commission, a civilian organization approved by the U.S. government in June 1861, and then located in Washington, D.C., came into being at a meeting of fifty-five women in New York City in late April. Made up for the most part of upper-crust white Anglo-Saxon Protestants, the Commission's president throughout the war was the Reverend Doctor Henry Whitney Bellows—a New England patrician, graduate of Harvard, and prominent Unitarian minister. Doctor Bellows, minister of All Souls Church in New York City at the outbreak of the war, proved to be a moving force within the association.

The Sanitary Commission, supported mainly by private funds, was dedicated to "preserving and restoring the health and of securing the general comfort and efficiency of troops, to the proper provision of cooks, nurses, and hospitals, and to other subjects of like nature."[3] In short, this organization would play a role in supplying food, blankets, clothing, medicine, and medical supplies. And, in 1864, the Commission would extend its concerns to the conditions in prisoner-of-war camps.

Despite its humanitarian concerns for those taken captive in the war, some Sanitary Commission members (not surprisingly) harbored snobbish, condescending opinions of the incarcerated Southerners. At least one Commission member noted pointedly that the majority of Confederate prisoners of war were bereft of meticulous enunciation. "Most of them were unlettered farmers' sons," observed Mary A. Livermore, "innocent of the alphabet. Their speech was almost unintelligible at times; for they talked a *patois,* made up in part of negro gibberish and in part barbarous English."[4] One critic has written: "The low and at times obviously prejudiced opinion of enemy soldiers by Sanitary Commission members becomes more striking when one considers the cloak of humanitarianism which encased their work."[5]

Personal prejudices, however, were but a minor hindrance to the Commission's operation. There was, more importantly, from the beginning an uneasy alliance between the Sanitary Commission and the War Department. The Commission would soon discover that the Medical Bureau of the War Department was rife with confrontations that involved egos, jealousy, turf battles, and political intrigue. Because the Medical Bureau had considerable influence on the treatment of Confederate prisoners of war, the status, efficiency, and morale of that office merit a brief comment. Historian William Y. Thompson has concluded that "the American volunteer soldier, entering the battles of the Civil War, faced an entirely different situation [from today's modern soldier]. Ahead lay death from enemy bullets. Behind him plodded a medical bureau, inadequately equipped in materiel, spirit, and vision to protect him from destruction by disease."[6]

The court-martial of 34-year-old William A. Hammond, Surgeon General of the Medical Bureau, illustrates the power of politics on the decision making process within the War Department. Doctor Hammond was a progressive, intelligent, innovative physician whose reputation seemed to fly in the face of the older, lethargic officers of the Medical Bureau. Hammond, with the enthusiastic support of the Sanitary Commission, was appointed to the post of surgeon general in the spring of 1862. Lacking any semblance of tact and convinced that his decisions were above criticism, Hammond was inevitably headed for a fatal showdown with the secretary of war. It came in February 1864 when a court-martial found Hammond guilty of "conduct unbecoming an officer and a gentleman."

Hammond's indictment was a transparent frame-up of a medical officer who was willing to take on the entrenched and inflexible members of the Medical Bureau's old guard. The heavy hand of Secretary Stanton was apparent to all who observed the proceedings. To complicate matters, Hammond's naïveté led him to believe unrealistically that he could receive a fair hearing. Alas, his most powerful enemy was the secretary of war—the man who was, in effect, the judge and jury in the case.

Hammond was dismissed from the service and denied a pension and the right to hold any office under the government of the United States.[7] The significance of his dismissal is that control of the Medical Bureau was now returned to unimaginative and unenergetic officers who could trace their military roots to the War of 1812. The triumph of the old guard in this case would have long-lasting effects. Now older physicians, clinging to antediluvian medical theories, were assigned to the important posts.

Therefore, in a system that was undeniably flawed, the progressive views of the best young doctors (such as Major Sanger) often were pushed aside. Clearly, this was an end to new ideas at a time when medical innovations could have played a somewhat important role in America's bloodiest war. The Medical Bureau lapsed into a lethargic state that would remain in place until the sudden crisis of the Spanish-American War in 1898. Thus by July 1864 when the first Confederate prisoners of war arrived in Elmira, the War Department's Medical Bureau was firmly in the hands of tired, recalcitrant military officers.

Even before the court-martial of Hammond, Doctor Bellows and the other leaders of the Sanitary Commission had found Secretary Stanton to be consumed by passion and rancor. On May 9, 1862, in a letter marked "Confidential" to Senator Preston King of New York, Bellows voiced his concerns over Stanton's delaying tactics and the selection of "political favorites" for the positions of medical inspectors. "If this delay," Bellows angrily concluded, "were due to doubt & uncertainty whom to nominate—it would be excusable. But we have reason to believe that it is wholly due to political & personal considerations, which are wickedly out of place, in the selection of *Medical* officers."[8]

Four days later, following a strained meeting with the secretary of war, Doctor Bellows wrote: "I am sorry to say that the impression of Stanton is that of a man with a brain in a very dangerous state of irritability & one, who in the use of his vast power, forgets the rights & the position of his officers who chance to be in private life. . . . I fear [Stanton possesses] an internal temper & cerebral condition which will come to some disagreeable end—if it continues to increase."[9]

Two years later relations between Secretary Stanton and Doctor Bellows remained strained. Now, over the War Department's objections, the

Sanitary Commission decided to proceed with an inspection and report on the condition of prisoner-of-war camps in the North and South. In charging that the Sanitary Commission, in making its subsequent investigation, was deceived, William B. Hesseltine has concluded that the Union's commissary general of prisoners falsely responded to questions regarding rations, blankets, clothing, shelter, and fuel. "Hoffman returned favorable answers to these questions," Hesseltine has observed, "and sent a copy of the rations he had ordered issued April 20, without mentioning the further reduction which Stanton had already approved."[10]

Colonel Hoffman's response came in the form of a letter to General Meigs. "With the above information I hope, [G]eneral," Hoffman concluded with a clichéed sense of piety, "you will be able to satisfy the Sanitary Commission that the prisoners of war in our hands are treated with all the consideration and kindness that might be expected of a humane and Christian people." He went on to say that "[i]f our enemies, instead of following our example, deliberately destroy the lives of their prisoners by denying them food and shelter they heap shame upon themselves in the eyes of the civilized world."[11]

In failing to inform the Sanitary Commission of a further reduction in rations (circular of June 1, 1864), Colonel Hoffman was clearly guilty of deception. And if Hoffman deceived the Commission in the hope of thereby inviting a positive report, he succeeded. The Sanitary Commission's report first reached the public through the *Daily National Intelligencer* in early October. The individual (apparently not a member of the newspaper's staff) who filed the story with that newspaper stated that a copy of the report reached him "in connection with . . . [my] official duties in the army." According to the *National Intelligencer's* account, the Commission found that "very fatal severity of treatment towards prisoners of war is proven against 'Rebel Authorities,' and proven beyond peradventure. The testimony is varied, authentic, ample, and its perusal shocks and exasperates."[12]

On October 19 the *National Intelligencer,* however, printed a lengthy editorial criticism of the Sanitary Commission's report for ignoring mistreatment of Confederate prisoners of war and in exaggerating the evil intent of the South. The newspaper, in questioning as to whether the Commission's conclusions were "authentic and trustworthy," stated that Sanitary Commission members "in making their report had not been careful to exclude from it the suspicion of all preconceived opinions or partisan bias in dealing with the facts elicited by their inquiries." In short, the newspaper cited the possibility (and probability) that the Commission members had been taken in by false information from the War Department. In conclusion, the *National Intelligencer* stated: "We insert in another part of today's paper a letter from a lady [Mrs. Mary Rhodes; see chap. 5], in which she gives an account of what she heard and saw at Elmira, New York, respecting the sufferings of the insurgent prisoners at that point. . . . The Sanitary Commission, we hope, will inquire into the accuracy of the impressions recorded by the writer."[13]

It should come as no surprise that the *New York Times*'s reaction to the Sanitary Commission's report was quite different from that of the *National Intelligencer*'s. The *Times* cited those who conducted the study as men whose "personal character place them so far beyond suspicion, that among men of intelligence . . . their word would not be called in question." According to the *Times,* "the investigation was at once formal, searching and unprejudiced." The newspaper then informed its readers that "these Commissioners come to the solemn conclusion, that during their captivity in the military prisons of the South, the great mass of our loyal soldiers *'were hungry day and night,* and suffered the pangs of famine with its dreams and delusions.'" The *Times* concluded that the Commission's report "may be considered as an epitome of the opposing social systems which have from the beginning, prevailed North and South; and there appears to be sound philosophy in the conclusions of the Commissioners, that 'the social theory may yet be fully established, *which attributes the alienation of the Southern people to a simple difference of feeling on a question of humanity.'"*[14]

In complete agreement with the *Times,* the *Advertiser* in late October ran a story that originally appeared in the *New York Herald.* Denying mistreatment of Confederates imprisoned in Elmira, the *Herald* had labeled as "pure fabrication" copperheads' claims of "the starvation, abuse and neglect of the rebel prisoners at Elmira, N.Y." According to the *Herald,* prisoners' rations at Elmira "are amply sufficient." And, in admitting that there was an unusually high level of illness in the camp, the newspaper declared that prisoners' sickness emanated "from causes beyond the control of the authorities, and of a temporary character, and there is no lack of medical attendance or supplies." Finally, in an indignant declaration that was embraced by the great majority of Northerners, the journal concluded: "Doubtless the malicious and groundless statements will be widely copied in the rebel papers, and be made the excuse for the infliction of still greater barbarities upon the unfortunates who are captured and fall into their hands."[15]

The belief that Elmira was a humane prison camp prevailed in some circles well beyond the immediate postwar years. In 1892, at a meeting of ex-prisoners of war in Scranton, John T. Davidson spoke on the fate of Confederate prisoners of war in Elmira. Davidson, a captain of the guard detail at Camp Chemung in 1864 and 1865, said that the mortality rate at Elmira "was large, owing to the fact that there was a decided change of climate, water, and the manner of living."[16] And, in what amounted to an emotional peroration, Davidson claimed that "the horrors of a prison camp, when the inmates are crowded into small quarters, poorly clad, half-fed, uncomfortably housed or sheltered, cruelly treated, with little or no medicine and no hospital accommodations, in a climate to which none are acclimated, away from home and friends, surrounded by the deadliest enemies, is a condition from which all men may well pray to be forever delivered, but none of these things can apply, with a shadow of truth, to the prison camp at Elmira."[17]

Davidson thus echoed three decades later what was accepted by most Elmirans in the autumn of 1864. And at times the generally favorable opinion that prison conditions were good in Elmira was backed by an authoritative voice. Almost a month to the day after the *National Intelligencer's* request that the Sanitary Commission look into the conditions that Mrs. Rhodes had described, Miss Dorothea Dix stepped off a train at Elmira's railroad depot. Her fame as a crusading reformer preceding her, she was greeted by a distinguished group of Elmira's leading citizens.

Dorothea Dix served during the war as the civilian superintendent of Women Nurses for the Union. She gained national notoriety in 1843 when she petitioned the Massachusetts legislature to remedy the horrible condition of the mentally ill in that state. Physically frail, wracked with persistent lung problems, she proved to be a person of seemingly endless willpower and energy. Her mission was to inspect hospital and camp conditions in Elmira.

It is not known who dispatched Miss Dix to Elmira, but it is probable that the Sanitary Commission (an organization whose compassion and concern she shared) recommended her. What is known is that Miss Dix's initial request to inspect Elmira's prison camp was rejected by Maj. Gen. Ethan A. Hitchcock, commissioner for exchange of prisoners. Hitchcock, a West Point graduate, was a soldier/scholar who thoroughly enjoyed the works of Shakespeare, Chaucer, Hegel, and Spinoza. Nevertheless, he carried out his duties in the War Department with an edgy zeal that bordered on contempt for the Confederacy. One account states that General Hitchcock's rejection of Miss Dix's request was "based on security, but two days later he changed his mind."[18] The *Advertiser* noted that her "visit is at the instance of the government, which avails itself of her life-long experience in connection with the amelioration of the condition of the criminal as well as the sick and wounded."[19]

The *Advertiser* reported that Miss Dix "was highly gratified at the manner in which the government provides for the prisoners of war in this place." She "visited the several hospitals, including the rebel hospital, in company with Col. Tracy, commandant of the post. She was invited by him to examine the beef, pork and vegetables furnished to the prisoners, and expressed herself satisfied with them all, as well as the general care bestowed upon them. Her only wish seemed to be that our prisoners in the South should be as well provided for as those at Elmira are now."[20]

Coinciding with Miss Dix's Elmira visit was a highly favorable weekly inspection report that was submitted by Capt. William P. Jordan of the 29th Maine to Colonel Tracy on November 20. Conduct, clothing, state of mess [house] and kitchen, hospital diet, and general health of prisoners were judged to be "good." Cleanliness was "much improved since last report," and state of quarters was termed "very fair." Bedding was such that "most of the men have blankets but no straw." Food was termed "quality of, good," and "quantity of, plenty." Sinks were listed as "fair," and "drainage, fair, except at the pond." Policing of the grounds and hospital were noted as being "very good." Captain Jordan's report concluded by stating that "attendance of sick appears very good," and "vigilance of guard, very good."[21]

On November 25 Dorothea Dix filed with the War Department an official report on her Elmira visit. Her account noted that she "visited the prisons [*sic*] and hospitals at Elmira, in both which the rebels are receiving all necessary care, and provision fully adequate to all necessities; health, good; sick-call, moderate; serious illness, but few cases; mortality, low; prisoners, about 8,000; probably 7,400 fully able for field service."[22] Miss Dix's conclusion that the mortality rate was low raises the question as to what in fact she was not shown. During her 2-day stay, twelve Confederate prisoners of war died. This brought Elmira's November death toll at that point to 128. Death would claim seventy-nine more prisoners in November to bring the mortality number for the month to 207. Only Camp Douglas in Chicago, with 217 deaths, surpassed Elmira in November.[23]

Significantly, at the time of Miss Dix's visit to Elmira, an angry feud was festering between Colonel Tracy and Major Sanger. If Dorothea Dix was aware of this contentious disagreement between these two strong-willed officers, there is no evidence of it in her report on Elmira to the War Department. The dispute undoubtedly was fueled by the criticism of Elmira officials after the exchange catastrophe of October. Although no documented evidence establishes the initial differences between the two men, it is highly probable that their acrimonious relationship began with complaints listed by Major Sanger in mid-September. At that time Sanger told a medical inspector from the Department of the East that he was prevented from obtaining medical supplies and this made it virtually impossible for him to properly administer the camp hospital. The camp's chief surgeon also stressed that hospital facilities (specifically water closets, dispensary offices, and storerooms) were inadequate.

On September 24 Surgeon William J. Sloan of the Medical Director's Office, Department of the East, instructed Sanger to list all essential requisitions necessary for hospital alterations, repairs, and improvements "for my approval, and the action of the general commanding the department. . . . I will urge everything essential to a good and proper administration of your department."[24]

For the five-week period following Sloan's letter it was Major Sanger, a recalcitrant man, who seemed to ignore Surgeon Sloan's advice and support. And it remained puzzling to some ranking members of the medical staff of the Department of the East as to why Sanger remained inexplicably silent through the month of October—a critical period when he could have sought guaranteed support. It would not be revealed until mid-November that the September 24 letter Sanger received from Surgeon Sloan had originally been "submitted to the commanding officer of the camp, Colonel Tracy, who stated that Colonel Hoffman, Commissary-General of Prisoners, Washington, gave all orders in relation to their management, and that all requisitions must be submitted to him [i.e., Colonel Tracy] for this action."[25]

Surgeon Charles McDougall (U.S. Army, medical director, Department of the East) at that time supported Colonel Tracy's position. In keeping with this, McDougall reasoned that the overriding objective was "to procure the necessary supplies and relieve the medical department of responsibility or censure."[26] This sort of ambivalence did not enhance Sanger's position. What is clear at this point is that Colonel Tracy, not Major Sanger, would determine the volume of supplies for the prison hospital. It would appear, then, that one cannot hold Major Sanger solely responsible for the camp's failure to acquire needed medical supplies and structural improvements.

In mid-October, Major Sanger, in hopes of being relieved of his duties in Elmira, sought the ear of a ranking military figure in a distant place. He wrote to Brig. Gen. John L. Hodsdon, adjutant general of the State of Maine, and requested that he be granted a military position in Maine. Citing his absence of more than three years from his home state, Sanger specifically requested a recruiting position in Augusta. Then came a most chilling passage: "I now have charge of 10,000 Rebels a very worthy occupation for a patriot, particularly adapted to elevate himself in his own estimation, but I think I have done my duty having relieved 386 of them of all earthly sorrow in one month."[27]

There is no evidence that General Hodsdon responded specifically to Major Sanger's incredibly shocking claim, and it is safe to assume that the general did not share the contents of the letter with other military authorities. Sanger's indictment by his own hand (even if exaggerated) would never come to light during his lifetime. It does much, however, to serve his critics in their contention that he exhibited a callous, brutal attitude toward the Confederate prisoners of war at Elmira. Taken literally, it reveals (his critics would argue) the inner core of a man who was a cold, calculating, self-serving medical officer whose lack of compassion led him to deny his patients at Elmira his salutary medical skills.

In an oblique way, Sanger's disturbing revelation corroborates the charges of former prisoner Walter D. Addison. A ward master in one of the camp's hospital barracks, Addison remembered that opium pills were dispensed to patients "no matter what the nature of the disease." Addison, citing the cavalier method of issuing drugs, recalled an incident that involved Major Sanger and a Surgeon Van Ness: "On one occasion three persons so being treated were were [sic] sinking, the surgeon-in-chief, a Doctor Sanger, was called in, he directed Dr. Van Ness to write four or five drops of Fowler's solution of arsenic. He wrote forty-five, and the patients in a very short time breathed their last. No investigation ensued. No reprimand. Dr. Van Ness continued his position." There was, according to Addison, a desire on the part of Union officers to kill Confederate prisoners. "All in authority in Elmira," he claimed, "seemed to be of this opinion."[28]

In his capacity as a hospital clerk, prisoner Anthony M. Keiley would in part agree with Addison. In the year following the war, Keiley wrote that "in six weeks he [Sanger] made more widows and orphans than the siege of Troy."[29] And Keiley charged that Sanger refused to sign any report that stated the cause of death as anything related to malaria. This, according to

Keiley, was because "in the medical department in a Yankee prison-camp . . . [there are] opportunities of plunder. . . . Vast quantities of quinine were prescribed that were never taken, the price (eight dollars an ounce) tempting the cupidity of the physicians beyond all resistance; but the grand speculation was in whiskey, which was supplied to the dispensary in large quantities, and could be obtained for a consideration in any reasonable amount."[30] Keiley would also cite "that the better class of officers in the pen were loud and indignant in their reproaches of Sanger's systematic inhumanity to the sick." And, according to Keiley, it was the soaring September death rate that eventually brought about Sanger's departure from Elmira.[31]

If the observations of Addison and Keiley are true, they would incline one to interpret Sanger's mid-October letter to General Hodsdon literally, not ironically. Yet when one examines the postwar opinion of prisoner James B. Stamp, one sees a decidedly different view of the prison's hospital structure. "The medical and hospital departments of Elmira prison," Stamp recalled, "are worthy of commendation. In addition to surgeons for the various hospitals, there was one for each of the five sections of the camp." Although he did not mention Major Sanger by name, Stamp related to "a full line of medical stores, which were in charge of competent druggists, and accessible at all hours of the day and night. The strictest rules of cleanliness were enforced in the management of the hospitals."[32]

If Stamp did not specifically defend the controversial Doctor Sanger, prisoner John S. Hutchinson did. Hutchinson arrived in Elmira in early July 1864 and procured a job in the prison hospital. "Dr. E. F. Sanger, Surgeon in charge of the hospital," Hutchinson would inform the publisher of the *Southern Historical Society Papers* in 1883, "showed me great kindness, for which I have ever been grateful." During the early summer days of 1883 Hutchinson journeyed to Bangor, Maine, where he would have "the pleasure of meeting with the Doctor [Sanger], and while conversing with him, the subject of the mortality among the prisoners, both North and South, came up." In a revealing gesture, Sanger provided Hutchinson with a complete record of the Elmira census and mortality rate that he had kept in his personal journal.[33] Hutchinson, at that time a pastor of the Methodist Church in Fredericksburg, Virginia, found Sanger to be pleasant and congenial. Those who remember Elmira's chief surgeon in a different light might perhaps agree with the poet that Hutchinson was seeing Sanger "in the gray disguise of years."

Yet what cannot be ignored by Sanger's critics is that he did in fact keep a personal journal of those who died in Elmira. Indeed, the ghosts of Elmira's Confederate dead were singed into his conscience. There is good reason for this. Sanger had, of course, taken the Hippocratic oath. He was a man who possessed a passionate interest in medicine, and he was at the beginning of the war eager to serve as a U.S. Army officer. Also, it must be remembered, that although he lost part of a leg during the siege of Port Hudson in 1863, he continued to serve as an army surgeon. And, perhaps most importantly, at Elmira Sanger would provide the most salient voice in calling for improvements in every aspect of prison camp life.

Yet Sanger, if his words were to be taken at face value, put on paper a shocking confession that could have resulted in a court-martial. This lends credence to his critics who claim that he was a devious, vindictive man bent on making survival difficult for Elmira's Confederate prisoners of war. To condemn Sanger for stating that he "relieved 386 of them [Confederate prisoners] of all earthly sorrow in one month" is, however, to ignore his acrimonious relationship with Colonel Tracy. It was Tracy who blocked Sanger's efforts to improve hospital conditions. And it was Tracy who would demand an investigation of Sanger's administration of the prison hospital. Clearly, Sanger's aggressive mannerisms had much to do with his claim in his letter to General Hodsdon. Perhaps more importantly, his words reflect a bitter, ironic, indirect protest at the role which he had been forced to assume: to be responsible for the health of the prisoners and to be denied access to the very medical supplies which he needed in order to do the proper job.

One can charge Sanger with being self-serving, abrasive, abrupt, rude, and most certainly untactful in his human relations. His complaints against Tracy certainly can be thought of in some respects as intended to lend cover to his own faulty management of the prison hospital. Yet it must be noted that between August 13 (a week after his arrival) and October 17 Major Sanger issued nine written reports that listed in great detail the life-threatening shortcomings of the prison camp. And his accounts eventually led to action. No other officer, in the duration of the camp, did so much in such a short period of time. Undoubtedly, the single greatest irony of the Elmira prison camp is this: the officer who most vociferously called attention to the unsanitary conditions and other major shortcomings of Barracks No. 3 became the nearest thing to a scapegoat in this very sad story.

In many respects Doctor Sanger thus remains an enigmatic figure. Yet one thing is certain—he intensely disliked Colonel Tracy. It is also clear that both men possessed an audacious faith in their respective judgments. As early as mid-October 1864 the clash between the two officers was made known to Washington when Tracy informed the commissary general of prisoners that the "mortality in this camp is so great as to justify, as it seems to me, the most rigid investigation as to its cause." Tracy, completing his first month in Elmira, called for an examination of the causes of disease—including diet, clothing, and stagnant Foster's Pond. And then came the request that exposed the ill-feeling within the camp's administrative structure—he called for an investigation of "the competency and efficiency of the medical officers on duty here." Tracy concluded that "an investigation, conducted by competent men, would do much to discover the cause and remedy the evil."[34]

In submitting Tracy's report to Secretary Stanton, Hoffman recommended that a medical inspector be dispatched to Elmira in order to determine the causes of illness within the prison camp. This recommendation came at a time when the chill of the October weather seemed to symbolize the dissension between the post commander, an imperiously rigid, autocratic figure, and the camp's chief surgeon, a deeply cranky and cheerless man. A decade after the war Sanger would caustically refer to Tracy as an officer "who liked the smoke of the frying pan better than the smoke of battle."[35] Clearly, Tracy was Sanger's implacable foe and the clash between these two proud and prickly men obviously affected the treatment of the prisoners of war confined at Camp Chemung.

Colonel Tracy, his feud with Major Sanger aside, finally took action on the construction of additional winter barracks at Camp Chemung. What motivated Tracy was that in early October 9,063 prisoners of war were quartered in the prison camp, and only 3,873 of those men slept in barracks. The remaining 5,190 Confederates were assigned to 1,038 tents.[36] On October 3 the War Department approved the project for additional quarters when Colonel Hoffman ordered Tracy to initiate the construction of shed barracks within the prison camp.

Lumber for the project was to be purchased with money from the prison fund, and the camp's prisoners of war would make up the labor force. Able prisoners who had taken the oath of allegiance would receive preference for jobs on the project. Thirty-five barracks (100 feet by 22 feet by 12 feet) were proposed for construction. Accommodating 120 prisoners of war in three-tiered bunks, each building would contain two coal stoves and a kitchen of 22 feet by 20. The floor of each building was to be elevated in order to prevent prisoners' burrowing with the intention of escaping.[37]

"The bunks extended the length of the ward on each side," prisoner Marcus Toney would recollect forty-two years later in his Civil War memoir, "leaving an aisle in the center and two stoves in each ward." Toney recalled that each bunk was "wide enough to sleep two medium-sized men." With two blankets per bunk, "in extreme weather four slept in the space of two, using one pair of blankets to sleep on, which gave three for cover." Recalling the severely cold winter nights of January and February 1865, he noted that "[t]wo of . . . [the prisoners] slept with their heads toward the east, and two with heads toward the west, and of course had to be on their sides; and when ready to change positions, one would call out, 'All turn to the right'; and the next call would be, 'All turn to the left.' The turns had to be made as stated, or there would be collisions. Of course the men did not disrobe in extreme cold weather, and on awakening in the morning their feet would be in each other's faces."[38]

The decision not to initiate construction of additional winter quarters until the beginning of the camp's fourth month of existence is highly questionable. Colonel Hoffman had known since his July 20 visit to Elmira that the camp needed additional barracks. If he needed a reminder, it came on August 28 when Lieutenant Colonel Eastman officially informed him of this fact. With the camp's original barracks filled far beyond capacity since August 1, Hoffman's lack of action merits considerable scrutiny.

It was common knowledge within the chain of command from the time of the camp's inception that prisoners of war would be housed at Elmira during the winter months. Yet the War Department, fully aware that a sufficient prisoner-of-war workforce was available from the very beginning of the camp's existence, did not move on the construction of additional barracks until the chill October nights made their presence known in Elmira. This late construction start quickly became an ominous omen in that delay in other important matters was now taking on a suspicious pattern of regularity. Stanton and Hoffman, two men bent on retaliation, are clearly culpable in delaying the construction of additional winter quarters. Their decision would result in the deaths of hundreds of those imprisoned at Camp Chemung.

As for the matter of Foster's Pond, it was October 17 when Tracy notified Colonel Hoffman that the "continued prevalence of disease and death in this camp impels me to call the attention of the authorities to . . . a stag-nant pond of water within the inclosure. Nothing else that I can see pro-duces the large mortality among the prisoners. . . . The medical officers attribute the larger proportion of the sickness prevailing to the effects of this body of impure and malarial matter." The Elmira post commander then proposed a 6,000-foot drainage trench that would run from the river to the pond. After discussing the cost of the project, Tracy poignantly reminded Hoffman that Lieutenant Colonel Eastman's August 17 recommendation of a drainage system for the pond was acknowledged by an August 20 telegram calling for a full report on the matter. Tracy then drove home the point that Eastman submitted a thorough report to the Office of the Com-missary General of Prisoners on August 21. The Elmira post commander then offered this sober conclusion: "It seems to me that a due regard for the lives of the prisoners confined here requires that some method of introduc-ing a running stream of water through this camp should be adopted."[39]

Two days later Hoffman passed Tracy's extensive report on up the chain of command to the office of Maj. Gen. Henry W. Halleck, chief of staff of the army. In doing so, Colonel Hoffman included the August 17 and August 21 reports of Lieutenant Colonel Eastman.[40] The inclusion of East-man's reports is a revelation of considerable significance. Eastman's letter of August 21 had remained dormant in Hoffman's files for two months. As with the delay of construction of additional winter barracks, this failure to respond to a potentially lethal condition in Elmira resulted in the unneces-sary deaths of hundreds of prisoners of war. Indeed, historian James I. Robertson, Jr., has concluded that, in ignoring the urgent requests of East-man, Tracy, and Sanger, "Hoffman and his colleagues in Washington assumed an almost sadistic apathy toward the [Elmira] prisoners."[41]

On October 23, 1864, with the blessing of the secretary of war, Colonel Hoffman informed Tracy that construction of a sluice for the purpose of funneling fresh water through the pond had been approved.[42] Privately, Union officers such as Capt. Bennett F. Munger and Lt. Frank Wilkeson must have wondered why in the name of humanity nothing had been done before this time, and survivors of Elmira would wonder openly in their post-war memoirs.

On October 27, 114 days into the prison camp's existence, work on a drainage sluice commenced at Camp Chemung. A wooden pipe con-structed of 2-inch plank with a six-inch-square opening was laid for approx-imately a mile upstream from the camp. The joints were joined together and heavily pitched with tar to prevent leaks. The project called for 125 to 150 prisoners of war to provide the labor. Colonel Tracy estimated that the excavation and laying of the pipe would be completed within twelve to fifteen days. Unfortunately, the severe weather of November and December prevented a speedy completion of the project. Another source of delay was the unanticipated problem of excavation. The workforce ran into quicksand in some areas and extremely coarse gravel in other sectors of the pipeline's course. To make matters worse, occasional flooding required several days of extensive pumping.

Sixty-seven days after its beginning, at a cost of $2,000, the project was completed. On that day, January 1, 1865, Colonel Tracy reported to the Office of the Commissary General of Prisoners "that the conduit for conducting a stream of water from the Chemung River through the prison camp . . . works like a charm."[43] Between the time of the camp's opening and January 1, 1865, however, 1,263 Confederate prisoners of war died in Elmira. The delay of addressing the condition of Foster's Pond can be directly traced to the commissary general of prisoners.

At the time that Colonel Tracy was beginning the drainage project, there was cause for celebration in Elmira. Lieutenant Colonel Eastman had returned to town and the *Advertiser* happily reported that it was "glad to see Lieut.-Col. Eastman once more upon our streets. We [congratulate] him upon his restoration of health."[44] Eastman had returned to Elmira from his position as military commander at Fort Mifflin, Pennsylvania, to serve as the grand marshal for Elmira's October 25 pro-Lincoln torchlight parade that enthusiastically moved through streets festooned with the colors of the United States. He would return to that Pennsylvania post on October 26 and remain there until November 1865.

Horace Greeley, the flamboyant publisher of the *New York Tribune* and one of the featured speakers at the pro-Lincoln rally, was granted permission to walk about inside the prison camp. "The baker, the preacher, and Horace Greeley," prisoner Marcus Toney recalled years later, "were the only visitors I saw previous to the surrender of General Lee. Mr. Greeley made some sneering remark about Southern chivalry, so when the time came that I should choose between General Grant and Mr. Greeley for President [in 1872] I voted for General Grant."[45]

A prolonged late October rainstorm canceled the weekly grand review of the troops at Camp Chemung. "The river was on the rise last evening," the *Advertiser* reported on the afternoon of October 29, "at midnight having come four feet above the low water mark. . . . The high water may test the strength of the fence about the prisoners [sic] camp, at Barracks No. 3. But all needful precautions have been taken against any such event."[46] Captain Munger's October 30 inspection stated that a "severe rain-storm has prevailed during the week, making the camp muddy and raising the water in the pond so that crossing to that part of the camp beyond it was prevented for one day." Munger concluded: "Another supply of clothing is needed, as the weather is becoming cold and many are still poorly clad."[47]

In November cold, icy rainstorms eventually turned to snow. "November blasts," the *Advertiser* waxed eloquent, "and snows have almost come upon us unawares this year. . . . November is the pioneer of winter, advancing with its sharp winds and freezing blasts to cut every blade and leaf of remaining green to level the waste and make a bed of winter to sleep upon."[48]

Bad weather was not the only impediment that confronted Camp Chemung. Delays in the construction of additional winter quarters also posed a serious problem. Tracy reported to Hoffman on November 6 that construction had been delayed because of a lack of lumber.[49] November also revealed problems with the older barracks in the camp. Tracy (four days earlier) had informed the War Department of the poor condition of the roofs on the older barracks. A special work crew of prisoners was assembled and the roofs were repaired.[50] On November 20 six of the new winter barracks were completed.

In mid-November the *Advertiser* related to Elmirans that the prison camp "is being made comfortable as need be, for the inmates. New barrack buildings have been erected to take the place of summer tents, and stoves have been introduced to impart the necessary warmth. . . . No pains will be spared to make living in the rebel camp desirable, warm and healthful during the inclement season now rapidly approaching."[51]

Despite the *Advertiser's* reassuring observations, some citizens of Elmira were not satisfied that all was well within the confines of Barracks No. 3. William F. Corey, an officer at the Second National Bank of Elmira and an administrator of the Volunteer Relief Association of Elmira, was one of the more prominent citizens who voiced emphatic dissent. "I am glad," Corey stated in a November 14 letter on bank stationery to a ranking officer of the U.S. Sanitary Commission, "that the Commission is about to do something for the Prisoners here." Corey then responded to the Commission's intention to ship supplies to Elmira: "Aware that Dr. Sanger has made a requisition for articles needed in his department, I presume that the consignment you mention is intended exclusively for the Hospital."[52]

Corey then indicted the administrators of the camp, stating that "there is too much truth in reports prevailing as to unnecessary suffering in the prisoners's camp here. There has been an outrageous negligence on the part of officials." Thousands of Confederates, he maintained, remained in tents and were without sufficient clothing and blankets and the prison hospital was "correspondingly destitute of necessaries." He concluded with this devastating charge: "Out of about 10,000 prisoners there have been 800 & 900 deaths since August and the surgeon in charge is of the opinion at least one third of this human life might have been saved by proper hospital supplies and regulations."[53]

It is quite apparent that Corey, a man who did not have access to the camp, had a primary source—Major Sanger. Sanger, claiming in a letter a month earlier that he was responsible for Elmira's high death rate, was at the same time serving as a conduit of information for Corey's local relief group and (indirectly) the U.S. Sanitary Commission. In doing so, Major Sanger presented Colonel Tracy in an unfavorable light.

Sanger's critics have argued that Elmira's chief surgeon was motivated by his dislike of Tracy. Yet it is undeniable that Sanger was privy to the questionable decisions of the War Department and the poor judgment of Colonel Tracy. Elmira's chief surgeon had firsthand knowledge of (1) the delay to correct the unsanitary condition of Foster's Pond; (2) the late start of construction of additional winter quarters; (3) the questionable October transfer of 1,264 prisoners of war, and (4) the reduction of rations (especially beef). Apprised of this information, William F. Corey concluded that there "has been an outrageous negligence on the part of officials" in Elmira.

On November 11, three days before Corey posted his letter to the Sanitary Commission, Colonel Hoffman was relieved of his position in Washington and assigned to the post of inspector and commissary general of prisoners for the western part of the nation. His new position took him to cities such as Chicago, Cincinnati, Indianapolis, St. Louis, and Columbus, Ohio. Hoffman's replacement was Brig. Gen. Henry W. Wessells, a man known for his advocacy of economy. Wessells would serve as commissary general of prisoners until February 1, 1865, when Hoffman returned to the post.

With General Wessells now in command of prisoners of war, orders to inspect and reject nonstandard beef continued through the autumn and winter months. Captain Munger, in his weekly inspection of the camp, noted that a "portion of the beef is very lean. Cows milked through the season and too poor for a respectable farmer to winter, are slaughtered, and the beef issued to prisoners."[54] Munger stated that in many instances a 92-pound side of beef would yield only 45 pounds of cooked meat. If Munger's calculation is correct, the thirty head of cattle contracted for slaughter each day to fulfill the daily beef order provided just over 5,500 pounds of meat.

Since there is no documentation on the amount of meat accepted and rejected on a daily basis, one can only estimate the impact of Special Orders No. 336. On days, for example, when 2,000 pounds of beef were rejected, this reduced the total to 3,500 pounds of uncooked meat. When cooked, the weight of the beef was reduced to 1,750 pounds. With the camp's average census at 8,100 prisoners of war, the average ration of beef amounted to 3.4 ounces per person. On days when there was no rejection of beef, the cooked meat amounted to 2,750 pounds, affording each prisoner 5.4 ounces of beef. It is highly unlikely that the Confederates often received 5.4 ounces of meat. To exacerbate matters, there was a glaring paucity of vegetables. Tracy, in a November 30 report to General Wessells, stated that "since October fresh vegetables—15 pounds of potatoes and 8 pounds of onions per hundred men—have been issued to the entire camp every three days in five."[55]

The prison camp, gripped by the bitterly cold days of late November and early December, began to show tangible signs of malnutrition, and survivors of Elmira (with understandable emotions) recalled that insufficient rations started to take their toll. Prisoner James Huffman would recollect late in his life that many Confederates "moped about, pining away for want of sufficient food to eat, losing their humanity, eating almost anything a brute would eat—as rats, gangrene poultices and the like." Elmira's prisoners of war, Huffman remembered, "were known by their pallid color and lifeless movements. Most of them died there, not from disease but pining away for lack of more food, some even sending word to their friends at home that they were being starved to death. These poor men grew so lean that they seemed to have no flesh at all, before their spirits left their bodies."[56]

Prison camp survivor Marcus Toney told of men turning to rats for food. "I am glad," Toney would readily admit, "that I did not have to go on this diet; but I have tasted a piece of rat, and it is much like squirrel."[57] Rats,

Selling rats for food at five cents apiece. This became a thriving marketing enterprise inside the camp. CHEMUNG COUNTY HISTORICAL SOCIETY

dogs, and cats inside Barracks No. 3 were pursued with considerable zeal by the hungry prisoners. A rat, five chews of tobacco, and a loaf of bread were equal in a currency exchange that pathetically portrayed the utter depravity of the camp's status. The demand for rats being steady, many enterprising prisoners inside the camp made the selling of the rodents a thriving avocation.

Catching and selling rats became a business for some of Elmira's prisoners. An Elmira survivor, R. B. Ewan, some forty-three years later, recalled the "sport of running . . . [rats] out of their holes." "Our Mart of Trade," he remembered, "was about in the center of the ground, and at 10 o'clock every day dressed rats on boards and tin plates, and sick prisoners' rations, were here offered for five cents and sometimes more."[58] Because Ewan served as a nurse in the prison hospital, he did not have to resort to eating rats.

The accounts of Huffman, Toney, and Ewan understandably are subject to the charge of being the bitter and exaggerated memoirs of men who perhaps found it impossible to be objective. Defenders of the prison camp point to the claims of Colonel Tracy and Lt. Col. Stephen Moore (the camp's executive officer and eventual successor to Major Colt) that rations for the prisoners of war were more than adequate. Outside sources such as the *Advertiser* and Dorothea Dix's inspection report frequently stated that the prisoners were well fed. And, long after the prison camp became part of Elmira's history, two prominent local authors would maintain that the administration of Camp Chemung was above reproach.[59]

It was on December 1, two weeks and three days after William F. Corey wrote his critical letter, that a Dr. Turner arrived in Elmira in hopes of inspecting the prison camp. Turner, a member of the U.S. Sanitary Commission and superintendent of the New York Inebriate Asylum, was met by Corey and introduced to Colonel Tracy. "I hesitated about admitting him," Tracy informed the War Department on December 3, "but deeming it important that the inspection should be made and the report published for the purpose of correcting the impression that seems somehow to have got abroad that the prisoners here are cruelly treated, I concluded to admit him, with the understanding, however, that no report is to be made until my action is approved by you." Tracy concluded by determining that "Doctor Turner is a gentleman of fine literary and scientific attainments and well qualified to make this inspection and report."[60]

Three days later, in a quick, terse, stern response, General Wessells informed Tracy that an inspection of a military prisoner-of-war camp by civilians was "highly improper, and the publication of a report cannot be permitted unless under direction of the Department of War."[61] Tracy was admonished by Wessells, and there was no published report of Dr. Turner's inspection of the camp; therefore, Turner's conclusions will forever remain a source of speculation. Unlike Dorothea Dix, Dr. Turner's visit to Elmira is unrecorded by the *Advertiser*. One can assume that he conversed with Major Sanger and William F. Corey. What was said has been lost to history.

Perhaps Sanger revealed to Dr. Turner the details of his disagreement with Colonel Tracy. Since it was quite clear at this time (the first week of December) that Major Sanger's days in Elmira were numbered, it is probable that his remarks to any concerned person at that time were uninhibited. What precipitated Sanger's departure was a lengthy report he submitted on November 1 to the surgeon general of the United States.

The report, signed by Sanger and nine of his assistant surgeons, was a damning document that stated the "ratio of disease and deaths has been fearfully and unprecedentedly large and requires an explanation from me to free the medical department from censure." Sanger next told of 2,011 admissions to the prison hospital through the months of August, September, and October, and a death rate during that period of 24 percent. Sanger then said that between August 13 and October 17 he had submitted nine written reports (to the post commander) "calling attention to the pond, vaults, and their deadly poison, [and] the existence of scurvy to an alarming extent." Next he had recommended a ration of fresh vegetables daily for the scurvy patients.[62]

The camp's chief surgeon then spoke of a "great delay in filling my requisitions for the hospital" and "the sickness and suffering occasioned thereby." Next he stated that Foster's Pond "remains green with putrescence, filling the air with its messengers of disease and death, . . . and the hospitals are crowded with victims for the grave." Sanger then told of prisoners being "hurried in to their rations of bread, beans, meat, and soup, to half gulp it down on the spot or to carry it hastily away to their quarters in old rusty canteens and impoverished dirty dippers and measures."[63]

Major Sanger then turned to his petulant relationship with Colonel Tracy when he stated that while Eastman was in command, he (Sanger) reported directly to the post commander. With Tracy in charge, "all direct communication has been cut off, and I am ordered by him [Tracy] to report to a junior military officer in camp, who has merely a forwarding power." Sanger then noted: "[I]n the administrative duties of a large hospital department the surgeon in charge must have direct communication with the commander, who is the only authorized executive officer."[64]

Sanger next reported serious delays in receiving medicine and other supplies. He also told of a camp inspector who "enters my wards at all times, instructs my ward-masters and nurses, finds fault to them of my management, and quizzes them in regard to the medical officers." Major Sanger concluded by stating that, much to the chagrin of the medical officers on duty, a camp inspector "changes the beds of the patients, corrects and changes their diet, [and] directs the washing of my patients without regard to my rules. . . . I have entered a written protest without avail. I cannot be held responsible for a large medical department of over 1,000 patients without power, authority, or influence."[65]

On November 12, a day marked by a blustery mix of snow and freezing rain, Surgeon William J. Sloan of the Department of the East (New York City) arrived in Elmira to determine the validity of Major Sanger's report. "The statements made to the Surgeon-General by Surgeon Sanger in his report of November 1 were not exaggerated," Sloan stated on November 14 in his opening sentence of a lengthy report on his Elmira visit, "although an undue warmth of language may have been exhibited, from the difficulties he had to encounter from the delays attending the filling of his requisitions and the little attention paid to his remonstrances."[66] Upon listing a number of proposed improvements for the camp and hospital, Surgeon Sloan concluded that Sanger "complained with justice of the perplexities arising from the delay in furnishing the supplies," and that Tracy, "while maintaining the incorrectness of these complaints, admitted the tardiness of the quartermaster." Then, in a comment laced with anger and disgust, Sloan stated: "The quartermaster justified himself by asserting the scarcity of lumber and straw, an excuse, it seems to me, which can be hardly sustained in that region of New York, in close proximity to the lumber and grain districts and on the lines of canals and the great Erie railroad."[67]

"I was informed," Sloan continued, "that everything being referred to the Commissary-General of Prisoners [General Wessells], the requisition of lining the buildings to make them comfortable for the winter was disapproved and the stopping of cracks and open places ordered. A personal inspection convinced me that this measure would not remedy the evil. The winters are exceedingly cold and bleak at Elmira, and the buildings were hastily erected of green lumber, which is cracking, splitting, and warping in every direction." Surgeon Sloan summed up his report by saying: "I feel confident if these suggestions [lining the inside of the barracks and installing larger stoves] are presented to the Commissary-General of Prisoners and the commanding general of the department, their force will be manifest and the proper steps will be taken immediately."[68]

It is clear that Surgeon Sloan saw Colonel Tracy as the source of the problem. The report presented the Elmira post commander as one who was obstructing Major Sanger's administration of the prison hospital. Yet Tracy had recommended on October 24 that the hospital wards be sealed, and three days later the War Department rejected his proposal. Nevertheless, Sloan's highly critical analysis finally moved the commissary general of prisoners to action.

In ordering Surgeon Thomas M. Getty to inspect conditions at Elmira, General Wessells, on November 23, noted: "Unfavorable reports [from Elmira] are continually received at this office, and it is desirable to correct existing evils." Wessells then clearly questioned Tracy's administrative ability when he told Getty to "make to the commanding officer such suggestions for immediate action as you deem advisable, and if possible ascertain his ability to carry them out."[69] On December 7 Wessells informed Tracy that Surgeon Getty's recommendations that the hospital wards be sealed and woodstoves be replaced with coal stoves in all prison barracks were now officially approved.[70] Ten days later Tracy reported to Wessells that the work had begun on Getty's recommendations.

Through his report of November 1, Major Sanger—an officer much despised by Confederate prisoners of war and Union officers alike—moved the War Department to better prepare the living quarters of Barracks No. 3 for the ensuing winter weather. And Colonel Tracy, through his call (October 3) for additional winter quarters and his demand (October 17) that the unsanitary condition of Foster's Pond be corrected, set in motion two projects that would improve the status of the camp.

Yet the dissension between Tracy and Sanger continued to hamper the flow of requisitions to the camp hospital. Colonel Tracy adamantly persisted in demanding that all of Sanger's requisitions be subject to approval (or rejection) by the post commander. In short, Tracy, not Sanger, would determine what requisitions were necessary to maintain the prison hospital. Further, Tracy insisted that each requisition was to be accompanied by a certificate signed by the surgeon in charge. Colonel Tracy also ordered that "Sanger and all Medical officers will remain on duty 8 a.m. until 12 [noon] and from 2 p.m. until 5 p.m. each day."[71]

Next, in a move that demoralized most members of the prison camp's medical staff, Tracy placed Sanger under virtual house arrest. The December 11 order stated that Sanger "will immediately take up his quarters at Prison Camp. Lt.-Col. Moore will assign him quarters at the Camp. There must be no time when he cannot be found at Camp unless absent by permission of Lt.-Col. Moore."[72]

The house arrest of Sanger marked the culmination of the bitter, glacially hard relationship between the prison camp's chief surgeon and Elmira's post commander. It is apparent that they took each other's measure and the result was a lasting, acrimonious working condition that poisoned procedures between the post commander's office and the prison hospital. What has never been revealed is the genesis of their fractious feud. It has remained one of the prison camp's mysteries. What is clear, however, is that, at least in their official relationship, neither officer grasped the fact that the military is a strange pastiche where you must work with people you don't like.

On December 22 Maj. Anthony E. Stocker arrived in Elmira; on that day he replaced Major Sanger as chief surgeon of the prison camp. On Christmas Eve, Sanger informed Surgeon General Joseph Barnes that Stocker was now in charge of the prison camp's hospital. In informing Barnes that he was awaiting orders, Sanger requested that he be assigned to the army of General Sherman or Maj. Gen. George Henry Thomas.[73] Two days after Christmas Sanger left Elmira for Cincinnati. On December 30 he received orders to report immediately to Detroit where he would serve as chief surgeon under Maj. Gen. Joseph Hooker in a large military hospital of the Army of the North. He would never again return to Elmira.

For four months and sixteen days Eugene F. Sanger was the center of the storm in Elmira. Short of temper, free of self-doubt, and lacking in compassion, Major Sanger was viewed as the villain of the piece by hundreds of Confederates who survived their ordeal in Elmira. Others who have chronicled the history of the camp also relate to Sanger in negative terms. Most certainly his demeanor and his terse and often unkind opinion of others made him liable to criticism. His contempt for Colonel Tracy was marked by an Olympian arrogance that could be taken as his failure to accept the chain of military command. A decade after the war Sanger would imply publicly that Tracy made decisions that seriously impaired the operation of the prison hospital. "Camp hygiene [hospital management] is a great study," he would write in a newspaper article, "which during the war was left by our bravest and ablest generals, to the medical staff. It would have been better at Elmira, but notwithstanding this drawback, the losses were not as large as among some of our own regiments in malarial regions."[74]

Major Sanger remains the Elmira prison camp's single most controversial figure. A physician of uncommon skill, he was vain, vindictive, petty, and self-centered. And his reports often were those of a man driven by a prickly, almost primordial sense of self-righteous determination. As Surgeon Sloan so aptly put it, they were marked by "an undue warmth of language." Yet it was his persistence that had much to do with eventual improvements in the camp's living quarters and general sanitation. Most puzzling about this man are his carefully kept personal written record of Elmira's dead and his shocking statement that he was responsible for the camp's high death rate.

CHAPTER 7

"The Brutal Stanton... Turned a Deaf Ear to the Tale of Their Sufferings"

"Today is Christmas," a morose Wilbur Grambling noted in his prison diary, "but it seems no more than any other day."[1] The unseasonably warm temperature on that particular Christmas Day produced a depressing quagmire of slush and mud. But few felt any holiday spirit, for the severe weather conditions of late autumn and early winter had resulted in frostbite and pneumonia.

To make matters worse, during the final week of December, the last stages of construction of additional winter barracks had temporarily come to a halt because of inclement weather. Additional hospital buildings within the camp were, with the final sealing of the structures' sides, near completion, and thirty coal stoves were slated to be installed (one at each end of the newly constructed barracks) on December 26. But as recently as late November and early December, more than 2,000 Confederates had been quartered in tents and a December 25 inspection report related that 900 prisoners of war were still sleeping in tents.[2]

Some 900 men in tents on December 25 had to be a matter of concern for Maj. Anthony E. Stocker, the prison camp's new chief surgeon. Stocker certainly must have realized that a tent with a single woodstove afforded insufficient protection from the cold weather for four men each with only one blanket. Although there is no written evidence, Major Stocker must have concluded that the delay in constructing additional quarters in Elmira had taken a terrible toll among the sick and wounded.

Major Stocker, a prominent physician in Philadelphia at the outbreak of the war, was the grandson of a French officer who fought under the Marquis de Lafayette in the American Revolution. Born into Philadelphia's upper class on March 5, 1819, Stocker completed his study of medicine in the early 1840s. He then served as a young surgeon in the Mexican War, and in 1848 returned to Philadelphia to resume his practice of medicine. In May 1861 he wrote to Secretary of War Simon Cameron, requesting a commission as a surgeon in the army. His service as an army surgeon in the Mexican War qualified him for an exemption from military duty in 1861, but the patrician Stocker's patriotism dictated that he should again serve. Secretary Cameron, a fellow Pennsylvanian, saw to it that Dr. Stocker was granted a commission with the rank of major on August 3, 1861.

In September 1861 Major Stocker became a member of the Army of the Potomac when he reported to Brig. Gen. George A. McCall's division, a unit within Maj. Gen. George Gordon Meade's brigade. General Meade would gain national fame later in the war when he defeated Robert E. Lee's Army of Northern Virginia in July 1863 at Gettysburg. Stocker apparently ran afoul of General McCall on May 10, 1862, when he was arrested and charged in extremely vague terms of unsatisfactorily performing his duties "in relation to the care of the sick of this division recently sent to Washington."[3] This ambiguous indictment had to do with Major Stocker's actions while he was in charge of a train of wounded soldiers. Specific counts against Stocker were never listed.

Major Stocker's offense drew the attention of General Meade, who, in a personal letter on May 14 to General McCall, advocated that Stocker must be notified of the specific charges and be granted an opportunity to argue his innocence.[4] Five days after Meade's letter, Stocker was ordered released from arrest until a general court-martial could be scheduled. During the interval, he resumed his duties. On May 27 Major Stocker was granted a qualified release from General McCall's division. Soon after this, court-martial proceedings were dropped; but Stocker was told he would have to remain in his present post for a period of time. Stocker continued to serve in McCall's division until August when he was transferred to the military hospital at Craney Island, Virginia, where he served as medical director until that base was closed the following December. From there, Major Stocker was ordered to Fortress Monroe in Virginia and this was followed by an assignment as surgeon in charge of Chesapeake General Hospital, also in Virginia.

As with Major Sanger, Stocker was not above requesting special consideration for specific assignments. While at Craney Island, he wrote Surgeon General William Hammond to request a position at Chestnut Hill near his hometown of Philadelphia. And, on December 23, Major Stocker requested that Brig. Gen. Lorenzo Thomas, adjutant general of the United States, consider him (Stocker) for a position of medical inspector. "I know," Major Stocker pleaded, "that one word from you can secure it for me. . . . Will you not say a good word for me, and get the appointment for me?"[5]

Stocker's requests reveal more than a trace of arrogance. For one thing, in writing Hammond, Thomas, and (earlier) Secretary Cameron, he did not hesitate to address his requests to the very top echelon of the military's power structure. Thus, it must have come as a deeply personal disappointment to Stocker when he was denied both the post at Chestnut Hill and a position as medical inspector. As with Sanger, the emoluments of the military were denied Major Stocker. The disappointment of his unsuccessful requests aside, Stocker faced a more serious problem in August 1863 when he once again faced the possibility of a court-martial. On being relieved of his post at Chesapeake General Hospital on August 9, Stocker curtly requested a prompt hearing.[6]

Stocker was charged by Surgeon R. H. Gilbert, medical director of the Department of Virginia, "in relation to the arrangement of the Hospital under his [Stocker's] charge." The military court of judges, viewing the counts against Stocker as vague and minuscule, cleared the surgeon of all charges in a final court-martial verdict. On September 28 Maj. Gen. John G. Foster notified the surgeon general's office that Major Stocker was "not only found . . . not guilty of the charges preferred against him, but, in the language of the Court [it was] found 'That the charges preferred against Surgeon Anthony E. Stocker . . . by Surgeon R. H. Gilbert . . . are frivolous, and apparently dictated by unworthy motives.'"[7]

Restored in good standing, on October 4, 1863, Major Stocker was relieved of his duties at the Chesapeake General Hospital. Following a twenty-day leave, he was assigned to Key West, Florida, where he served as medical director until October 1864. While at Key West, Stocker contracted yellow fever, a disease that seriously impaired his ability to carry on as medical director. In October, a debilitated Surgeon Stocker returned to Philadelphia where he remained until December when he was ordered to replace Major Sanger at Elmira.

If Chief Surgeon Stocker, after his assumption of his new duties at Elmira, made any serious assessment of the conditions of the prison camp, he left no record of this, for one finds no documentation bearing his name in the matter of requests, improvements, shortcomings, supplies, quantity of medicine, quality of food, or hospital accommodations. Unlike Major Sanger, Stocker did not call attention to any serious problems that perhaps developed during the cold, winter months of January, February, and March 1865. Yet it was during these months that 1,202 Confederate prisoners of war, 40.3 percent of Elmira's overall death toll, died in Barracks No. 3.[8]

What was Stocker's official explanation of the camp's alarming death toll? His failure to record the events of January, February, and March leaves him open to critical speculation—i.e., was he part of a conspiracy of silence? Did Colonel Tracy, perhaps feeling that he was impugned by Sanger's scathing and candid reports, instruct Major Stocker to refrain from writing detailed accounts of the prison camp hospital's status? Critics of the camp's management would at best find Stocker's lack of documentation to be suspiciously mysterious.

In fewer than ten days after his arrival, Major Stocker would be apprised of the fact that the death toll at Elmira for December was 269. This brought the total number of prison camp deaths at Elmira to 1,263.[9] Curiously, Stocker's thoughts on this alarming statistic are not revealed in any official communiqué. On the positive side, Major Stocker must have taken comfort in the report of January 1, 1865, that all prisoners of war were finally quartered in barracks. At that time the only individuals still sleeping in tents inside the compound were Union guards. This situation had a month earlier drawn editorial fire from the *Army and Navy Journal,* which claimed "that the troops on duty at Elmira, New York, are during this inclement weather, living in tents" and "that even in that land of plenty they receive no vegetables." The editorial stated that its purpose was to use these facts to illustrate "the idea we have advanced, that many soldiers desert because they feel that they are not receiving their just rights and dues."[10]

The editorial drew an immediate response from Elmira in a letter dated January 2, 1865, (quite possibly by Colonel Tracy's hand). "I have no hesitation," the terse reply stated, "in stating that there has been no case of desertion at Elmira on account of ill usage, or for the causes stated in your journal. When men have deserted, it has not been for the want of supplies, or care, for the Government has been most munificent and watchful towards them." Desertion took place at Elmira, the response bluntly concluded, because Union recruits at that post "were the lowest and meanest class, assisted and encouraged by traitors at large."[11] With criticism of his treatment of the prisoners of war coming from Southern newspapers, and now the *Army and Navy Journal* calling attention to the living conditions of the Union guard detail, Tracy must have felt like the Light Brigade at Balaclava.

On Friday, January 6, another winter blast, the heaviest of the season, struck Elmira. Freight and passenger train service was temporarily suspended by the severity of the storm, and as the temperature plummeted, a northwesterly wind whipped through Barracks No. 3. Prisoner Arthur H. Edey of the 5th Texas recalled in a late-winter letter to Confederate president Jefferson Davis that "summer coats and pants were no protection from the bitter relentless winds and snows of Elmira."[12] The lack of proper clothing for the winter season (already a major concern of the prisoners) would become yet another controversial issue in Elmira.

Official weekly reports of provision of clothing for Confederate prisoners of war at Elmira ranged from a few positive observations to mostly negative comments.[13] The prison camp was frequently supplied with additional clothing, shoes, and blankets in amounts that often fell short of specific requests. In the belief that Confederate prisoners would remain in Elmira (and other prisoner-of-war camps in the North) for the winter season, some individuals, concerned with the prison population's welfare, attempted to provide additional clothing and blankets to cope with the cold weather.

As early as August 22, 1864, "Noah Walker & Co.," a Baltimore clothing retailer, notified the then post commander at Elmira, Lieutenant Colonel Eastman, that it possessed an abundant number of clothing packages, ordered by relatives of prisoners of war at Elmira, that were posted for delivery to Elmira. The problem, Noah Walker & Co. stated, was that the War Department restricted all deliveries of clothing to prison camps. The Baltimore clothing company also stated that it had many orders that remained unfulfilled because of stringent government rules. The letter concluded by requesting Eastman to render a decision on what to do with clothing ticketed for Elmira.[14]

Three days later Eastman requested of the commissary general of prisoners "further instructions relating to the issue of clothing to prisoners of war. The friends of the prisoners are sending clothing almost daily for their use, and I have some doubt if it can be issued under Circular No. 4." East-

man then noted that the prisoners of war at Elmira "are in need of clothing, and if it be permitted to issue all that is received it will save the Government considerable expense, and I recommend that it be done. . . . I send
with this application from Noah Walker & Co. . . . to know if they can
send clothing to prisoners when ordered by their friends. Shall I answer in
the affirmative?"[15]

Circular No. 4 that Eastman put in question dictated that clothing
might be furnished to "destitute" prisoners of war by near relatives—solely
with the approval of the post commander. The outer garments must be
gray, and only one suit and one change of underwear would be allowed.[16]
On September 8 Colonel Hoffman informed Eastman that Circular No. 4
must be complied with in regard to evidence that the clothing was provided
by near relatives.[17]

There is no record that the Noah Walker clothing firm ever received a
response from the War Department. What is known is that Lieutenant
Colonel Eastman refused to allow the shipment of any clothing from Baltimore. Eastman's action in this matter remains a mystery to some and a
salient example of deliberate cruelty to others. Perhaps Eastman, seriously
ill at that time, did not have the energy to work his way around Circular
No. 4 and allow clothing from Baltimore to be shipped to Elmira. It certainly appears that a healthy, alert, concerned post commander could have
figured a way to procure the additional clothing.

In what may have been a separate attempt to send clothing to Elmira, a
Baltimore relief organization consisting of private citizens in early September sent a representative to Elmira to broach the possibility of providing a
clothing shipment for prisoners at Barracks No. 3. Although it is not known
whether this group was affiliated with Noah Walker & Co., one possibility
is that the Noah Walker firm turned its stocks of clothing marked for Elmira
over to an independent relief group. John J. Van Allen was appointed by the
Baltimore group to determine the needs of the prisoners in terms of clothing, money, food, and other necessities. He lived just twenty miles north of
Elmira in Watkins (presently Watkins Glen, New York).

Van Allen, a man who had studied at a business school in Elmira in his
younger days, would recall in 1876 that he journeyed to Elmira and sought
permission from Lieutenant Colonel Eastman to enter the camp in order to
assess the needs for clothing, blankets, medicines, and money. According to
Van Allen, Eastman received him with courtesy and kind attention, and,
Van Allen would claim, Eastman informed him that the prisoners of war at

Elmira "were very destitute of clothing and blankets; that not [sic] one-half of them had even been captured during the hot summer months with no other than thin cotton clothes, which in the most instances were in tatters."[18] A more realistic view suggests that the Elmira post commander, a veteran of thirty-five years of military service, was not about to relate to Mr. Van Allen, a total stranger, the actual conditions of the prison camp.

War Department regulations prevented Eastman from allowing Van Allen to enter the prison camp. Upon being denied access to the camp, Mr. Van Allen next contacted, by letter, the secretary of war. Stanton's response, Van Allen declared, alluded to a bureaucratic labyrinth by which clothing could be sent to Elmira, which was so complicated that the Baltimore relief group abandoned the project. "I was actually forced to give the matter up in despair," a disappointed John J. Van Allen recollected. "The brutal Stanton," years later he bitterly declared, "was inexorable to all my entreaties, and turned a deaf ear to the tale of their sufferings."[19]

Stanton's refusal to honor Van Allen's request, stated the editors of the *Southern Historical Society Papers,* was consistent with his insolent response to a proposal to raise money in England to alleviate the status of prisoners of war held in Northern prisons. The secretary of war's response, according to the *Southern Historical Society Papers,* was "that the United States Government *was rich enough to provide for its prisoners, and needed no foreign help."* The journal's editors concluded that "the United States Government *was* amply able to provide for its captives; but it chose to adopt a system of cold-blooded cruelty, and to seek to avoid the verdict of history by the most persistent slanders against the Confederate authorities."[20] Indeed, to some Southern critics, Stanton was a demented Ahab.

The abortive Baltimore efforts were actually paralleled by two separate proposals that were presented to the Department of War. The first came on August 11 from W. H. Winder, a resident of New York City. Winder, a brother of Brig. Gen. John H. Winder (the Confederate commissary general of prisoners), initiated a *quid pro quo;* i.e., Confederate prisoners of war would be provided with winter necessities in return for substantial amounts of cotton to be shipped from the South to Northern ports.

Winder, in an unfortunate choice of words, informed Stanton that "prisoners, Federal and Confederate, . . . [were] suffering great and unnecessary hardships to an extent to cause great sickness and mortality, most of which might be averted by a very simple process or arrangement." It is hard to imagine that Winder's words were not taken by the touchy Stanton as a reflection on the U.S. War Department's management of prison camps. In outlining his proposal for providing clothing and other necessities (for both Confederate and Union prisoners of war) in exchange for cotton, Winder concluded that this "simple arrangement on some such basis would do so much to relieve such sad distress as now prevails that it cannot fail to receive favorable attention from every one having a proper heart and power to act thus."[21] The "sad distress as now prevails" again reflected on the prisoner-of-war policy of the United States's secretary of war.

Unfortunately for Winder, the feeling at the highest levels of the Union's Department of War was one of distrust of the Confederacy. In short, the South could not be trusted to carry out the provision of human-itarian aid to those confined in Southern prisons. "There is but one way by which relief can reach them [Union prisoners of war]," Maj. Gen. Ethan A. Hitchcock, the U.S. commissioner for exchange, bluntly concluded, "and that is through the success of the Federal armies."[22] Hitchcock's chilling, unvarnished words sounded the death knell for Winder's proposal.

In September 1864 yet another proposal similar to Winder's was brought forth by a New York City resident, M. M. Broadwell, who claimed that he had connections in high places in the Confederate capital of Richmond. Despite General Grant's interest in Broadwell's proposal and some initial movement on the part of the War Department, nothing came to fruition. With the failure of Winder and Broadwell, Judge Robert Ould, the Confederate agent of exchange, now took up the cause of bringing about an agreement between the Union and the Confederacy on the ques-tion of providing winter clothing and other necessities for prisoners of war. On October 6 Judge Ould initiated matters by writing a letter to Maj. John E. Mulford, U.S. assistant agent of exchange.

Perhaps Mulford's familiarity with the town of Elmira had something to do with his being somewhat receptive to Ould's overture. Mulford, a man with a humanitarian bent, was a native of Havana, New York (presently Montour Falls), a Schuyler County village eighteen miles north of Elmira. At the outbreak of the war, his patriotism led him to raise a com-pany that became the first to report to Albany in response to President Lin-coln's call for 75,000 men.[23] Yet Major Mulford's willingness to consider a proposal that would alleviate suffering in all prison camps did not guaran-tee an agreement between parties North and South.

In his letter to Mulford, Judge Ould called attention to the fact that thousands of prisoners of war would be held by both sides through the winter of 1864–1865. Ould reasoned that in the name of humanity certain measures could be taken to provide relief and comfort for those held in captivity. Presenting a rough sketch of an exchange of food, blankets, and clothing, he made it clear that these supplies were to be considered ancillary provisions that were to be dispensed in addition to regular rations and other articles. Judge Ould wisely sent a copy of his carefully worded Mulford letter to Secretary Stanton with a brief explanation that this was the view of the Confederate government.[24]

In referring the matter to Grant, Stanton instructed his general to take action "as you may deem best adapted to the relief of our soldiers held as prisoners by the rebels. . . . It is the desire of the President that no effort consistent with national safety and honor be spared."[25] It was General Grant's understanding that a release of all soldiers would come only with an exchange of prisoners. Stanton, ever the Machiavellian manipulator of War Department affairs, understood full well that Grant viewed any prisoner exchange as something inconsistent "with national safety and honor."

The individual, it must be said, with the final word—President Abraham Lincoln—firmly opposed an exchange of prisoners. What Lincoln would agree to was an exchange of supplies that would bring relief to prisoners of war on both sides. Thus, what began in October was a series of communiqués that included the thoughts of Grant and Lee at one level and Ould and Mulford at another. Grant and Lee quickly agreed to implement any approved plan to supply prisoners of war with clothing and other necessities. The details were hammered out by Judge Ould and Major Mulford.

In the course of negotiations, it was Judge Ould who came up with the idea that the South provide for a large shipment of cotton to the North. The cotton would be sold and the money realized from the transaction would be used to purchase clothing, blankets, and other necessities for Confederate soldiers held in Northern prisons. Grant was receptive to Ould's proposal. On November 11, 1864, Judge Ould informed General Grant that the Confederacy would place on board a Union vessel 1,000 bales of cotton. The transaction would take place in the harbor at Mobile, Alabama. The cotton was to be transported to New York City where it was to be sold at market price, and the proceeds to be used for the purchase of supplies for those confined to Northern prison camps.[26]

The U.S. transport *Atlanta,* under a flag of truce, was designated to sail into Mobile Bay, take on the cotton, and carry the cargo to New York City. A paroled Confederate officer, in the custody of a Union general, would receive the *Atlanta*'s freight at New York City and make arrangements for the sale of the cotton. The Confederate officer would then, in turn, see to it that purchases of supplies for Southern prisoners of war transpired. This came to be known as the Ould-Grant agreement.

The simplicity of the plan raised hopes for the success of the operation. At this point, however, a series of delays, orchestrated by Secretary Stanton, all but eliminated any possibility of provisions (especially overcoats and blankets) arriving in Northern prison camps before the beginning of the winter season. On November 16, four days after Grant and Ould had reached a final agreement, the secretary of war objected to the Confederate officer (Maj. Gen. Isaac R. Trimble) who was proposed by Judge Ould to handle matters in New York City. Three weeks later it was decided that Confederate Brigadier General William N. R. Beall, paroled from Fort Warren in Boston Harbor and in the custody of Union Brigadier General Halbert E. Paine, would manage the transaction of cotton for provisions. With the cotton (515,700 pounds) sitting on the wharfs in Mobile for close to three weeks, the U.S. transport *Atlanta* still had not received final orders from the War Department to pick up the designated cargo.

It was at this time that Union post commanders, in their efforts to procure winter clothing, began filing requests with the War Department for supplies that included blankets and overcoats for those confined in their respective prison compounds. Colonel Tracy, in response to a December 1 request, received on December 7 a shipment of clothing that only partly filled his requisition. On December 12 Tracy was told of the Ould-Grant agreement, and at the same time informed that three Confederate officers were to be dispatched to Elmira to issue the clothing that would be purchased from the sale of cotton. Two days later, in a letter dated December 12, Tracy was advised by General Wessells that "a large amount of cotton has been shipped for New York . . . the proceeds to be applied for the purchase of clothing . . . for the comfort of rebel prisoners of war." With the belief that the cotton was on its way to New York City, Tracy accepted the remainder of Wessells's message: "In view of this fact it is desirable that no more clothing shall be provided by the Government than is absolutely demanded by the ordinary dictates of humanity. You will please report your views on this subject."[27]

Colonel Tracy now instructed Lt. Col. Stephen Moore (Maj. Henry V. Colt's replacement as commander of Camp Chemung) to inform a committee of prisoners of war that arrangements must be made for the reception of provisions that soon would be shipped by General Beall. Tracy, going on the false assumption that the cotton was on its way to New York City, approved a letter written to General Beall by a committee of three prisoners of war.

The three Confederates—Arthur H. Edey (Company A, 5th Texas), William Key Howard (Company E, 4th Virginia Cavalry), and Joseph A. Barstow (Company C, 24th Virginia Cavalry)—speaking for their fellow prisoners of war, informed Beall on December 15 that there were no Confederate officers confined at Elmira. The three Confederates then requested that General Beall inform them as to how individuals were to be selected to be authorized to receive and dispense supplies that would be ticketed to come to Elmira from New York City. Edey, Howard, and Barstow then related to Beall that qualified and responsible men within the prison camp could assume the responsibility of issuing all supplies that came from the purchase of the cotton.[28]

Arthur H. Edey, the man who would later inform Jefferson Davis that the summer clothing worn by the prisoners of war at the time of their capture offered "no protection from the bitter relentless winds and snows of Elmira" (see endnote 12), and his two Confederate compatriots had visions of winter clothing arriving soon. Their letter was in response to General Beall's December 9 circular that requested Confederate prisoners of war to determine what supplies (clothing, blankets, and rations) were most needed in Elmira.[29] There is no recorded evidence that Beall responded to the letter of the three Elmira Confederates. What is known is that prisoners at Elmira were fearful of a cold winter and eager to receive adequate clothing. Like Tracy, they believed that necessary supplies would arrive soon.

At the War Department, however, General Wessells, a man who had been a prisoner of the Confederacy and who readily accepted the idea of retaliation, knew very well that the cotton shipment was still on the docks in Mobile. He was also aware that it would be weeks before the cotton would arrive in New York City. In his December 12 letter to Tracy, which stated that the government would not provide clothing because it would be coming soon from another source, Wessells apparently had deliberately misled the Elmira post commander. Colonel Tracy and the other military administrators of Northern prison camps were unaware that Secretary Stanton and General Wessells had decided on a course of action that resembled a dual strategy of deception and delay.

Through the remainder of December Colonel Tracy waited for the arrival of more clothing. On January 5 the frustrated and angered Elmira post commander informed Wessells that since mid-December he (Tracy) had been going on the assumption that a large amount of cotton was on its way to New York City. The proceeds from the sale of that cotton, Tracy continued, would ensure the purchase of clothing, blankets, and other supplies earmarked for Elmira. In light of this fact, the Elmira post commander had assumed that "it was not deemed advisable to provide any more clothing for prisoners than was absolutely demanded by ordinary dictates of humanity. . . . We have heard nothing further in relation to the subject since. A number of prisoners will soon be destitute of trousers and other articles of clothing."[30]

Tracy then tersely informed General Wessells that Elmira's December 1 prison clothing requisition remained unfilled. Still due to be sent to Elmira were 1,000 jackets, 2,500 shirts, 3,000 pairs of trousers, 8,000 drawers, 7,000 pairs of socks, and 1,500 caps. Colonel Tracy most emphatically requested "that these amounts . . . be furnished immediately for issue to prisoners, unless the Department is advised that supplies will be speedily forwarded by the rebel authorities."[31] Tracy's frustration and the shortage of clothing at Elmira were just two of the appalling results that can be traced to the subtle, premeditated plotting of the devious Secretary Stanton. General Wessells, in this instance acting as Stanton's agent of deception, willingly played his role in a shameful bureaucratic shell game that kept the truth from Tracy and his staff of camp administrators.

On January 19 Wessells, in a transparent display of sophistry, informed the frustrated Tracy that December clothing requisitions for Elmira could not be forwarded until Tracy had responded to a December 12 letter from the commissary general of prisoners "which explained the necessity of strict economy in the issue of clothing to rebel prisoners at the present time, and requested that you would report your views on the necessity of such issue at Elmira, N. Y. No reply to this letter has been received, and the requisitions are still in this office." Then, in a passage that clearly reveals that the War Department withheld by design winter clothing from Elmira, Wessells stated: "The clothing received by you was sent to Elmira by mistake, and was not part of that required for by you. It was reported as issue before the error was discovered." The commissary general of prisoners then added that no further clothing supplies would be shipped to Elmira until the cargo of cotton arrived in New York City.[32]

Tracy fired off an immediate response. "I would offer in explanation," the Elmira post commander stated, "that about the same date (December 12) we received instructions from Brigadier-General Paine . . . to forward immediately through him, to the agent of the rebel authorities, a report from the prisoners of war at this depot of the supplies necessary to render them comfortable." Tracy, upon explaining that the report was forwarded at once to Paine, then informed Wessells that he (Tracy) "did not deem it necessary to make any further report before the arrival of the supplies from the rebel authorities." Colonel Tracy closed by stating that he "forwarded [to the Office of the Commissary General of Prisoners] this day [January 21] requisition in duplicate for such clothing as will be absolutely necessary within the next four weeks."[33]

A response from the War Department to Tracy came six days later. Maj. George Blagden, assistant to the commissary general of prisoners, informed the Elmira post commander that "the cotton for the purchase of supplies for rebel prisoners has arrived in New York, [and] it is supposed that clothing will be forwarded by General Beall [the paroled Confederate officer] nearly or quite as soon as it could be furnished by the Quartermaster's Department." Major Blagden then concluded that Colonel Tracy's clothing "requuisitions will be held for the moment."[34]

This meant that Tracy would have to wait until General Beall cleared his sale of cotton and began distributing the supplies he was able to purchase from New York City merchants. Of equal importance, Blagden revealed that clothing requisitions ticketed for Elmira were deliberately being withheld by the War Department through the months of December and January. Since the purchases from cotton were to be supplemental, clearly this was a violation of the terms of the agreement. Again, the heavy hand of Secretary Stanton, with the furtive support of General Wessells, came into play.

Deprived of sufficient rations (the inspection and rejection of beef remained a daily drill at Elmira) and of clothing and blankets that remained in warehouses in Washington, the prison camp's January death rate reached 285. This brought the prisoner-of-war death total in Elmira to 1,548.[35] How many of these deaths were the result of a shortage of clothing and blankets cannot be determined. What is known is that the obligation of the belligerents to feed and clothe the prisoners of war in their respective charge was ignored by Stanton and Wessells.

On February 1, 1865, William Hoffman again assumed the post of commissary general of prisoners—this time with the rank of brevet brigadier general. One of his first acts was to inform Brig. Gen. Halbert E.

Paine (the Union officer responsible for the custody of General Beall) that clothing from the cotton transaction had to be distributed primarily to the largest of the Union-administered prisoner-of-war camps—Point Lookout (Maryland), Fort Delaware (Delaware), Camp Chase (Columbus, Ohio), Camp Douglas (Chicago), Camp Morton (Indianapolis), Rock Island (Illinois), Alton (Illinois), Johnson's Island (Sandusky, Ohio), and Elmira. General Hoffman also listed two prison hospitals—one near Nashville, and the other near New Orleans.[36] All told, 62,000 Confederate prisoners of war were to receive relief from the cotton transaction.

The saga of the cotton transaction was marked from the beginning with misfortune. The project took a turn for the worse in December when a number of troubling factors began to emerge. First, the price of cotton began to fall. Had the cotton been shipped in mid-November, it would have brought a sale price (at $1.35 per pound) of $696,195. By December 1 the sale price of the cotton shipment had dropped to almost $630,000. To make matters worse, the cotton remained in Mobile through the month of December.

In part the reason for the delay in transferring the cotton to the *Atlanta* can be traced to the poor status of the communications between Union and Confederate officers in the Mobile area. Also, poor weather conditions and a shallow channel in Mobile Bay forced Confederate officials to resort to cumbersome, slow-moving barges in the transfer of the cotton. The barges had to make their way to the *Atlanta* from the city of Mobile thirty miles to the north at the head of the bay. Finally, on January 13, the commander of the *Atlanta* decided to set out for New York City. Because the ship's capacity could not hold the entire shipment of cotton, the *Atlanta* steamed out of Mobile Bay with only 870 bales on board. The other 130 bales were eventually shipped to New York City in April on another Union vessel.

When the *Atlanta* arrived in New York City on January 24, there was still more delay. General Beall had been given little opportunity to prepare for the *Atlanta's* arrival because, on January 3, Stanton had ordered him to be placed under arrest for "conspicuous and offensive" conduct. Released from his jail cell in Fort Lafayette (New York Harbor) on January 25, the beleaguered Confederate officer now began his task of selling the cotton and purchasing supplies. By then a rapidly declining cotton market yielded General Beall just under $332,000—less than 50 percent of what was anticipated by Ould in November. To make matters worse, the 170 bales of cotton that arrived in New York City in April netted General Beall a little less than $.30 per pound and a total of only $23,994.76. The hopes of those who had envisioned larger amounts of clothing and blankets were dashed.

The policies of Secretary Stanton account clearly in part for this miserable failure to properly execute a perfectly logical plan. The Confederacy's considerable cotton resources, in part, could have been used in exchange for relief for Southerners held in Northern prisons such as Elmira. It was a sensible idea. Had a plan similar to the Ould-Grant agreement been adopted earlier, much suffering in Northern camps would not have taken place. Thus, cotton, scarce in the North and abundant in the South, could very well have served as a commodity of merciful dimensions. Unfortunately, the preclusion of suffering is something that the secretary of war did not view as a matter of concern.

Three Confederate officers—Lt. Col. H. J. Price, Maj. John P. Thompson, and Maj. Daniel S. Printup—arrived in Elmira on February 7 for the sole purpose of distributing supplies that General Beall would send to Elmira. "Their presence in our city will . . . produce quite a stir," the *Advertiser* reported. "They are stopping at the Brainard [House] and are quite the observed of all observers. Last evening they were allowed the freedom of the hotel under guard, and were introduced to quite a number of our citizens. They wear the usual Confederate uniform, for officers of their rank."[37]

Two days after their arrival, they toured Barracks No. 3 in preparation for the task of distributing clothes and other supplies. On February 15 they were moved under guard from the Brainard House to one of the officers' barracks in front of the prisoners' camp. From the officers' barracks, they were allowed to move to other areas of Elmira only with the written approval of Colonel Tracy. The initial three boxes of clothing from Beall's office in New York City had arrived in Elmira on February 7.

The Confederate officer appointed to supervise the distribution of clothing at Camp Chemung was Major Printup, a man who practiced law before the war. Printup was described by the *Advertiser* as being "a regular fire eater and secessionist."[38] Although the newspaper did not elaborate, it can be assumed that Charles Fairman had met with Printup. Colonel Tracy communicated with Printup on a daily basis and concluded that the Confederate officer would be reluctant to take the oath of allegiance but "at least he has no confidence in the success of the rebellion and is in favor of peace and reunion."[39] This is hardly the definition of a "fire eater."

Whatever Major Printup's views were, he went about the business of receiving and distributing supplies. The first shipment he received contained clothing for prisoners of war recovering from smallpox. As additional boxes arrived, Printup and his two fellow Confederate officers duly recorded the name and rank of every Elmira prisoner receiving articles of clothing. It was during the initial stages of his duties in Elmira that Major Printup came forth with a startling revelation when he informed General Beall that one J. Gladke, a local clothing merchant, offered to supply "a large lot of clothing made up expressly for the prisoners." According to Printup, Gladke put together $5,000 worth of clothing with the understanding that he would be permitted to sell it, but then was prohibited from doing so by local military authorities. Printup then explained to Beall that Gladke was willing to produce more clothing on a grander scale and his (Gladke's) finished product appeared to be "of good quality & seems to us fully within the prices asked."[40]

Major Printup's reference to a local clothing merchant with a substantial supply of goods that could readily be purchased by military authorities for Elmira's prisoners of war sheds light on yet another piece of evidence that resembles a policy of deprivation. With permission from Washington and with a prison fund that was, on February 1, 1865, just over $127,000, Colonel Tracy could have made a move to alleviate some of the suffering the prisoners experienced during the months of December and January. But Tracy, a man guided by legal principles and a rigidly fixed canon of military procedures, apparently had no trouble in following inflexibly the dictates of the War Department. And the War Department had no desire to move swiftly on the clothing question.

Although there is no evidence that Colonel Tracy notified Washington that a local merchant was capable of supplying clothing, Secretary Stanton and General Wessells, or, later General Hoffman, are hardly likely to have allowed any transaction to take place. And the return of Hoffman, a notoriously tightfisted bureaucrat in the same vein as Wessells, to the post of commissary general of prisoners guaranteed the continuation of a prison clothing shortage in Elmira. He held to a churlish guideline that he articulated in a November 15, 1863, letter to the prison camp commander at Camp Morton: "So long as a prisoner has clothing upon him, however much torn, you must issue nothing to him, nor must you allow him to receive clothing from any but members of his immediate family, and only when they are in absolute want."[41] Indeed, Hoffman's stringent measures were borne out in late March when Major Printup notified General Beall that the camp's acute clothing shortage remained a grim reality.[42]

It was at the conclusion of the war that a great upwelling of stories claiming that General Beall was the one to be faulted for the shortage of blankets and winter clothing in Northern prison camps began to circulate among Confederate prisoners. In a letter that appeared in a great number of Southern newspapers, Beall responded to this charge. Addressing his September 14, 1865, remarks to "The Confederate Prisoners of War," he explained in considerable detail how and why certain delays took place. Steering clear of any criticism of Secretary Stanton, Beall cited falling cotton prices, poor weather conditions, and "some inefficient U.S. quartermaster on his own authority." Responding specifically to charges that he "gave contracts to Union men," an incensed General Beall concluded: "In reply I have but to say that I looked upon my duties and obligations as too sacred to admit of my consulting anything save the interest of the prisoners."[43]

The shortage of clothing in Elmira and other prison camps was paralleled by a steady stream of stories in Northern newspapers that continued to carry reports of ill treatment of Union prisoners of war.[44] And more talk of retaliation was generated in some Northern publications. On January 28, 1865, the *Army and Navy Journal* published a lengthy letter from an individual who claimed to have served as an officer at a camp that housed Confederate prisoners of war. He stated that Southern captives were treated in a humane manner, and then spoke of the brutal treatment of Union soldiers held in Confederate prison camps. In calling for retaliation, the writer enthusiastically noted that tactic "is the usual and most effective means in our hands to remedy the ill treatment of our prisoners in the hands of the enemy. It is, therefore, to be made use of." The writer then proposed the organization of a special prisoner-of-war depot, suggesting that it "might well be known as 'Camp Retaliation.'"[45]

Two weeks later the *Philadelphia Medical and Surgical Reporter,* a journal dedicated to healing, addressed the question of retaliation when it proclaimed the laws of civilization demand the humane treatment of prisoners of war. The publication went on to state that it "is with feelings of sadness that we are compelled to record the fact that these principles have been departed from in this nineteenth century of the Christian era, and in our own country." In stating that Union prisoners of war were being subjected to brutal treatment, the journal noted that Congress was entertaining a proposition that called for retaliation. The *Philadelphia Medical and Surgical Reporter* then made it clear that "we have no desire to see our responsible

Government demean itself to the level of savages. . . . No, God forbid that we should be partakers of their evil deeds!"[46] While not calling for reciprocation, the journal made it clear that the South was guilty of maltreatment of Union prisoners of war. The publication's citing this view of the Confederacy certainly did not assuage those in the North who called for retaliatory measures.

Congress did not establish an official policy of retaliation. No "Camp Retaliation" was constructed. The subject, however, does raise this intriguing observation: Unbeknownst to the vast majority of those individuals who collectively composed Washington's arrayed powers—i.e., the Senate and House of Representatives, the federal judiciary, and officials of cabinet rank—an unstated policy of retaliation was in place in Elmira, and perhaps in other Northern prisoner-of-war camps. Editors and the public in general were unaware of any such policy on the part of the War Department. It was a surreptitious strategy that was far removed from the public cant and known only to those who were privy to classified documents in the arcane inner reaches of the Department of War.

The key to the existence of such a strategy can be found in Camp Chemung's weekly inspection reports and the military correspondence that went back and forth between Elmira and Washington. What would evolve from these documents were hard facts that reveal a policy of delay that brought death and illness to a prison camp located in a rich agricultural section of New York State that was untouched by the shot and shell of war.

Flowing from this, inevitably, would be a collective prisoner-of-war memoir (albeit at times emotional, bitter, and distorted) that would depict Elmira as a gothic backwater of despair, disease, and death. For the prison camp's survivors, the haunting image of Elmira would remain with them well into the next century in the form of a miasmic pond, stacks of white pine coffins, insufficient rations, inadequate clothing and blankets, poor hospital facilities, and bone-chilling nights in tents in late autumn and early winter. All of these things came about as a result of administrative decisions that were inextricably interwoven and implemented in Elmira and Washington by men who, singly and in combination, carried out a policy that resulted in an appallingly high death rate.

Therefore, with much justification, the great majority of the survivors of Barracks No. 3 would remember that terrible place as "Helmira." Defenders of the Union military's administration of the prison camp would look upon the survivors as embittered individuals who were bent on skulk-

Roll call during late winter/early spring of 1865. The barracks in this picture replaced the tents that were used from July through December 1864. CHEMUNG COUNTY HISTORICAL SOCIETY

ing about and whispering poison in people's ears. Yet all denials of ill treatment would pale in the light of military documents (128 volumes), i.e., the *Official Records,* that were published in an incremental process between 1880 and 1901.

The camp's survivors would remember the brutal weather conditions of the autumn and winter months. Prisoner John N. Opie would recall winter mornings when "the men crawled out of their bunks, shivering and half frozen, when a scuffle and frequently a fight, for a place by the fire occurred. God help the sick or the weak, as they were literally left out in the cold."[47] In his old age, prisoner James Huffman would talk of "weather . . . so extremely cold that some of the men froze their feet while standing on the snow and ice at [morning] roll call."[48]

On January 16 Wilbur Grambling wrote in his prison diary: "Weather broken and quite cold. We have had no coal to keep the fire today."[49] Indeed, the dearth of clothing and blankets during the months of December and January lends a distinct poignancy to these remembrances. And official military documents would confirm the Confederates' bitter recollections. Capt. Bennett F. Munger's December 4 report stated: "One thousand six hundred and sixty-six [prisoners of war] are entirely destitute of blankets, or have blankets nearly worthless."[50]

Prisoners' accounts of the biting winter weather in Elmira project very little exaggeration. The severe winter of 1864–65 was such that it became a major story in Elmira's newspapers. Aside from the customary "January thaw," there were very few fair and moderate days during that particular winter season. The *Advertiser* spoke of January 16 "as being one of the wildest and most blustery days of the season. We were favored with . . . blustery, blinding snow squalls which seem to have swept pretty generally through this part of the state."[51] On February 7 and 8 a great winter storm paralyzed Elmira with eighteen inches of snow. This was followed by several days of extremely cold temperatures. On February 11 the *Advertiser* reported that snow in the wooded areas near the town was two and a half feet in depth.[52]

The presence of the prison camp and the harsh winter conditions, however, did not prevent the citizens of Elmira from enjoying a lively social season. In noting the town's Grand Carnival on ice, the *Advertiser* reported that "everybody loving the delightful pastime of skating will be on hand to see the novel sights of the evening embracing curious costumes, outlandish rigs and beautiful dresses. The grand masquerade will be enlivened with music and fireworks."[53]

Elmira's Grand Carnival was followed the next evening by the Grand Military Ball—a spectacular social event that was attended by Elmira's polite society and featured Colonel Tracy and the ranking officers of his staff—at the Brainard House. Describing it as "a most elegant affair," the *Advertiser* reported: "Brave men and fair women mingled in the mazy dance and such a display of the beauty, *elite*, fashion and courtesy of the town has been seldom witnessed. The ball room was tastefully decorated with festoons and wreathes of evergreens with army badges . . . so as to give a gay and bright appearance mingled with the sterner emblems of war."[54]

All this was in marked contrast to the sorry reality of Barracks No. 3. Sixteen Confederate prisoners of war died the day of the Grand Military Ball. The Elmirans who attended the glittering event at the Brainard House most likely accepted editor Charles Fairman's assessment of Elmira's Confederate captives. Three weeks before the military ball, Fairman had assured his readers that all was well inside the prison camp. "They are now all comfortably housed in wooden barracks," he reported in a detailed account of the camp's status, "and are kept warm and have an abundance to eat. . . . The sick are well taken care of. . . . With the exception of the discomforts of absence from home, they have nothing to complain of."[55]

Six days after the Grand Military Ball, the February death toll revealed that 426 Confederate prisoners of war died in Elmira during that month. In February death would claim an average of just over 15 individuals per day. This brought the number of deaths in Barracks No. 3 to 1,974. Only Camp Chase in Ohio with a February death rate of 499 men had a higher figure than Elmira's.[56]

Despite the *Advertiser's* claim that satisfactory conditions existed inside Barracks No. 3, the camp's death toll does not attest to good hospital care. And Major Stocker's mysterious silence does not suggest that he tried very hard to lower it. A dreaded disease that did contribute toward the prison camp's death rate was smallpox. The initial presence of that lethal illness in Elmira occurred in late October. Brought in from Fort Morgan in Mobile Bay, Alabama, the disease would ravage the Elmira prison camp for the next six months.

With the presence of smallpox came a creation of an ersatz "smallpox hospital" consisting of rows of "A" tents that housed three patients and a woodstove in each dwelling. By early January, with the spread of the disease prompting authorities in Washington to further action, General Hoffman's office informed Colonel Tracy that temporary buildings were to be constructed in order to isolate smallpox patients, and a smallpox hospital was constructed in mid-February in a remote corner of the narrow peninsula between Foster's Pond and the Chemung River (the "trans-Mississippi department").

Before the construction of a smallpox hospital, however, the attempts to stop the spread of the disease in Barracks No. 3 were futile. Among the precautions taken was the order to burn the clothing of patients who recovered from the disease. In spite of this and other precautions, smallpox raged through the months of January, February, and March. The disease spread fear through the camp—and for good reason, as its lethal presence exacted between 300 and 400 lives. Yet there was at least one prisoner, Enos Lyons, who had no fear of entering the smallpox hospital. "I had the disease at the age of six in Ireland," Lyons would write in 1912 to author Clay Holmes.[57]

Prisoner Marcus Toney's recollection of his stay (January 25–29) in the smallpox hospital sheds some light on what a patient experienced in that isolated area of the camp. Toney would recall:

> I walked across the lake [Foster's Pond] on the ice, and commenced my search at the head of a row of tents, trying to find some bedfellows who had as light an attack as mine. . . . I found a tent with two patients . . . and I crawled in. We did not see a doctor while there, but once a day a waiter brought some tea and bread. . . . My bedfellows could not eat or drink anything, and I had all the rations, yet I could not get enough. The second night one of our bedfellows died. . . . We had about eight blankets, but could not keep warm; and to make the situation worse, the men who died were dragged out and left in front of the tents, and in whatever position a man was when death overtook him in that position he froze. Some with arms and legs extended presented a horrible sight.[58]

If Marcus Toney's account is accurate, then Elmira's "smallpox hospital" was a misnomer. The place was nothing more than several rows of tents that housed diseased individuals in a marginal area of the camp that was on the most part ignored by the medical staff. Any attempt to care for smallpox patients properly in the camp was evidently nonexistent. If one accepts Toney's recollection, it vividly illustrates the absolute necessity for the camp's acquiring better hospital facilities. In some respects Toney's memory of his hospital stay is supported by a January 24, 1865, inspection report. On that day Medical Inspector G. H. Lyman (U.S. Army) filed a report of his inspection of prison hospital conditions at Elmira with the surgeon general's office.

On February 4 Col. Madison Mills, medical inspector general (U.S. Army), sent a copy of Lyman's report to the commissary general of prisoners. The report stated that Elmira's prison hospital accommodations remained insufficient, and 200 ill prisoners were being deprived of a hospital bed because of a lack of space. The report recommended additional hospital wards and provisions for hot water bathing for the sick. Next it was suggested that there be a fresh change of clothes for hospital patients. After calling for improved ventilation and additional hospital barracks, the report concluded that overcrowding could result in an increase in disease.[59]

This report, a reflection on Major Stocker's handling of hospital affairs, most certainly lends credence to the argument that the prison hospital remained inadequate. Weaknesses that Major Sanger had months before brought to the attention of Colonel Tracy and to authorities in Washington remained in place. Since Tracy allowed conditions to remain as they were, he must bear some of the responsibility. As post commander, he did have access to prison funds that could bring about improvements, and he could have submitted to Washington a strong request for hospital improvements. This was not done. In fairness to Tracy, perhaps it is best to conclude that the War Department would quite probably have denied any request for additional prison hospital improvements at Elmira. Major Stocker's silence also warrants censure. Throughout his tenure in Elmira, Stocker never came forth with a "Sangeresque" response to the prison camp's inadequacies.

In conjunction with a shortage of clothing, severe winter weather, smallpox, and insufficient hospital facilities, the gnawing presence of hunger continued its devastating effects on the Confederates. The reduced rations order of June 1, 1864, was still in effect the following winter, and Special Orders 336 continued to curtail the daily supply of beef. A lack of a sufficient amount of food resulted in severe weight loss, an acute weakness in physical strength, a lack of resistance to disease, and the continued presence of scurvy. The threat of scurvy became so acute that on February 13 General Hoffman took action when he ordered the sutlers at all Northern prison camps be allowed to sell vegetables to the prisoners of war. Post commanders were put on notice "that this privilege is not abused."[60]

For those prisoners of war who could not afford to purchase vegetables from the camp sutler, rats, of course, continued to be taken for food. Some Confederates, going beyond the killing of rats for food, ventured into prohibited areas. Prisoners occasionally would capture a dog or a cat, kill it, and cook it over a fire that was commonly used for cooking rats. The dog of the camp's baker fell victim to a small group of Confederates. Those who ate the dog claimed it "tasted like mutton."[61] The baker, a citizen of Elmira who came into Barracks No. 3 daily to bake bread, filed a complaint with prison commander Lt. Col. Stephen Moore. The offenders were brought before Moore and punished.

Punishment for killing and eating a dog consisted of something known as the "barrel shirt." A whiskey barrel was a common choice for punishment. One end to the barrel was removed and a hole was cut in the other end so as to get the head through. For a designated number of hours, a prisoner was ordered to "wear" a barrel with a placard proclaiming "I eat a dog," or "Dog Eater." It was not uncommon to see twelve to fifteen men parading about in all kinds of weather with barrel shirts. Perhaps the most denigrating barrel shirt placard stated: "I stole my mess-mate's rations."[62]

Numerous other violations called for the barrel shirt, and precedent for this type of punishment was established during the first weeks of the camp's existence. According to one camp survivor, Major Colt was taken in by a forgery scheme that eventually led to punishment by the barrel shirt. Colt was the keeper of all money sent to the prisoners. Prisoners with money held by Colt filled out a request form that was presented to the sutler for the purchase of food and other items. A prisoner serving as a clerk in Colt's office gained access to a large number of blank request forms and passed them on to a small group of Confederates who in turn began forging Colt's signature. The forged request forms were given to dozens of prisoners who then presented them to the camp's sutler. When an angry Major Colt discovered the forgery scheme, justice was swift. Prisoner R. B. Ewan years later remembered: "The Major [Colt] had more than 60 of these counterfeiters wearing pork-barrel shirts six hours a day for 10 days."[63]

While hunger and desperate measures to procure food persisted inside Barracks No. 3, the U.S. House of Representatives, on December 21, 1864, came forth with a resolution that considered all the correspondence in reference to the question of the exchange of prisoners of war.[64] What followed was a month of Union War Department correspondence that reached across the line to the Confederacy. Finally there was an exchange agreement, and on February 4, 1865, orders from the War Department directed Colonel Tracy to make preparations for the transfer from Elmira to points south of 3,000 prisoners of war.[65]

In groups of 500, the Confederates would be scheduled to leave over the next several weeks. This was the beginning of an operation that would eventually phase out the Elmira prison camp. It also was the initial indication of the North's assumption that the war's logistical hourglass was running against the Confederacy. Washington was aware that Gen. Robert E. Lee's Army of Northern Virginia was exhausted. An exchange of prisoners, beginning in February, would have no bearing on the outcome of the war.

A cautious Colonel Tracy, keenly aware of Elmira's disastrous October 1864 transfer, responded by reminding General Hoffman that the ill-fated transfer of 1,264 prisoners of war in October 1864 was carried out by the Northern Central Railroad. The journey to Baltimore took forty hours and resulted in five deaths. Tracy, noting that the run should have been made in fifteen hours, suggested that it would be most desirable to send the prisoners of war on the Erie Railroad to New York City and then on to Baltimore by either railroad or steamer.[66]

Colonel Tracy's suggestion of using the Erie Railroad was rejected, and the first 500 Confederates, after taking the oath of allegiance, marched out of Barracks No. 3 on February 13 at 4:30 in the afternoon. Their destination was the railway depot and a Northern Central Railroad train that would take them to Baltimore and then by boat to Point Lookout, Maryland, and finally to City Point, Virginia. The *Advertiser* presented a vivid picture of the event when it noted:

> The sick and disabled were removed in a long line of baggage wagons and stowed away in the cars comfortably as could be arranged for them. A few so ill to be unable to sit up were tenderly cared for in the Hospital ambulance, in which they were carried to the train. There were many stout, healthy looking ones among the entire number, but as a general thing the sick and complaining who were able to be moved or travel were those selected for the first five hundred exchanged. They looked hopeful even through the diseases under which many were laboring or recovering from. The glad prospect of home once more, even in its devastation and desolation, seemed to light up the countenances of all, and the sick and weary took a fresh cling to life, that they might have strength to greet loved ones once more. The sight, if a sad one, best illustrated the effects and terrible results of a most unrighteous and unjust rebellion of which they were the suffering victims. They were living testimonies of the suffering and losses for which the Southern leaders have made themselves accountable.[67]

In mid-February General Hoffman expedited the exchange process by directing Colonel Tracy to prepare a roster of all prisoners of war at Elmira who desired to be exchanged.[68] On February 20 an additional 500 prisoners of war left Elmira on the Northern Central Railroad. Through the months of February and March 3,042 Confederates were transferred from Elmira to points south.[69] During the month of March 491 prisoners of war died at Elmira. This staggering number resulted in an average of just under sixteen deaths per day for the month. Only Camp Chase, Ohio, with 499 deaths the previous month, had a higher single monthly death toll of any Union-administered prison camp throughout the war. On April 1 the camp's census stood at 5,054. Elmira's death toll had now reached 2,465 prisoners of war.[70]

In mid-March the prison camp was hit with a natural disaster in the form of a flood that inundated Barracks No. 3. Springlike weather made its presence known at the end of the first week in March. Rapidly melting snow raised the level of the Chemung River to the point where, on March 11, the water rose three feet above normal as a result of an ice jam. The following day the river continued to slowly rise to even higher levels, and late in the evening of March 15 it was decided that the lower areas of Barracks No. 3 should be evacuated. At one o'clock on the morning of March 16 rafts were used to carry the sick from the smallpox hospital and the regular prison hospital to higher ground. All sick prisoners were placed inside the barracks of the 19th Veteran Reserve Corps across the street from the prison camp. Coffins containing the bodies of those Confederates who had died on March 15 were removed from the dead house. All this was done without incident.

Prisoners in the higher areas of the camp were ordered to stay in the second and third tiers of their bunks. Some remained in their bunks for as long as forty-eight hours. In what must be considered a minor miracle, there was no loss of life. Prisoner James Huffman would recall: "All the prison walls were swept away except the side next to Elmira [the east side of the prison], and if there had been much current some of the buildings on the hill would have gone. . . . As soon as the water began to fall and before it left the cook houses, some of the boys waded in and got some choice hams intended for Yankee officers, but we feasted on them all the same."[71] Colonel Tracy, in his report to Hoffman on the consequences of the flood, stated that some barracks were weakened to the point where they would have to be taken down.[72]

In the days that followed the flood, talk turned to the collapse of the Confederacy. The *Advertiser* began to carry a continuing story that related to Union military advances and the impending surrender of General Lee's beleaguered Army of Northern Virginia. Rumors of the war's end ushered in the month of April. Grant and Lee, the two great mythic figures of the Civil War, were now about to play out the final act of a struggle that had emotionally and physically drained the nation. General Grant had isolated the city of Richmond and was moving on General Lee's forces at a remote place in southern Virginia called Appomattox Courthouse. There, on Palm Sunday, April 9, 1865, Robert E. Lee surrendered to Ulysses S. Grant.

The following day the *Advertiser* informed its readers that Lee's surrender was the "last great crowning event."[73] Three days later Wilbur Grambling scribbled in his prison diary: "Seems to be settled that Gen. Lee and Army has surrendered to Grant. Some seem to rejoice while others lament the capture of so noble an army."[74] The war was over. Some 5,000 men in Barracks No. 3 now began to count down their remaining days in Elmira.

CHAPTER 8

"But the Great Question Is, at Last, Who Was Responsible for this State of Things?"

On April 12, 1865, a man registered at the Brainard House under the name of John Harrison. He had journeyed to Elmira from Montreal, Canada. The significance of this is that Montreal was a center of Confederate activity during the war, and this guest of the Brainard House, a Marylander, had served in the South's military forces for four years. His Elmira mission, mysterious and highly improbable of any degree of success, was to gain access to Barracks No. 3 in order to make sketches of the camp. He also sought information on the guard details and the time of day when there was a changing of the guard. Outlandish as it may seem, his task was to determine the possibility of an escape on a grand scale of the just over 5,000 Confederates housed in the camp at that time.

On April 13 the Confederate visitor by way of Montreal bribed a Union officer and was admitted to Camp Chemung where he completed a number of sketches of the prison. On that same day the Confederate, a well-groomed man and a bit of a fashion plate, purchased a new suit of clothes at a local clothing store. He was told that alterations would be completed within a few days.

On Saturday, April 15, as he entered the Brainard House's dining room for breakfast, talk of the assassination of Abraham Lincoln filled the air. He immediately went to the hotel's telegraph office and sent this message to

New York City: "J. W. B. If you are in New York, telegraph me. John Harrison."[1] Upon leaving the telegraph office, he heard that it was John Wilkes Booth who had shot President Lincoln. He immediately attempted to retrieve his telegraph message to New York City, and, failing to do so, promptly left Elmira and lived under cover in various parts of Europe and Egypt for the next two years.

"John Harrison" in reality was John Harrison Surratt, the son of Mary E. Surratt—the woman who was destined to be found guilty on extremely questionable evidence and executed for her part in the assassination of President Lincoln. Mary E. Surratt's crime was that she allowed the men who conspired to murder Lincoln and other high officials (Vice President Andrew Johnson, Secretary of State William H. Seward, and Lt. Gen. Ulysses S. Grant) to rent rooms in her Washington boardinghouse. Her Southern sympathies and a deep religious conviction that the Lord would punish the North also figured in the case against her. Mary E. Surratt's son, along with Booth and seven others, were immediately implicated by the government. John Harrison Surratt was part of Booth's circle and one of those who entertained a crackbrained scheme to kidnap Lincoln and take him to Richmond. The government's suspicions merited his being placed on the wanted list.

Surratt and Booth were part of what historian Bruce Catton has called "a weird set of dimwitted incompetents who could hardly have carried out a plan to rob a corner newsstand."[2] Yet, tragically, they succeeded in murdering Abraham Lincoln. Surratt, after serving as a member of the Vatican's Swiss Guard, eventually was tracked down in Egypt and returned to the United States in 1867. He was initially indicted and tried as a conspirator in the assassination of Lincoln. His trial ended in a hung jury, and an attempt to retry him failed. He lived out his life in Baltimore where he died in 1901.

Part of Surratt's defense was that he was in Elmira at the time of the assassination, a claim confirmed by the Elmira clothing clerk who had sold Surratt a suit of clothes on April 13. Four others testified that they had seen Surratt in the lobby of the Brainard House on the day of the assassination. Proof that Surratt had registered at the Brainard House, for some unexplained reason, turned out to be missing.[3] His presence in Elmira at the time of Lincoln's murder caused a bit of a stir in the form of rumors that a man who was in league with John Wilkes Booth had stayed at the Brainard House. "There was considerable excitement in town," the *Advertiser* reported on April 24, "over the arrest of some one on Saturday [April 22] who had some connection with the Booth assassination. But the whole stir probably arose from the arrest of some deserter, who was brought here in irons and assigned to our military authorities."[4]

The assassination of Abraham Lincoln left a stunned and angered nation in mourning. The North's newspapers voiced a collective irony when they spoke of the shock, grief, and disbelief in the midst of the joy and triumph of a restored Union. Inside Barracks No. 3, prisoner Marcus Toney, on April 15, jotted in his diary that the assassination of President Lincoln "has been another dark day for us."[5] Years later Toney would recall: "Immediately after hearing this [the news of Lincoln's assassination], one indiscreet prisoner yelled out, 'It is a good thing; old Abe ought to have been killed long ago!' The guards immediately rushed him, and I thought that he would get the bayonet; but they trotted him to the headquarters of Major Beall, who ordered him tied by the thumbs."[6] Tension between the guards and the Confederates continued at a fever pitch through the day and night of April 15. Although threats of shootings and the use of the bayonet were frequent, the day passed without an additional incident.

On April 24, with the trauma of the assassination lessening ever so slightly, the *Advertiser's* Charles Fairman was among a small delegation of Elmirans who were granted permission by Colonel Tracy to enter Barracks No. 3. As he passed through the main gate, Fairman immediately noticed the cosmetic refinements of the camp in the form of flower gardens, attractive lawns, and walks. He attributed much of the camp's pleasant atmosphere to the officers in charge. He then assured his readers that Barracks No. 3 was "the finest Camp in the United States. Certain we are that in all its decorations and adjuncts, except the miserable and misguided rebels who infect it, it is the most beautiful spot in Elmira, or within a hundred miles of Elmira."[7]

Turning next to those who administered the camp, Fairman stated that Colonel Tracy and Major Stocker were "due the principle [*sic*] share of the credit for the condition of this camp. Dr. Stocker is a man of remarkable energy, enterprise and intelligence. After witnessing the results of his administration, we feel that at least no better man could have been selected by the government for the discharge of his manifold and responsible duties." He then concluded with what was by that time a familiar anomaly: "One of the brightest pages in the history of our nation will be that one which records the enlightened and generous humanity with which it has treated its prisoners of war, amid the barbarous provocations which would have tempted a less conscientious and christian power to do otherwise."[8]

The total number of deaths in Elmira for April was 267—a number that once again was the highest monthly figure for any Northern camp. Elmira's April figure brought the camp's death toll to 2,732 prisoners of war. The camp's census on April 30 was 4,754.[9] Major flood damage to railroad trestles on the Northern Central line prevented any prisoner-of-war exchange in Elmira for April. Upon the completion of bridge repairs in early May, the Northern Central Railroad once again was able to move large numbers of released Confederates to Baltimore where connections could easily be made for points south. In May 1,037 Confederates were released from Elmira, and 131 prisoners of war were received. Some 131 Confederates died in May to bring the camp's total number of dead to 2,863. With the census on May 31 for Barracks No. 3 at 3,610, the end of the camp's existence was in sight.[10]

With the phasing out of Barracks No. 3, Colonel Tracy faced other pressing problems. Drunkenness and disorderly conduct on the part of Union soldiers escalated in Elmira in the spring of 1865. The numerous saloons that thrived in the vicinities of Barracks Nos. 1 and 3 created special problems for the post commander. On March 25 a desperate Colonel Tracy, in his effort to curtail what many of Elmira's citizens considered the nefarious flow of ale, beer, and intoxicating liquor, ordered both barracks commanders to station guards around all saloons in the vicinity of Barracks Nos. 1 and 3. No enlisted man from any regiment would be allowed to enter. The post commander made it clear that the order would be enforced and the barracks commanders would be held responsible.[11]

In spite of Tracy's edict, the carousing and lawless behavior of Union soldiers persisted through April and May. In early June Elmira's beleaguered post commander notified the War Department that approximately 5,000 men were waiting in Elmira for discharge and payment. "Liquor is being sold in immense quantities," Tracy lamented, "and the streets are full of riotous and drunken men, making life and property insecure." He then queried: "Can authority be granted me to suppress the sale of liquor in this City?"[12]

It was during these days that large groups of intoxicated soldiers gathered night after night on the Lake Street Bridge for the sole purpose of harassing civilians and officers with abusive language and physical threats. On a night when a military patrol attempted to clear and secure the bridge, shots were fired and five soldiers were wounded. The confrontation culmi-

A soldier's pass that was issued during Elmira's unruly days immediately following the conclusion of the war. Note the "Not good in drinking saloons" stipulation.

GEORGE FARR COLLECTION

nated in two companies of troops being called out to secure the Lake Street Bridge for the remainder of the evening.[13]

On June 5 Tracy, obviously weary of managing a prison camp and an increasingly incorrigible Union barracks, submitted his letter of resignation to the War Department. In calling for the immediate consideration of his request, the Elmira post commander explained that he had an opportunity at that moment to join a law firm in New York City.[14] On June 17 Col. J. R. Lewis of the 1st New York, Veteran Reserve Corps, replaced Tracy as post commander. Noting Tracy's departure, the *Advertiser* observed that his duties as post commander "have been conducted with great good sense and energy."[15] Free from his obligations in Elmira, Benjamin Franklin Tracy was now about to resume a law career that would lead to national fame.

Colonel Tracy's tenure in Elmira, a matter of controversy, would remain with him for the rest of his life. Among other things, he would be remembered for his festering feud with Major Sanger. Tracy's relationship with Sanger, however, was not as egregious as his issuing of Special Orders No. 336—the edict that curtailed the prison camp's daily ration of beef. Although he exhibited poor judgment in this matter, there is no concrete evidence that Tracy in any way took part in a policy of retaliation. On the positive side, he was adamant when it came to correcting the unsanitary condition of Foster's Pond. Also, he pushed for the construction of additional barracks. Perhaps his finest hour was his stand on the clothing question, and his sharp differences with the War Department during the months of December (1864) and January and February (1865). If nothing else, Tracy's position on this question exposed the devious plotting of Washington. Summing up Tracy's performance, the balance sheet is mixed at best.

Through the final weeks of the prison camp and beyond, Elmira continued to be a scene of lawless behavior on the part of Union soldiers who were in the process of being mustered out of the service. Their behavior was now a major cause of concern for Elmirans. Despite its great joy that four years of bloody war had come to an end, fear and apprehension gripped the town. Amidst this ambivalence, the *Advertiser* dutifully carried accounts of the Confederate exodus from Barracks No. 3.

On June 23 prisoner James Huffman departed from Barracks No. 3 for his journey back to Virginia. He arrived home seven days later "to find destruction, waste, and poverty. . . . There was no money; the start must be made from the bottom. I went to work with a will."[16] Huffman, like thousands of his prison comrades, had returned to a Southland whose composition had changed; i.e., the ravages of war and the crumbling status of the "peculiar institution" made it clear that the economic and social landscape of what was the Confederacy would never be the same. Nevertheless, on the day Huffman left Elmira, prisoner W. R. Lauden of the 50th Virginia wrote a letter home that stated he was happily looking forward to "a cup of good old whiskey & a glass of good old wine."[17] Indeed, with the joy of leaving prison and the anguish of returning to a devastated homeland, Huffman and Lauden must have regarded June with ambivalent emotions.

Time was now running out on existence of the Elmira prison camp, and the rate of departure foretold the closing of the camp by no later than mid-July. Three hundred Confederates left Elmira on June 30 to bring the total number of prisoners of war released in that month to 2,509. Fifty-four prisoners of war died in Elmira in June; this raised the camp's death toll to 2,917. The prison's census was now down to 1,047 men.[18]

In the pewter morning light of July 11, 256 Confederate prisoners of war downed a quick breakfast, rechecked their personal belongings, and waited for the order to assemble for the two-mile trek through the dusty streets of Elmira to the railroad station. This group made up the final contingent of prisoners to leave Barracks No. 3. They were now returning home to shake off the stupor of prison and the wanton barbarism of war.

Prisoner Marcus Toney (center, in white duster and hat) was among the final group of Confederates who left Elmira on the afternoon of July 11, 1865. CHEMUNG COUNTY HISTORICAL SOCIETY

Like many of those who preceded them during the spring and early summer, a number of these men were little more than walking corpses who were going home to die. Wilbur Grambling, perhaps the camp's most diligent diarist, had departed from Elmira less than two weeks before the camp's closing. He would be dead at age twenty-seven in 1870—"reportedly from a respiratory ailment incurred during his prison days."[19]

Some of that final contingent were too feeble to do anything more than wait for their train. Others visited some of Elmira's shops and restaurants. One of them, Marcus Toney, would recall: "After getting out of prison I first went to a restaurant and then to a clothing store, and fixed myself for traveling. I got a shave also, the first one in many months."[20] As the train pulled away from the station, it is most likely that home, the status of their health, and the indelible memory of the prison camp were the cerebral companions of Elmira's last freed Confederates.

Some 142 prisoners of war, many of them scarecrow figures and all too ill to travel, were transferred to Elmira's Union hospital. Sixteen Confederates died between July 1 and 10 to bring Elmira's total number of dead to 2,933.[21] This number, officially recorded by Lt. Col. Stephen Moore, includes 24 civilians who died in the camp and the seven unknown Confederates. A final total of 2,950 includes 17 Confederate deaths in Elmira's Union hospital between July 12 and September 1.[22]

A total of 12,122 Confederate prisoners of war were housed in Elmira.[23] Elmira's 2,950 dead resulted in a 24.3 percent death rate. It was the highest death rate of any prison camp in the North.[24] Estimates accepted by most historians show that the overall death rate of prison camps in the North was 11.7 percent; the overall death rate of prison camps in the Confederacy was 15.3 percent.[25] During the Elmira prison's 369 full days of existence, the death rate averaged eight per day.

Clearly, responsibility for Elmira's death toll can be traced to a small cadre of decision makers. Many of the camp's survivors would claim that those who made the decisions at Elmira were devious men, treacherous and scheming. Others would argue that a mosaic of questionable decisions was carried out by perversely deficient officers. And almost all of Elmira's survivors agree that the villain of the piece was the secretary of war. Indeed, Secretary Stanton's unrestrained and autocratic exercise of power, arbitrarily and cruelly executed, encouraged a policy in Elmira that by any standard was marked by obfuscation and delay. The result was a camp where the scale of human suffering was extremely high, and this will forever remain the sad legacy of Elmira's Barracks No. 3.

To the very end the supporters of the military decision making in Elmira saw the prison camp as a veritable haven for the Confederates. The optimism that continued to bubble up in the *Advertiser,* however, fails to account for the camp's high death rate. On the final day of the camp's existence, the newspaper boasted: "Improvements have been going on up to the time of the discharge of the last prisoners of war; these have made the place a small Eden."[26] This ludicrous pronouncement seems a final proclamation of a newspaper that for the entire year of the camp's existence attempted to promote the public's lack of an understanding of the facts of prison life by devious, emotional circumlocutions. Collectively, the *Advertiser's* incantations of the camp's positive status served as a numbing insight into the newspaper's failure to cope honestly with the horrible conditions of Barracks No. 3. For some, that the *Elmira Advertiser* chose not to acknowledge and speak out against the treatment of the prisoners of war comes with ill grace and remains very much a shameful element in this story.

In mid-July the *Advertiser* noted that the saloons just east of the camp on Water Street were being torn down. "They have served many purposes,

"Citizens" and "unknowns" were included in Lt. Col. Stephen Moore's final official count of those Confederates buried in Elmira's national cemetery.

BRENT MOORE

both good and evil," the journal concluded with an obvious sigh of relief, "and were the landmarks of a large, brisk and thrifty trade with soldiers."[27] Throughout the war, much to the town's continued astonishment and dismay, the overwhelming presence of the military had given rise to a large number of disorderly saloons, eating houses, and houses of ill repute. Those accommodations, like the prison camp itself, would now become part of Elmira's Civil War history.

Eight days after the closing of Barracks No. 3, fifteen officials from the city of Philadelphia toured the prison camp. Meeting on business in Williamsport, Pennsylvania, the officials decided to extend their trip to Elmira before going on to Niagara Falls, New York. Elmira's mayor provided carriages for a grand tour of Barracks No. 3. Through the courtesy of Lieutenant Colonel Moore, the Philadelphia delegation was shown through all the buildings of the camp, and told how the Confederate prisoners of war were cared for and treated in Elmira. At the conclusion of their day, the visitors were received by their fellow Philadelphian, Major Stocker.[28]

It is reasonable to conclude that the Philadelphia officials came away from the prison camp more inclined to view the place as "a small Eden" rather than "Helmira." They most likely were the last group of public officials to be given a detailed visit of Barracks No. 3. Shortly after their tour, and contrary to claims in local newspapers that the camp would be torn down, Barracks No. 3 was converted into a military center solely devoted to mustering out Union soldiers. In February 1866 the Union military operation in Elmira came to an end.[29] Barracks No. 3 was dismantled and all materials were auctioned off to the highest bidder.

In the years that immediately followed the war, soldiers of the United States and the Confederacy would begin telling their stories of life in Civil War prisons. In books, articles in magazines and newspapers, letters to the editor, and talks at gatherings of people who wished to learn about the soldier's lot during the war, the stories collectively constituted a gothic tale of misery and death. It was also during this postwar period that national cemeteries were created in incremental pieces of legislation by the Congress of the United States. On June 23, 1874, as part of a rush of last-minute legislation, the Forty-Third Congress established "Woodlawn National Cemetery at Elmira, New York."[30]

Newspaper editors throughout the United States remained relatively silent on the prisoner-of-war question until January 1876 when a thunder-

Lt. Col. Stephen Moore, the son of a military officer, served as an officer with the 3rd New Jersey before being assigned to the Elmira prison camp on October 1, 1864. Known among his fellow officers as a courtly and refined gentleman, he succeeded Major Colt as prison camp commander on December 1, 1864. Following the war, he eventually settled in Wellsville, New York, and for many years owned and managed summer resorts in New York State's Finger Lakes area. CHEMUNG COUNTY HISTORICAL SOCIETY

clap of charges and countercharges in the House of Representatives rocked the nation. Initiating a confrontation that marked the opening of the Forty-Fourth Congress's first session was Congressman James G. Blaine, the legendary "Plumed Knight" from Maine. An adroit and redoubtable figure in the Republican party and future presidential candidate, he was hated and feared by his political opponents. The 45-year-old Blaine, a master of parliamentary tactics, rocked the Democratic majority by proposing an amendment to an amnesty bill that would restore full political rights to all Southerners.

The Plumed Knight, aggressive and resolute as ever, proposed to change the bill with an amendment that would deny the general amnesty and restoration of rights to Jefferson Davis, late president of the so-called Confederate States of America. After some parliamentary dexterity on Blaine's part, the amendment was brought up for debate on the floor of the House. Blaine, whom his political enemies considered to be a waver of the "bloody shirt," began by recalling the horrors of Andersonville and placing the blame upon Jefferson Davis.

Rising to respond to the Blaine amendment was Benjamin H. Hill of Georgia. A tall, powerfully built man, Hill had served in the Confederate

Senate and was one of a small minority of Georgia politicians who opposed secession. He and his fellow Southerners were infuriated by Blaine's incendiary rhetoric. What had ignited their fury was Blaine's reference to Andersonville. "And I here, before God," Blaine declared in rich cathedral tones, "measuring my words, knowing their full extent and import, declare that neither the deeds of the Duke of Alva in the Low Countries, nor the massacre of Saint Bartholomew, nor the thumbscrews and engines of torture of the Spanish Inquisition begin to compare in atrocity with the hideous crimes of Andersonville."[31]

Goaded by Blaine's comments, Hill waded in with a 2-hour speech that amounted to an angry disclaimer of any charge that Andersonville was the atrocity that Blaine said it was. Addressing Blaine, Hill said that the horrors of Andersonville could not be attributed to any deliberate act on the part of the Confederacy. The situation at Andersonville, Hill argued, grew out of the exigencies of war and the harsh policies of the North. Congressman Hill then produced what he termed a letter which he claimed was written by a Union military surgeon who served at the Elmira prison. When asked by Congressman Thomas Platt of Owego, New York, where he procured the letter, Hill responded that the letter was published in the *New York World*. The full text of the surgeon's letter was reprinted three months later in the *Southern Historical Society Papers*.[32]

Excerpts from the letter read by Hill alluded to the ills of the camp, i.e., severe weather, a lack of winter clothing, the contaminated pond, inadequate shelter, smallpox and the shortcomings of the smallpox hospital, and malnutrition. The final segment of the medical officer's letter read by Hill stated: "They [Confederate prisoners of war at Elmira] were allowed to starve. . . . At Andersonville, as I am informed by brother officers who endured confinement there, as well as by the records at Washington, the mortality was twelve thousand out of say forty thousand prisoners. Hence it is readily to be seen that range of mortality was no less at Elmira than at Andersonville."[33]

With tempers now at the boiling point, Congressman Platt stated: "I desire to say that I live within thirty-six miles of Elmira, and that those statements are unqualifiedly false." Hill shot back: "Yes, and I suppose if one rose from the dead the gentleman would not believe him." Platt responded: "Does the gentleman say that those statements are true?" Hill replied: "Certainly I do not say that they are true, but I do say that I believe the statement of the surgeon in charge before that of a politician thirty-six miles away. . . . That gentleman, so prompt to contradict a surgeon, might perhaps have smelled the small-pox but he could not see it, and I venture to say that if he knew the small-pox was there he would have taken very good care to keep thirty-six miles away. He is a wonderful witness."[34]

Next Congressman Hill raised the point that continued to gnaw at the nation's conscience: "But the great question is, at last, who was responsible for this state of things?"[35] This is a question that was never answered by the Civil War generation, and it is an issue that continues to divide those who address it today.

The following day the acrimonious exchanges continued to fly like shrapnel across the House floor. This in spite of Congressman James A. Garfield's regret of "the course that the debate has taken, especially that portion which occurred yesterday."[36] Garfield—a former college professor, president of Hiram College in Ohio, Civil War general who experienced combat, and (in 1876) a Republican powerhouse in the House of Representatives—would be elected president of the United States in 1880. Andersonville and the trial of Capt. Henry Wirz were brought up. Wirz, the commander at Andersonville, was the only Civil War military figure to be convicted and executed for war crimes.

Garfield called attention to Benjamin Hill's remarks that appeared in a morning newspaper. "When the gentlemen from Maine [Blaine]," Hill was quoted as saying, "speaks again let him add that the atrocities of Andersonville did not begin to compare with the atrocities of Elmira, of Fort [Camp] Douglas, or of Fort Delaware, and of all the atrocities, both at Andersonville and Elmira, the confederate government stands acquitted from all responsibility and blame." Garfield wondered "what influence of the supernal or nether gods could have touched . . . [Hill] with madness for the moment and led him to make that dreadful statement."[37]

Hill was then confronted with a telegraphic communication from Benjamin F. Tracy to Thomas C. Platt. Tracy, in denying any cruel and inhumane treatment of the prisoners in Elmira, cited several points—many of them questionable. The former Elmira post commander, clearly stung by Hill's remarks, noted that there was no deadline and no prisoner of war was shot for attempting to escape. He then claimed that the quantity and quality of food was excellent. In making this claim, he noted that large sums of money went for purchasing vegetables that supplemented the regular ration. Tracy also declared that the quality and quantity of beef was good, and the bread was as good as could be found on a congressman's dinner table.

Turning next to the burial of the dead, he noted that separate graves and markers were accorded to those who died in the camp. The hospital facilities, Tracy said, were very good and hospital supplies were abundant. Next he claimed that quarters for prisoners of war afforded comfort during Elmira's extremely cold winter months. He then stated that the camp was well policed and kept clean. Tracy concluded his response to Hill's criticism of Elmira by noting that "the mortality [in Elmira] which prevailed was not owing to neglect or want of sufficient supplies or medical attention, but to other and quite different causes."[38] Failing to elaborate, the former Elmira post commander left that vague and murky statement to stand on its own.

The debate now crossed party lines. Charles C. B. Walker, a resident of Corning, New York, and the Democratic congressman who represented Elmira, took the floor in support of Tracy's remarks. "I was almost daily at Elmira during the war," Walker stated, "and I know that [C]onfederate prisoners had the same care and treatment that the Union soldiers had, and I never heard a complaint."[39] Walker's observation was followed by great applause. There was, however, a discordant observation in Elmira that Walker had not come forth more quickly. On the day after his response to Hill, the *Advertiser* chided: "We are sorry that Mr. Walker did not give his contradiction of official statement sooner in the House. No man knows better than he the absolute falsity of the accusation."[40]

Immediately following Walker, Garfield declared that "the lightning is our witness. From all quarters of the Republic denials are pouring in upon us." He then proceeded to read a communiqué from Capt. John J. Elwell, the quartermaster at Elmira at the time of the prison camp. "By authority of the Secretary of War," Elwell's brief message stated, "I furnished 15,000 [*sic*] rebel prisoners at Elmira with the same rations—coffee, tobacco, coal, wood, clothing, barracks, medical attendance—as were given to our own soldiers. The dead were decently buried in Elmira cemetery. All this can be proved by democrats [*sic*] of that city."[41]

Congressman Hill now began to retreat from his criticism of Elmira. He stated "that there was no purpose on my part by any of my remarks on yesterday to charge inhumanity upon anybody at Elmira or anywhere else. I only read the evidence from official sources as I understood it." And, after a brief but angry exchange with Blaine, Hill said: "I do not undertake to say to what special cause the mortality on either side was attributable, I say it was attributable to those horrors inseparable from prison life everywhere; and I simply entered my protest against gentlemen seeking to stir up those old past horrors on either side, to keep alive a strife that ought to be buried. That is all."[42] His remarks were greeted with applause.

The amnesty debate then moved away from the prison camp question and eventually concluded with no resolution to the question. It was not until June 6, 1898, that Congress restored full citizenship to the few survivors of the Civil War who were still not pardoned. But in January 1876 the verbal animosity on the floor of the House of Representatives was accompanied by a crescendo of partisan rancor in newspapers across the nation. Pandora's box was opened, and, in many cases, only the most tenuous connection with the prisoner-of-war issue was evident in histrionic editorials in the North and South. For the next several days the press, ostensibly with a deep emotional investment in the politics of the day, dredged up every imaginable bromide that could be even remotely associated with the prison camp question.

In Maine, the *Portland Daily Eastern Argus* used the debacle as an opportunity to attack Blaine when the newspaper claimed that the Plumed Knight's intention was "a deliberate effort to stop the flow of centennial feeling, and to harrow up the Democrats and render harmony impossible among the majority in the house[*sic*]."[43] The *New York Tribune* saw a curious irony in Hill's remarks when it noted: "It was no doubt a strange revelation to more than one veteran Northern Democrat to see the Government of the United States arraigned for sufferings of Union prisoners in the South, to hear an ex-Confederate Senator quote history to prove that the policy of the South was humane and that of the United States brutal."[44]

In Mississippi, the *Natchez Daily Democrat and Courier* saw Blaine as the villain: "Ex-Speaker Blaine has gone again into the 'bloody shirt' business. . . . If we of the South wished to keep fresh in the memories of the people the horrors incident to our late war and, indeed, to every war, our representatives, too, could point to issues of cruelty, on the part of the North, rivaling Andersonville in hardship, and without the excuse of necessity that certainly palliates, if it does not excuse, the treatment of Union prisoners."[45] And the *Nashville American* saw Congressman Hill's speech as "a remarkable effort—remarkable no less for the painstaking, convincing way in which he met every one of Blaine's statements and arguments, than for the earnest and eloquent peroration, glowing with patriotic and fraternal sentiment, which appears to have fairly electrified the House."[46]

The New York Times specifically took exception to Hill's charges against Elmira when it stated: "The slander upon Elmira, whose prison was so kindly looked after, even by ladies in the city and neighborhood, that

Union soldiers made complaints that those in the field had less care, was indignantly repudiated by some, laughed at as a weak invention by others."[47] In Charleston, South Carolina, the editor of the *News and Courier* saw Blaine as a political opportunist, "a shrewd politician who aspires to the Republican nomination for President. To strengthen his chances . . . he bitterly opposes the restoration to Mr. [Jefferson] Davis of his civil rights, taking the ground that he is responsible for the ill-treatment of Federal prisoners at Andersonville, and is, therefore, unworthy to enjoy with Ben Butler, Charles Francis Adams, Boss Tweed and Peter Cooper, the honors of American citizenship."[48]

The editor of the *Atlanta Constitution,* perhaps remembering General Sherman's destruction of that city, observed that "Mr. Hill showed, moreover, that the sufferings of the [C]onfederates in northern prisons had been greater than those at Andersonville."[49] A *New York World* reporter, sniping at the pervasive corruption of the Grant administration, wrote: "It is very possible that Mr. Hill's address was in some respects exactly what Blaine hoped for when he began the discussion. It enabled the Republicans to go back to the days of their honesty and purity and ignore the knavery and corruption of the present."[50]

In addition to this volatile editorial colloquy, letters containing emotionally charged indictments found their way to editors' desks. One such missive to a Rochester, New York, newspaper vehemently proclaimed that "rebel prisoners [in Elmira] were treated with all possible care, kindness and consideration. . . . Every man who could and would work at anything was allowed three good meals and ten cents a day. The idle received but two meals, but were permitted to carry away a quart of soup for the third, if they pleased, and such soup, too, as very few of us have the good fortune to find, except at home."[51]

On January 14 a letter in the *Advertiser* expressed "surprise that the citizens of Elmira seem disposed to pass without response the serious and damaging charge made against them upon the floor of Congress by the representative from Georgia." The writer suggested: "Let us hold a public meeting over this matter. . . . Mr. Platt and Mr. Walker have done their part in rebuking this bold slander—now let us do ours by putting into their hands our indignant protest against this wanton assault upon our fair fame."[52]

And in late January, word came from Maine when Dr. Eugene F. Sanger responded to Congressman Hill's comments. Filling two columns, Sanger's account of what occurred in Elmira appeared on the front page of the *Portland Daily Press*—the state's largest newspaper. In referring to what he termed "Hill's shameless defense of Andersonville," Sanger initiated an enthusiastic and thorough defense of the treatment of Southern prisoners of war in Elmira. Claiming that he possessed "a better knowledge of the internal workings of that camp [Elmira] . . . than all the statistics which either side may be able to accumulate," he stated that the unsanitary condition of Foster's Pond was remedied and proper barrack accommodations were furnished. He noted that the Confederates were allotted adequate rations and attributed the camp's multiple illnesses to the importation of germs that could be traced to what he called the "malarial regions of the South."

In alluding only obliquely to his trouble with Colonel Tracy, Sanger set his sights on the War Department and its frustrating penchant for delay. Obfuscation and red tape, he argued, clearly impaired rapid and efficient action. In saying this, Sanger, ever the blunt New Englander, implied that blame for much of what went wrong in Elmira should be placed on the War Department. He also stated that Elmira was a victim of false and negative newspaper reports—especially the account of "a female reporter . . . who [was] disappointed . . . because she did not find [inside the prison camp] the neatness of a gentleman's parlor, or a first class city hospital." There is no record that any other officer at Elmira ever referred to a newspaper report of "a female reporter." No such account was called to the attention of the post commander by the War Department. Sanger then concluded his statement with detailed references to the horrors of Andersonville.[53]

Capt. Robert R. Roberts Dumars, a ranking officer on duty at the prison camp during the entire year of its existence, also responded to Congressman Hill's charges. "There were at one time," Dumars stated in a letter that appeared on the front page of *The New York Times*, "as many as 10,000 prisoners here, and I assert . . . that they were better cared for and better fed, as a general thing, than were our Union soldiers in the field." He next stated that the Confederates were housed in comfortable quarters "except during a short time . . . in the early part of the Fall of 1864, when a portion of them had to put up with A tents." In claiming that "all the prisoners were supplied with sufficient blankets and clothing to keep them warm," Dumars, taking sharp exception to Hill's observations, concluded by reassuring the critics of the camp that the necessities of life (food, clothing, and housing) were provided in abundance.[54]

The heated exchanges of the amnesty debate and the adamant responses that followed fail to shed much light as to what actually happened at Elmira.

It is quite clear that the remarks of Tracy, Sanger, Elwell, and Dumars are in many respects at variance with what the records show actually took place inside Barracks No. 3. Their exculpatory statements were those of men who had a vested interest in presenting a positive account of what occurred inside the prison; i.e., they desired to live out their years with a plausible explanation of the camp's high death rate.

To those prisoners of war, however, who survived the ordeal of Elmira, the four officers' refutations of Hill's charges amounted to nothing more than rhetorical legerdemain. Elmira's survivors would remind those who listened that the death toll within the camp was heightened through the behavior of the War Department and those officers who carried out orders. As the postwar decades unfolded, those survivors spoke with the seductive aura of martyrdom. This certainly would influence the court of public opinion—especially in the American South.

The camp's survivors often would refer to those who decided the fate of Barracks No. 3 as inept administrators. Those survivors are supported by documents that reveal a lack of three essential elements—the practical virtues of good judgment, intelligence, and common sense. The best that can be said for the management of the camp is that it evolved from a series of administrative blunders, and those in charge were little more than bumblers.

A harsher appraisal will claim that what happened in Elmira is an illustration of the ghastly dynamics of war. That is, somewhere in the dark regions of the human spirit there is an atavistic desire to rend the enemy—and with this comes the corollary that it is the acceptable norm of wartime behavior. Men, who in any other worldly endeavor are civilized and kind, tend to abandon all reason in time of war. William Allen White, the sage editor and publisher of the *Emporia (Kans.) Gazette,* put it best when he said: "War brings men down to beasts quicker than whiskey, surer than women, and deadlier than the love of money."[55] The decision makers who shaped events in Elmira would seem to confirm this. And to those survivors who carried the memory of searing tragedy with them for the remaining days of their lives, the lesson of Elmira was clear: The leverage of the ruthless is considerable.

Admittedly, a lack of documentation makes some points almost unanswerable. Yet the camp's high death rate does invite speculation that Elmira was deliberately made into a death camp. Ranking officers within the War Department, prominent citizens, and Northerners of common circumstances voiced their outrage at the treatment of Union soldiers in prisons such as Andersonville and Libby. This was enjoined by the simmering passions emanating within the arcane recesses of Secretary Stanton's mind. All this points to a policy of retaliation.

When seeking proof to these claims, history counsels caution. What can be surmised is not the same as what can be proved. There is no definitive paper trail of evidence that specifically cites Elmira as a place of retaliation. Yet it can be said that the men who made decisions that determined Elmira's fate were enthusiastic supporters of retaliation. Never was there a clearer illustration of this essential fact than Secretary Stanton's reaction to a request for additional barracks at Camp Douglas in Chicago. "The Secretary of War," the assistant adjutant general wrote, "is not disposed at this time, in view of the treatment our prisoners of war are receiving at the hands of the enemy, to erect fine establishments for their prisoners in our hands."[56]

Deliberate delays in making major improvements within Barracks No. 3 contributed to Elmira's extremely high death rate. The consequences of denying additional rations, clothing, and blankets were great—and, in the minds of the camp's survivors, intended. This gives the charge of retaliation considerable credibility. Through a policy that by any standard was marked by delay and obfuscation, Secretary Stanton, a man of profound calculations, saw to it that a handful of his ranking officers (Hoffman, Wessells, Hitchcock, and others) implemented a policy of retaliation—a policy that turned Elmira into a death camp.

The verifiable facts constitute an enormous haystack, containing an abundance of tiny needles that reveal damning information. The unconvinced may continue to wonder whether that haystack contains a sufficient number of needles to support the retaliation argument. Yet all must recognize the following:

1. Stanton's call for retaliation in April 1864.

2. The support for retaliation among the War Department's ranking officers.

3. The reduction of rations by 20 percent on June 1, 1864.

4. The call for 10,000 prisoners to be housed in Elmira when the capacity of Barracks No. 3 was 4,000.

5. The lack of a medical staff until the fifth week of the camp's existence.

6. The long delay in reacting to Surgeon Alexander's July 14 report that called for hospital facilities, a medical staff, and proper drainage of Foster's Pond.

7. The total lack of a medical staff to treat the prisoners of war who had been injured in the Shohola train wreck.

8. Colonel Eastman's long delay in notifying the War Department of the danger of Foster's Pond, the immediate need for hospital facilities, and the need for additional barracks.

9. The circumstances surrounding Colonel Tracy's appointment to Elmira, and, in particular, the role of Henry J. Raymond.

10. Colonel Tracy's beef inspection order of October 3, an order that resulted in a significant reduction of beef on an almost daily basis.

11. The angry reaction of medical officers in Baltimore to the disastrous transfer of 1,264 prisoners from Elmira in October 1864—and Stanton's tacit rejection of any disciplinary action.

12. The late start in correcting the unsanitary condition of Foster's Pond.

13. The delay in construction of additional barracks.

14. The acrimonious clash between Tracy and Sanger, resulting in a demoralized medical staff and hospital decisions being made by unqualified officers.

15. Nine hundred prisoners still sleeping in tents in late December.

16. The deliberate withholding of winter clothing from Elmira during December and January.

17. The Cromwellian austerity of Hoffman's and Wessells's fiscal policies toward a conquered population.

There also remains a rather curious dimension to the tragedy of Barracks No. 3. The record of the camp's high death toll is a legacy that Americans today instinctively view as incompatible with their image of the United States. The awareness of this is troubling because it suggests more about the core of our character than we wish to admit. During the Civil War the politics of the War Department, functioning within a Machiavellian mind-set, justified a pattern of behavior that manifested itself in the form of delaying and/or rejecting relatively reasonable requests on the part of prison personnel. Americans needlessly inflicted pain and death upon Americans. Powerful men who claimed in public to have acted justly are now seen to have employed unjust means in private.

As Americans, we are not comfortable with this painful set of facts, and often ignore or refuse to face up to them. Perhaps we can best understand the tragic story of the Elmira prison camp in this light: The decision makers epitomized the grim fact that nothing distills individuals to their primal elements quite like internecine warfare.

Elmira, with its 24.3 percent death rate, was irrefutably the worst camp in the North. One can argue that record is, in a sense, even worse than Andersonville's. Although records relating to Camp Sumter at Andersonville in southwestern Georgia are incomplete, official records of that prison camp's post surgeon show that between March 1 and August 31, 1864, 7,712 Union prisoners of war died in the camp hospital. During the summer months of 1864 the Camp Sumter (Andersonville) census listed 31,678 prisoners of war.[57]

Today there are 12,914 graves in the National Cemetery at Andersonville. Some estimates place the total number of deaths even higher. With some 45,000 Union prisoners of war being incarcerated at Andersonville, the camp's death rate is generally agreed upon at 29 percent.[58] It was the largest of the Confederate prisons, and to this day the very mention of the prison's name conjures up thoughts of death, horror, wretched treatment, and man's inhumanity to man. The Georgia prison camp was a horrible place because inadequate transportation and an effective Union naval blockade were coupled with acute shortages of food, medicine, clothing, and building materials. Defective shelter, a lack of sanitation, and disease were pervasive. And yet all this was due to the inability of the Confederacy to produce enough food and to procure other essential necessities to sustain life. In short, Andersonville became the symbol of death through circumstances beyond the control of the South's decision makers.

The grim statistics of Andersonville are similar to those in Elmira. Yet the striking contrast between Andersonville and Elmira should be apparent even to the most casual observer. Elmira, a city with excellent railroad connections, was located in a region where food, medicine, clothing, building materials, and fuel were in abundant supply. None of this could be said of Andersonville. Hence, Elmira became a symbol of death for different reasons.

Decisions made by the War Department and carried out by ranking officers in Elmira were the major cause of the camp's high death toll. All these decisions were put forth by individuals who carried the imprimatur of one man—the secretary of war. The words of Richard Hooker, the sixteenth-century English theological scholar, bring to mind this fitting admonition: "That to live by one man's will became the cause of all men's misery." Consciously or unconsciously, Stanton created an Andersonville in the North. It is true that no prison camp managed by the U.S. Department of War matched the appalling death rate of Andersonville, but, clearly, a more compassionate and enlightened approach to operating the prison camp at Elmira could have prevented what must be considered a horrible tragedy in America's Civil War.

If the legacy of Barracks No. 3 is the responsibility of the War Department, today Elmira's national cemetery of the Confederate dead—like a tableau of silent witnesses—remains as testimony to the darkest chapter in the city's history. Laid out in barracks style, almost 3,000 Confederates are surrounded on all four sides by the graves of Union soldiers. The original wooden markers, withered over the years, eventually gave way to stone markers, which were permanently put in place by the U.S. government in 1907. Land contiguous to the two-and-one-half-acre plot was added in 1918 and again in 1939.[59] Additional land was purchased in 1987 when Judge Daniel J. Donahoe, an Elmiran and a veteran of the Second World War, organized and led a group of local citizens—most of them members of veterans groups such as the Veterans of Foreign Wars, the American Legion, and the Catholic War Veterans—in raising the sum of $20,000 in private funds. The money allowed for an additional 2.9 acres to be included as part of the cemetery's acreage.[60]

Woodlawn National Cemetery presently consists of ten and one half acres where over 9,000 veterans and their dependents are buried. A monument dedicated to the memory of those buried in the cemetery's Confederate section was commemorated in November 1937 by the United Daughters of the Confederacy. The Shohola monument marks the common grave of the Shohola dead. In the spring of 1997 a group of Elmira Southside High School students placed a marker dedicated to the memory of John W. Jones. It states: "Confederate soldiers were buried here with kindness and respect by John W. Jones, a runaway slave. They have remained in these hallowed grounds of Woodlawn National Cemetery by family choice because of the honorable way in which they were laid to rest by a caring man."

Two miles south of the cemetery, the east-west extremities of the former site of the prison camp on West Water Street on Elmira's west side are noted by two stone markers that were placed there in 1900 by members of the Lathrop Baldwin Post of the Grand Army of the Republic. The man who chaired the committee that put the two markers in place in 1900 was Melvin Mott Conklin, postmaster of the Elmira Post Office. Conklin, as a twenty-year-old Union soldier, it will be recalled, had served as a spy inside the prison camp.

The graves of Elmira's prisoners of war in the 2½-acre Confederate section of the national cemetery at Elmira. Just under 3,000 Southern prisoners are buried in Elmira. CHEMUNG COUNTY HISTORICAL SOCIETY

Three flags (Old Glory, the Stars and Bars, and the city of Elmira flag) fly above the monument that commemorates the site of Barracks No. 3.
BRENT MOORE

In August 1985 a monument citing the significance of the U.S. draft rendezvous and the prison camp was commemorated on a small plot of land that was part of the site of Barracks No. 3 and now is the property of the Elmira Water Board. In the summer of 1992 an original flagpole, located inside the camp 100 feet back from the main entrance, was moved to the site of the monument on the Elmira Water Board's property. Today it stands as the lone vestigial remnant of the Elmira prison camp. Located in a quiet middle-class neighborhood, the markers, the monument, and the flagpole are the sole reminders of what once existed in 1864 and 1865.

If there is a poignant nexus between the Confederate dead and Elmira today it exists in the person of Mrs. Dorothy Lewis Grant. Mrs. Grant and her husband came to Elmira in 1965 and purchased a home that they

The original flagpole that stood inside the prison camp 100 feet back from the main entrance. In 1992 it was moved to its present-day site next to the Barracks No. 3 monument on the grounds of the Elmira Water Board. The flagpole was reduced to its present height when a lightning bolt struck the top twenty-five feet of the pole many years ago.

BRENT MOORE

discovered was on the site of the prison camp. She then became aware of the fact that she had an ancestor buried in the Confederate section. Mrs. Grant's relative, John W. West of Company G, 34th Virginia, died of diphtheria in Elmira on October 22, 1864. In a 1993 WSKG public television documentary, Mrs. Grant reflected on the prison camp: "I found the whole concept of the prison camp very disturbing, and especially in the winter when I would look out and down from a height and see the . . . barren conditions, sometimes deep snow, ice everywhere, and consider what it meant to be living in a tent out there. I found that I had the ancestor buried in Elmira . . . in the Confederate section and he was my great grandmother's brother."[61]

During the serene summer months, descendants of the Confederate prisoners of war often make the trek north to the Woodlawn National

Cemetery to honor the memory of an ancestor who died at the prison camp. When they arrive, they see that the cemetery is peaceful and well kept. Two such visitors in September 1995 were James and Wanda Pollard of McDonough, Georgia. Wanda Pollard read a poem while her husband placed some red Georgia clay on the grave of Pvt. John Rigby of Company D, 35th Georgia. Private Rigby died in Elmira on May 4, 1865. "John Rigby," James Pollard said, "is my great-great grandfather. He was true to the end. In the end John probably knew he would never see Southern soil again, so I thought I would bring some Georgia soil to him." James Pollard concluded: "I hope I will see him someday at the last roll call."[62] He thus expressed a faith that served as a common bond between the 9,172 human beings who survived Elmira and the 2,950 who did not.

NOTES

CHAPTER 1

1. Catherine S. Connelly, "The Chemung Canal: 19th Century Freight-way," *Chemung Historical Journal* 1, no. 4 (June 1956): 150.
2. *Elmira (N.Y.) Gazette,* October 4, 1949.
3. Lois R. Tomlinson, "Highlights of the Canal Days," *Chemung Historical Journal* 1, no. 4 (June 1956): 170.
4. Eva Taylor, "'Rail-Road Guide'—A Literary Gem," *Chemung Historical Journal* 20, no. 3 (March 1975): 2469.
5. Ausburn Towner, *A History of the Valley and County of Chemung from the Closing Years of the Eighteenth Century* (Syracuse: D. Mason, 1892), 164 (hereafter cited as Towner, *A History*).
6. *Frank Leslie's Illustrated Newspaper,* September 12, 1857.
7. *Elmira (N.Y.) Daily Advertiser,* December 2, 1864.
8. *Frank Leslie's Illustrated Newspaper,* September 12, 1857.
9. Many Confederates who survived the camp and wrote of their experiences often referred to Elmira as "Helmira." The term can be found in any number of editions of the *Confederate Veteran*. On May 13, 1993, WSKG Public Television (Binghamton, New York) presented a one-hour documentary on the prison camp entitled *Helmira, 1864–1865: Andersonville of the North*. Written, produced, and narrated by Bill Jaker, the documentary eventually was presented on public television stations throughout the United States (hereafter cited as WSKG, *Helmira*).
10. *Elmira (N.Y.) Weekly Advertiser and Chemung County Republican,* March 9, 1861 (hereafter cited as the *Advertiser and Republican*).
11. Towner, *A History,* 200–201.
12. Edwin D. Morgan Papers, April 17, 1861, GK 11818, microfilm box 88, Manuscripts and Special Collections, New York State Library.

13. *Advertiser and Republican,* April 20, 1861.

14. *Buffalo Morning Express,* reprinted in the *Advertiser and Republican,* May 11, 1861.

15. *New York Courier and Enquirer,* reprinted in the *Elmira (N.Y.) Weekly Gazette,* May 9, 1861.

16. C. B. Fairchild, *History of the 27th Regiment N.Y. Vols.* (Binghamton, N.Y.: Carl & Matthews Printers, 1888), 6.

17. *Advertiser and Republican,* April 20, 1861.

18. Tina Hager and Cynthia Melendez, eds., *Elmira in the Civil War: Training Camp of the Blue, Prison Camp of the Gray* (Elmira, N.Y.: Chemung County Historical Society, 1991), IB.

19. Thomas E. Byrne, "Elmira 1861–1865; Civil War Rendezvous," *Chemung Historical Journal* 9, no. 4 (June 1964): 1248 (hereafter cited as Byrne, "Civil War Rendezvous").

20. *New York World,* June 2, 1861.

21. *Advertiser and Republican,* June 15, 1861.

22. Rev. Henry W. Bellows to Gov. Edwin D. Morgan, October 22, 1861, *United States Sanitary Commission Records,* Manuscripts Division, New York Public Library, Astor, Lenox and Tilden Foundations; microfilm file F775-3, box 628, Butler Library, Columbia University (hereafter cited as *Sanitary Commission Records,* Butler Library, Columbia University).

23. Robert Leckie, *None Died in Vain: The Saga of the American Civil War* (New York: HarperCollins, 1990), 173.

24. "Journal of Charles Condit Mosher," collection 37, box 14, folder 7, Seneca Falls (N.Y.) Historical Society.

25. Ibid.

26. *New York World,* June 6, 1861.

27. Ibid.

28. John G. Nicolay to Gov. Edwin D. Moran, June 24, 1861, Papers of the New York State Adjutant General's Office, BO462-84, old box 154, April 22, 1861–July, 1861, box 37, folder 1, New York State Archives.

29. Carol Vaughan, "Erin Day by Day in Civil War Era," *Chemung Historical Journal* 22, No. 1 (September 1976): 2626.

30. *Advertiser and Republican,* July 27, 1861.

31. Byrne, "Civil War Rendezvous," 1249.

32. *Elmira (N.Y.) Weekly Gazette,* May 16, 1861.

33. *Elmira (N.Y.) Daily Press,* August 16, 1861.

34. *Rochester (N.Y.) Daily Union and Advertiser,* reprinted in *Albany (N.Y.) Argus and Atlas,* July 6, 1861.

35. James M. McPherson, *Battle Cry of Freedom: The Civil War Era* (New York: Oxford University Press, 1988), 492.

36. Col. James Barnet Fry was appointed provost marshal general on March 17, 1863. Colonel Fry, an extremely able man, reported directly to President Lincoln and Secretary of War Stanton. In early April 1863 Fry proposed that each state become a federal "Draft Rendezvous."

37. Eugene Converse Murdock, *Patriotism Limited, 1862–1865: The Civil War Draft and Bounty System* (Kent, Ohio: Kent State University Press, 1967), 452–562. This is a lucid account of how the draft functioned in New York State. A July circular from the adjutant general's office proclaimed the adoption of Colonel Fry's proposal: "The following are announced as rendezvous for drafted men in the States named viz.: Buffalo, Elmira, Riker's Island, N. Y. City." On July 8 the commanding officers were informed: "Requisitions for camp and garrison, equipage, arms, equipments, and subsistence have already been sent to the proper supply Departments, for the service of your depot. Of subsistence ten days' rations for 3,000 men have been required for." "Letters and Telegrams Received, 1863–1865," RG 110, series 2343, box 43, National Archives (hereafter cited as National Archives, "Letters and Telegrams Received").

38. National Archives, "Letters and Telegrams Received," box 43; shortly after this, Albany was designated as New York State's third federal draft rendezvous.

39. Ibid.

40. *Elmira (N.Y.) Daily Gazette,* February 5, 1864.

41. *Elmira (N.Y.) Daily Advertiser,* August 26, 1864.

42. "Letters Sent, August 1863–February 1866," RG 110, series 2341, Letter Book 1, 101, National Archives (hereafter cited as National Archives, "Letters Sent"). A letter addressed to Thomas E. Byrne, Chemung County historian, and dated November 22, 1983, from Mrs. Jeannine J. Simonds of Orange Park, Florida, stated that her ancestor ("Samuel C. Severns/Severance") lost his life in the riot. According to Mrs. Simonds, her ancestor was "a volunteer in Michigan troops, [and] was killed in Elmira 25 Feb., 1864. His military records indicate there was a 'riot between soldiers of his regiment enroute to Washington and invalid soldiers stationed at Elmira.'" According to Mr. Byrne, there is

no evidence of "Samuel C. Severns/Severance" being buried in the Woodlawn National Cemetery at Elmira. Mrs. Simonds' letter and two newspaper accounts of this incident can be found in the file of the late Albert G. Hilbert at the Chemung County Historical Society. For many years Mr. Hilbert served as the Chemung County Historical Society's staff historian. One newspaper account, dated "Aug. 1923" carries the headline "Famous 'Battle of Chemung' Fought on Water Street At Baldwin During Civil War, Several Soldiers Meeting Death." The article does not cite a specific number of dead and wounded, but it clearly does not agree with Eastman's official report of one dead and four wounded. The other newspaper article, also claiming that there were several deaths, is entitled "The Battle of Chemung" and appears in the *Elmira (N.Y.) Evening Star,* May 23, 1906. There are no known editions for February 1864 of Elmira's three newspapers—the *Advertiser, Gazette,* and *Press* (hereafter sources from Mr. Hilbert's file cited as Chemung County Historical Society, "Hilbert File").

43. "Papers of Brev. Brig. Gen. William Hoffman," RG 249, entry 16, box 1, National Archives (hereafter cited as National Archives, "Hoffman Papers").

44. U.S. War Department, *The War of the Rebellion: A Compilation of the Official Records of the Union and Confederate Armies* (Washington, D.C.: Government Printing Office, 1880–1901), 128 vols., series 2, vol. 4, 67–75 (hereafter cited as *O.R.,* with all references to series 2 unless otherwise noted).

45. Ibid.

46. Ibid., 266–68. On the day the cartel was agreed to, the Union held approximately 20,500 Confederate prisoners of war (National Archives, "Hoffman Papers," box 1).

47. Benjamin P. Thomas, and Harold M. Hyman, *Stanton: The Life and Times of Lincoln's Secretary of War* (New York: Alfred A. Knopf, a division of Random House, 1962), 73 (hereafter cited as Thomas and Hyman, *Stanton*).

48. Ibid., 374.

49. Prisoners of war continued to be exchanged with some degree of regularity until July 3, 1863. On that day the U.S. Department of War decreed that prisoner exchanges other than those approved by army commanders "are in violation of general orders and the stipulations of the Cartel, [and] are null and void." On July 4, 1863, Maj. Gen. George

Gordon Meade, commander of the Union army at Gettysburg, informed the War Department: "A proposition made by General Lee, under flag of truce, to exchange prisoners was declined by me." After Gettysburg, the exchanges of prisoners virtually came to a halt. John Shirley Ward, "Responsibility for the Death of Prisoners," *Confederate Veteran* 4, no. 1 (January 1896), 10–13.

50. *O.R.,* vol. 8, 767–68; National Archives, "Hoffman Papers," box 1.
51. *O.R..* vol. 7, 146.
52. Ibid., 152.
53. National Archives, "Letters and Telegrams Received," box 43.

CHAPTER 2

1. Undated account in an unnamed newspaper of one Lieutenant Dean, the officer in charge of building the fence that enclosed the prison camp, file 500-320, Chemung County Historical Society.
2. John Francis McDermott, *Seth Eastman: Pictorial Historian of the Indian* (Norman, Okla.: University of Oklahoma Press, 1961), 6–15 (hereafter cited as McDermott, *Seth Eastman*).
3. George W. Cullom, *Biographical Register of the Officers and Graduates of the U.S. Military Academy at West Point, N.Y.* (Boston and New York: Houghton, Mifflin, 1891), 435–36; Appointment-Commission-Personal File of Brev. Brig. Gen. Seth Eastman (1875), RG 94, series 3827, box 326, National Archives (hereafter cited as National Archives, "Appointment-Commission-Personal File").
4. *O.R.,* series 1, vol. 23, 237.
5. McDermott, *Seth Eastman,* 61; 93–94.
6. Ibid., 26.
7. For a vivid assessment of Eastman's painting of Indians, see ibid., 103–12.
8. Ibid., 103.
9. "The Forts of Seth Eastman," *Periodical* 7, no. 1 (spring 1976), 22.
10. National Archives, "Letters Sent," Letter Book 1, 151–52.
11. National Archives, "Letters and Telegrams Received," box 43.
12. Ibid.; *O.R.,* vol. 7, 152.
13. National Archives, "Letters Sent," Letter Book 1, 159.
14. Lonnie R. Speer, *Portals to Hell: Military Prisons of the Civil War* (Mechanicsburg, Pa.: Stackpole Books, 1997), 241.
15. National Archives, "Letters Sent," Letter Book 1, 162.

16. Ibid., 163–64; *O.R.*, vol. 7, 157.

17. National Archives, "Letters Sent," Letter Book 1, 168.

18. National Archives, "Letters and Telegrams Received," box 43; telegram from Brig. Gen. Edward A. Townsend: "The order concerning Barracks at Elmira being used for prisoners of war is revoked. Acknowledge receipt"; telegram from Colonel Hoffman: "I am informed that the order for setting apart barracks at Elmira for prisoners of war has been countermanded."

19. National Archives, "Letters Sent," Letter Book 2, 1.

20. *O.R.*, vol. 7, 394.

21. National Archives, "Letters Sent," Letter Book 2, 11. The following day the *Advertiser* reported: "Lt. Col. Eastman informs us that he has now accommodations for 10,000 rebels at barracks No. 3, which await their coming" *Elmira (N.Y.) Daily Advertiser,* July 1, 1864.

22. National Archives, "Letters Sent," Letter Book 2, 12.

23. National Archives, "Hoffman Papers," box 1; Special Orders No. 251, July 2, 1864, "General and Special Orders," RG 110, series 2351, vol. 3, 185–88, National Archives (hereafter cited as National Archives, "General and Special Orders").

24. *History of the DeWitt Guard, Company A, 50th Regiment National Guard, State of New York* (Ithaca, N.Y.: Andrus, McChain, 1866), 173–74.

25. National Archives, "General and Special Orders," vol. 3, 188.

26. *O.R.*, vol. 8, 997–1001; from the time of the camp's inception to the conclusion of the war, 180 prisoners of war who took the oath of allegiance were released from Elmira.

27. Not all prison workers took the oath of allegiance. In many cases, a prison job depended on the skills of the individual—e.g., an educated, literate prisoner who refused to take the oath often would qualify as a clerk in an office or the prison hospital.

28. R. B. Ewan, "Reminiscences of Prison Life at Elmira, N.Y.," *National Tribune Repository,* vol. 1 (January 1908): 15 (hereafter cited as Ewan, "Prison Life").

29. *O.R.*, vol. 7, 424.

30. Henry V. Colt was the brother of Samuel Colt, the famous inventor of the revolving breech pistol, the submarine battery (used in harbor defense), and the submarine cable.

31. These remarks were attributed to General Sherman in a letter published in the *National (Washington, D.C.) Tribune,* November 26, 1914.

32. *Elmira (N.Y.) Daily Advertiser,* July 7, 1864.

33. Clay W. Holmes, *The Elmira Prison Camp: A History of the Military Prison at Elmira, N.Y.* (New York: G. P. Putnam's Sons, 1912), 307 (hereafter cited as Holmes, *Elmira Prison Camp*).

34. Anthony M. Keiley, *In Vinculis; or, the Prisoner of War* (Petersburg, Va.: Vindex, 1866), 130 (hereafter cited as Keiley, *In Vinculis*).

35. *Elmira (N.Y.) Daily Advertiser,* July 7, 1864.

36. Ibid., July 11, 1864.

37. *O.R.,* vol. 7, 465.

38. Ibid., 466.

39. *Elmira (N.Y.) Daily Advertiser,* July 15, 1864.

40. Joseph C. Boyd, "Shohola Train Wreck; Civil War Disaster," *Chemung Historical Journal* 9, no. 4 (June 1964): 1254 (hereafter cited as Boyd, "Shohola Train Wreck").

41. August 25, 1946, newspaper article; name of newspaper not listed. Chemung County Historical Society, "Hilbert File."

42. *New York Tribune,* July 18, 1864.

43. *O.R.,* vol. 7, 489.

44. Boyd, "Shohola Train Wreck," 1260.

45. *Binghamton (N.Y.) Weekly Standard,* July 20, 1864.

46. Ibid.

47. *Elmira (N.Y.) Daily Advertiser,* July 19, 1864.

48. *New York Tribune,* July 18, 1864.

49. Keiley, *In Vinculis,* 155.

50. *New York Tribune,* July 16, 1864.

51. *O.R.,* vol. 7, 488–89.

52. National Archives, "Letters and Telegrams Received," box 43.

53. *Elmira (N.Y.) Daily Advertiser,* July 20, 1864.

54. Ibid., July 21, 1864.

55. Ibid., July 22, 1864.

CHAPTER 3

1. Thomas E. Byrne, "Elmira's Civil War Prison Camp: 1864–1865," *Chemung Historical Journal,* vol. 10, no. 1 (September 1964): 1287 (hereafter cited as Byrne, "Prison Camp").

2. Keiley, *In Vinculis,* 117–120 passim.

3. "Reminiscences of Walter D. Addison," Thomas Jefferson Green Papers, no. 289, 3–4, Southern Historical Collection, Wilson Library,

University of North Carolina, Chapel Hill (hereafter cited as Addison, "Reminiscences").

4. James Huffman, *Ups and Downs of a Confederate Soldier* (New York: William Rudge's Sons, 1940), 93 (hereafter cited as Huffman, *Confederate Soldier*). For an abridged account of Huffman's Civil War experiences, see James Huffman, "Prisoner of War," *Atlantic Monthly* 163, no. 4 (April 1939): 542–48 (hereafter cited as Huffman, "Prisoner of War").

5. James P. Jones and Edward F. Keuchel, eds., "A Rebel's Diary of Elmira Prison Camp," *Chemung Historical Journal* 20, no. 3 (March 1975): 2459 (hereafter cited as Jones and Keuchel, eds., "Rebel's Diary").

6. *O.R.,* vol. 8, 997.

7. *Elmira (N.Y.) Daily Advertiser,* July 13, 14, and 23, 1864.

8. Ibid., August 2, 1864.

9. *O.R.,* vol. 7, 568–69.

10. *New York Evening Express,* August 2, 1864.

11. *New York Evening Post,* August 2, 1864.

12. Ibid., August 3, 1864.

13. *Elmira (N.Y.) Daily Advertiser,* August 2 and 4, 1864.

14. Ibid., August 1, 1864.

15. National Archives, "Letters Sent," Letter Book 2, 22.

16. *New York Evening Post,* August 3, 1864.

17. Huffman, *Confederate Soldier,* 91–92 passim.

18. National Archives, "General and Special Orders," Letter Book 3, 204; *O.R.,* vol. 7, 568–69.

19. *Elmira (N.Y.) Daily Advertiser,* August 3, 1864.

20. National Archives, "General and Special Orders," Letter Book 3, 207.

21. Ibid., 216.

22. *Elmira (N.Y.) Daily Advertiser,* July 25, 1864.

23. Interview with the Reverend Robert Lester, a retired pastor of The Park Church, January 16, 1996. The Reverend Lester is a noted authority on the history of The Park Church and the life of the Reverend Thomas K. Beecher. The quotation of Dr. Myra C. Glenn is from her book, *Thomas K. Beecher: Minister to a Changing America, 1824–1900* (Westport, Conn. and London: Greenwood Press, 1996), 97. Dr. Glenn argues that the great paradox of The Park Church was the congregation's opposition to slavery and Beecher's antiabolitionist position. The Reverend Lester and longtime Chemung County historian Thomas E. Byrne take exception to Dr. Glenn's thesis.

24. Rev. Robert McNamara, "Elmira's Dachau for Confederate Prisoners," *Catholic (Rochester, N.Y.) Courier-Journal,* October 8, 1964, 3 (hereafter cited as McNamara, "Elmira's Dachau").

25. Keiley, *In Vinculis,* 166.

26. McNamara, "Elmira's Dachau," 3.

27. National Archives, "Hoffman Papers," box 1.

28. *Elmira (N.Y.) Daily Advertiser,* July 26, 1864.

29. Ibid., July 27, 1864.

30. "Medical Officers' Files," RG 94, box 506, National Archives (hereafter cited as National Archives, "Medical Officers' Files").

31. All biographical material on Eugene F. Sanger came from the following sources: *Military Order of the Loyal Legion of the United States,* Headquarters Commandery of the State of Maine, Circular No. 8, series of 1897, no. 146; *Bangor (Maine) Daily Whig and Courier,* July 26, 1897; *History of Penobscot County Maine, with Illustrations and Biographical Sketches* (Cleveland: Chase, 1882), 768–70; *General Catalogue of Bowdoin College and the Medical School of Maine: A Biographical Record of Alumni and Officers, 1794–1950* (Portland, Maine: Anthoensen Press, 1950); *Dartmouth College and Associated Schools General Catalogue, 1769–1940* (Hanover, N.H.: Dartmouth College Publications, 1940); *Sketches of the Alumni of Dartmouth College from First Graduation in 1771 to the Present Time, with a Brief History of the Institution* (Cambridge, Mass.: Riverside Press, 1867); National Archives, "Medical Officers' Files," box 506.

32. Regimental, 6th Regiment, July 27, 1861, box 40, folder 5, Maine State Archives.

33. Ibid., box 40, folder 7.

34. Ibid., folder 8.

35. Ibid., November 22, 1861, folder 9.

36. Ibid., October 22, 1862, folder 21.

37. Ibid.

38. Keiley, *In Vinculis,* 138.

39. Last will and testament of Eugene F. Sanger, November 30, 1896. Register, Office of the Register of Probate, County of Penobscot, State of Maine.

40. National Archives, "General and Special Orders," vol. 3, August 11, 1864, no. 281, 208; August 11, 1864, no. 283, 210; August 13, 1864, no. 285, 212; August 20, 1864, no. 292, 219; August 25, 1864, no. 296,

222; August 31, 1864, no. 303, 229; September 5, 1864, no. 308, 326; September 10, 1864, no. 313, 342.

41. Keiley, *In Vinculis,* 139.

42. *Elmira (N.Y.) Daily Advertiser,* August 19, 1864.

43. *New York Evening Post,* August 17, 1864.

44. *Elmira (N.Y.) Daily Advertiser,* August 19, 1864.

45. J. B. Stamp, "Ten Months Experience in Northern Prisons," *Alabama Historical Quarterly,* Alabama Department of History and Archives 28 (winter 1956): 496 (hereafter cited as Stamp, "Northern Prisons").

46. *Binghamton (N.Y.) Weekly Standard,* September 7, 1864.

47. Keiley, *In Vinculis,* 158–59 *passim.*

48. *Elmira (N.Y.) Daily Advertiser,* August 17, 1864.

49. *Rochester (N.Y.) Daily Union and Advertiser,* reprinted in the *Elmira (N.Y.) Daily Advertiser,* August 13, 1864.

50. *Elmira (N.Y.) Daily Advertiser,* August 30, 1864.

51. Keiley, *In Vinculis,* 158.

52. Towner, *A History,* 269–70.

53. Ibid., 270.

54. *Elmira (N.Y.) Daily Advertiser,* September 9, 1864.

55. *Elmira (N.Y.) Daily Gazette,* September 3, 1864.

56. National Archives, "General and Special Orders," vol. 3, 252.

57. Keiley, *In Vinculis,* 158.

58. *Elmira (N.Y.) Daily Advertiser,* August 19, 1864.

59. National Archives, "Letters Sent," August 22, 1864, Letter Book 2, 35.

60. *O.R.,* vol. 7, 560.

61. Ibid., 584.

62. Ibid., 692.

63. Marcus B. Toney, *The Privations of a Private* (Nashville and Dallas: M. E. Church, South, Smith, and Lamar, 1907), 98 (hereafter cited as Toney, *Privations*).

64. John R. King, *My Experiences in the Confederate Army and in Northern Prisons* (Clarksburg, W.Va.: United Daughters of the Confederacy, 1917), 36 (hereafter cited as King, *My Experiences*).

65. National Archives, "Letters Sent," August 17, 1864, Letter Book 2, 32.

66. *Elmira (N.Y.) Daily Advertiser,* August 22, 1864.

67. Jones and Keuchel, eds., "Rebel's Diary," 2459.

68. Ibid., 2461.

69. Ibid., 2459.

70. *O.R.*, August 18, 1864, vol. 7, 607.

71. *Military Order of the Loyal Legion of the United States,* Headquarters Commandery of the State of New York, Circular No. 7, series of 1915, no. 1144.

72. *O.R.*, vol. 7, 604–5.

73. Ibid., 603–4.

74. Ibid., 595.

75. Ibid., 1004–5.

76. Ibid., 676–77.

77. Ibid., 676.

78. Ibid., 682.

79. Ibid., 785.

80. *Elmira (N.Y.) Daily Advertiser,* August 18, 1864.

81. Records of the Commissary General of Prisoners, "Letters and Telegrams Sent," RG 249, Letter Book 1, 140, National Archives (hereafter cited as National Archives, Commissary General of Prisoners, "Letters and Telegrams Sent").

82. *O.R.*, August 28, 1864, vol. 7, 692–93.

83. Ibid., vol. 8, 997.

CHAPTER 4

1. From August 30 through October 7, 1864, no prisoners of war were received in Elmira. With the resumption of the reception of prisoners at Elmira on October 8, there would be no more transfers from Point Lookout, Maryland. From October through May 1865, the great majority of Confederate transfers to Elmira came from New Orleans and Fort Fisher, North Carolina.

2. *Elmira (N.Y.) Daily Advertiser,* September 1, 1864.

3. Ibid., September 14, 1864. On September 10, 1864, local tobacco production was described in the *Advertiser* as "large and thrifty, with few exceptions." Two days later "a good production" of corn was cited by the newspaper.

4. Bruce Catton, "Prison Camps of the Civil War," *American Heritage Magazine* (a division of Forbes) 10, no. 5 (August 1959): 8.

5. Observations of essential shortages in the Confederacy and an abundance of food, medicine, etc., in the North pervade in publications such as the *Southern Historical Society Papers* and the *Confederate Veteran;*

e.g., see "Memorial Day at Camp Chase, Ohio," *Confederate Veteran* 24, no. 8 (August 1916): 348–52.

6. *Elmira (N.Y.) Daily Advertiser,* August 29, 1864.

7. *New York Evening Post,* reprinted in the *Binghamton (N.Y.) Weekly Standard,* August 31, 1864.

8. F. S. Wade, "Getting Out of Prison," *Confederate Veteran* 34, no. 10 (October 1926): 379.

9. Huffman, *Confederate Soldier,* 100.

10. Letters of Capt. John S. Kidder, September 10, 1864, family papers of Harrie Washburn, Sharon Springs, N.Y. (hereafter cited as "Kidder Letters").

11. Ibid., September 25, 1864.

12. *Elmira (N.Y.) Daily Advertiser,* September 21, 1864.

13. Ibid., July 29-30, 1864.

14. *Rochester (N.Y.) Daily Union and Advertiser,* reprinted in the *Elmira (N.Y.) Daily Advertiser,* September 30, 1864.

15. *Philadelphia Press;* this is an 1884 newspaper account with a dateline "Elmira, July 16," file 404-B, Chemung County Historical Society.

16. Letter of Thomas C. Jones, January 26, 1904, file 500-320, Chemung County Historical Society.

17. "Kidder Letters," November 13, 1864.

18. Huffman, *Confederate Soldier,* 96.

19. Byrne, "Prison Camp," 1179.

20. National Archives, "Letters Sent," September 4, 1864, Letter Book 2, 39.

21. National Archives, "Medical Officers' Files," September 16, 1864, box 506.

22. *Elmira (N.Y.) Daily Advertiser,* September 24, 1864.

23. Benjamin Franklin Cooling, *Benjamin Franklin Tracy: Father of the Modern American Fighting Navy* (Hamden, Conn.: Archon Books, Shoe String Press, 1973), 7 (hereafter cited as Cooling, *Benjamin Franklin Tracy*).

24. Ibid., 3–12; *New York Times,* August 7, 1915; *New York Tribune,* August 7, 1915; *Owego (N.Y.) Gazette,* August 12, 1915.

25. Cooling's excellent biography of Tracy quite naturally dwells on the subject's role as secretary of the navy. It is the most detailed single account of Tracy's years in President Benjamin Harrison's administra-

tion. Other material on Tracy's postwar career is taken from the three newspapers cited in endnote 24.

26. WSKG, *Helmira.*

27. Cooling, *Benjamin Franklin Tracy,* 13–21; "Office of the Adjutant-General Volunteer Service Branch," RG 94, box 361, National Archives (hereafter cited as National Archives, "Volunteer Service Branch").

28. National Archives, "Volunteer Service Branch," box 361.

29. Charles Carroll Gray Diary, file 2569, N.Y., Southern Historical Collection, Wilson Library, University of North Carolina, Chapel Hill.

30. Carl Sandburg, *Abraham Lincoln: The Prairie Years and the War Years,* vol. 3 (New York: Dell Publishing, property of Harcourt, Brace, 1954), 492.

31. National Archives, "Volunteer Service Branch," box 361.

32. Ibid.

33. Ibid.

34. Ibid.

35. *New York Times,* March 31, 1864.

36. Letter of Sgt. W. S. Toland, 83rd New York, April 23, 1864, *O.R.,* vol. 7, 80–81.

37. Ibid., 81.

38. Ibid., 110–11.

39. Ibid., 113–14.

40. T. Harry Williams, *Lincoln and the Radicals* (Madison: University of Wisconsin Press, 1960), 344–45.

41. Ibid., 6–7.

42. Richard N. Current, *The Lincoln Nobody Knows* (New York: Hill and Wang, property of McGraw-Hill, 1964), 176.

43. David Donald, *Lincoln Reconsidered* (New York: Vintage Books, Alfred A. Knopf, a division of Random House, 1956), 71.

44. Alan Barker, in his insightful study of the Civil War, sees Stanton as a man whose "vanity was intolerable but Lincoln humored him and used him in the interests of victory." Alan Barker, *The Civil War in America* (Garden City, N.Y.: Doubleday, a division of Random House, 1961), 119–20.

45. *O.R.,* vol. 7, 150–51.

46. Ibid., 183–84. Retaliation had been a long sought-after policy of the War Department; see *O.R.,* vol. 6, 314–15; 446–47; 485–86; 510–11; 513–14; 524; 647–49.

47. National Archives, "Hoffman Papers," box 1.

48. James I. Robertson, Jr., "The Scourge of Elmira," in William B. Hesseltine, ed., *Civil War Prisons* (Kent, Ohio: Kent State University Press, 1962), 88 (hereafter cited as Robertson, "Scourge of Elmira"). Professor Robertson has concluded the Confederate prisoners of war at Elmira were deliberately starved.

49. Thomas and Hyman, *Stanton,* 373.

50. *O.R.,* vol. 7, 573–74.

51. Ewan, "Prison Life," 14.

52. Keiley, *In Vinculis,* 172–73 passim.

53. *O.R.,* vol. 7, 175.

54. "The Treatment of Prisoners during the War between the States," *Southern Historical Society Papers* 1, no. 3 (March 1876): 215.

55. *Listing of Confederate Soldiers Buried in the Woodlawn National Cemetery, Elmira, New York,* Technical Support Service, Department of Veterans Affairs, National Cemetery Systems, Washington, D.C. (hereafter cited as *Confederate Soldiers Buried in Elmira*).

56. *Elmira (N.Y.) Daily Advertiser,* September 29, 1864.

57. National Archives, "Letters Sent," January 17, 1865, Letter Book 2,154.

58. *O.R.,* vol. 7, 878.

59. Ibid.

60. *Confederate Soldiers Buried in Elmira; O.R.,* vol. 8, 998.

61. Holmes, *Elmira Prison Camp,* 295.

62. *Elmira (N.Y.) Telegram;* undated newspaper account, file 310–60, Chemung County Historical Society. For an excellent account of John W. Jones's role in the burial of the Confederate dead, see Joseph A. Douglas, "The Ironic Role of African Americans in the Elmira, New York Civil War Prison Camp, 1864–65," *Afro-Americans in New York Life and History* 23, no. 1 (January 1999): 18–22.

63. James Marion Howard, "A Short Sketch of My Early Life," Albertville, Ala. (June 12, 1917), 16, file 500-315, Chemung County Historical Society, name of publication not cited (hereafter cited as Howard, "My Early Life").

64. *Confederate Soldiers Buried in Elmira.*

65. *Elmira (N.Y.) Daily Advertiser,* October 10, 1864.

66. Byrne, "Elmira's Civil War Prison Camp," 1292.

CHAPTER 5

1. *New York Times,* October 2, 1864.
2. *Elmira (N.Y.) Daily Advertiser,* November 2, 1864; on that date the *Advertiser* endorsed Henry J. Raymond for New York State's 6th Congressional District seat in the U.S. House of Representatives.
3. William B. Hesseltine, *Civil War Prisons: A Study in War Psychology* (New York: Frederick Unger, 1971), 172; [property of Continuum International Publishing Group] (hereafter cited as Hesseltine, *Civil War Prisons*).
4. *O.R.,* September 12, 1864, vol. 7, 816.
5. Emery M. Thomas, *The Confederate Nation: 1861–1865* (New York: Harper Colophon Books, 1979), 199.
6. Hesseltine, *Civil War Prisons,* 183.
7. *New York Times,* November 1, 1864.
8. Jones and Keuchel, eds., "Rebel's Diary," 2460.
9. Anne Bruin Papers, 1862–1865, no. 2484, Va., Southern Historical Collection, Wilson Library, University of North Carolina, Chapel Hill.
10. *Elmira (N.Y.) Daily Advertiser,* October 1, 1864; October 7, 1864.
11. *New York Times,* October 9, 1864.
12. *Elmira (N.Y.) Daily Advertiser,* October 3, 1864.
13. "Kidder Letters."
14. National Archives, "General and Special Orders," vol. 3, 287.
15. *Elmira (N.Y.) Daily Advertiser,* December 2, 1864.
16. Photostat of Diven's letter to the *Elmira (N.Y.) Daily Advertiser,* December 14, 1878, file 404-B, Chemung County Historical Society.
17. Frank Wilkeson, *Recollections of a Private Soldier in the Army of the Potomac* (New York and London: G. P. Putnam's Sons, 1887), 226 (hereafter cited as Wilkeson, *Recollections*).
18. Toney, *Privations,* 96.
19. Keiley, *In Vinculis,* 145–46.
20. Ibid., 141.
21. Wilkeson, *Recollections,* 225.
22. Addison, "Reminiscences," 7.
23. Howard, "My Early Life," 14.
24. Stamp, "Northern Prisons," 496.
25. *Confederate Veteran* 12, no. 2 (February 1899), 65.
26. G. T. Taylor, "Prison Experience in Elmira," *Confederate Veteran* 20, no. 7 (July 1912): 327.

27. Toney, *Privations,* 98.
28. Berry Greenwood Benson Papers, 1843–1922, no. 2636, Ga., S.C., 199, Southern Historical Collection, Wilson Library, University of North Carolina, Chapel Hill (hereafter cited as "Benson Papers").
29. *O.R.,* December 30, 1864, vol. 8, 52–53.
30. Ibid., January 10, 1865, 52.
31. Ibid., January 15, 1865, 77.
32. Ibid., 65.
33. *Elmira (N.Y.) Daily Advertiser,* December 2, 1864.
34. Ibid., December 3, 1864.
35. Cooling, *Benjamin Franklin Tracy,* 33.
36. *O.R.,* vol. 7, 996–97.
37. Addison, "Reminiscences," 8–9.
38. Keiley, *In Vinculis,* 195.
39. Letter dated June 13, 1996, from Mel Traweek, Ph.D., to Ms. Constance Barone, director of the Chemung County Historical Society, file 500-320, Chemung County Historical Society; Washington Traweek was Dr. Mel Traweek's great-grandfather's first cousin.
40. *Montgomery (Ala.) Advertiser,* June 22, 1902; for detailed personal accounts of the escapees, see Holmes, *Elmira Prison Camp,* 168–253.
41. "Benson Papers," 445–46.
42. Ibid., 453.
43. Holmes, *Elmira Prison Camp,* 195.
44. Ibid., 196.
45. Ibid.
46. *Montgomery (Ala.) Advertiser,* June 22, 1902.
47. Ibid.
48. "Benson Papers," 446.
49. Holmes, *Elmira Prison Camp,* 197.
50. *Richmond Examiner,* reprinted in the *Elmira (N.Y.) Daily Advertiser,* November 17, 1864.
51. Toney, *Privations,* 95.
52. Jones and Keuchel, eds., "Rebel's Diary," 2460.
53. *Elmira (N.Y.) Daily Advertiser,* October 8, 1864.
54. Toney, *Privations,* 95.
55. *Confederate Soldiers Buried in Elmira.*
56. "How the 'Rebs' Escaped from Elmira," *Elmira Sunday Telegram,* June 22, 1951.

57. Wilkeson, *Recollections,* 228.

58. *O.R.,* vol. 7, 691.

59. Keiley, *In Vinculis,* 178.

60. Ibid., 182.

61. *Elmira (N.Y.) Daily Advertiser,* October 12, 1864.

62. Keiley, *In Vinculis,* 188.

63. *Elmira (N.Y.) Daily Advertiser,* October 12, 1864.

64. Ibid.

65. Keiley, *In Vinculis,* 191.

66. *O.R.,* vol. 7, 892–93.

67. Ibid., 893.

68. Ibid.

69. Ibid., 894.

70. Ibid.

71. Ibid., 892.

72. Ibid., 1094.

73. Ibid.

74. *Daily (Washington, D.C.) National Intelligencer,* October 19, 1864.

75. Ibid.

76. *Elmira (N.Y.) Daily Advertiser,* October 19, 1864.

77. *O.R.,* vol. 8, 998.

CHAPTER 6

1. Hesseltine, *Civil War Prisons,* 197.

2. *New York Times,* February 3, 1864.

3. *O.R.,* series 3, vol. 1, 224–25.

4. William Young Thompson, "Organization, Supply, and Relief in the United States Sanitary Commission" (Ph.D. diss, University of North Carolina, Chapel Hill, 1953), 160.

5. Ibid.

6. William Y. Thompson, "The U.S. Sanitary Commission," *Civil War History* 2, no. 2 (June 1956): 41.

7. In 1878 Dr. Hammond initiated a campaign to clear his name of the guilty verdict brought against him by the War Department. Both houses of Congress annulled the court-martial proceedings and verdict. On August 27, 1879, President Rutherford B. Hayes signed a bill that cleared Dr. Hammond of all charges. His name was placed on the army's list of officers with the rank of brigadier general. Solely inter-

ested in vindication, Dr. Hammond requested neither back pay nor future pay. An early pioneer in the field of neurology, he practiced medicine until his death in 1908.

8. *Sanitary Commission Records,* microfilm file F775-4, box 638, Butler Library, Columbia University.

9. Ibid.

10. Hesseltine, *Civil War Prisons,* 198.

11. *O.R.,* vol. 7, 398.

12. *Daily (Washington, D.C.) National Intelligencer,* October 7, 1864.

13. Ibid., October 19, 1864.

14. *New York Times,* October 16, 1864.

15. *New York Herald,* reprinted in the *Elmira (N.Y.) Daily Advertiser,* October 25, 1864.

16. Holmes, *Elmira Prison Camp,* 294.

17. Ibid., 297.

18. Louis E. Schroeder, "The Elmira Prison Camp: An Analysis of a Union-Controlled Prison During the American Civil War" (master's thesis, Axinn Library, Hofstra University, 1976), 87; Schroeder cites the Dorothea Dix papers, Wagner Library, Harvard University.

19. *Elmira (N.Y.) Daily Advertiser,* November 19, 1864.

20. Ibid., November 21, 1864.

21. *O.R.,* vol. 7, 1146.

22. Ibid., 1159.

23. Ibid., vol. 8, 999.

24. Ibid., vol. 7, 1091–92.

25. Ibid., 1135.

26. Ibid.

27. Eugene F. Sanger Papers, Records of the Office of the Adjutant General, Regimental Correspondence, 1861–1865, Maine State Archives; at the time these documents were examined, no file number had been assigned to these papers.

28. Addison, "Reminiscences," 6–7.

29. Keiley, *In Vinculis,* 144.

30. Ibid., 144–45.

31. Ibid., 145.

32. Stamp, "Northern Prisons," 494–95.

33. "Two Witnesses on Prison Morality at Elmira," *Southern Historical Society Papers* 11, no. 11 (November 1883): 524–25.

34. *O.R.,* vol. 7, 997.

35. *Portland (Maine) Daily Press,* January 24, 1876.

36. *The Medical and Surgical History of the Civil War,* vol. 5 (Wilmington, N.C.: Broadfoot, 1991), 56, formerly entitled *The Medical and Surgical History of the War of the Rebellion (1861–1865).*

37. *O.R.,* vol. 7, 918–19; only twenty-eight barracks were actually completed.

38. Toney, *Privations,* 103-04.

39. *O.R.,* vol. 7, 1003–4.

40. Ibid., 1004.

41. Robertson, "Scourge of Elmira," 90.

42. *O.R.,* vol. 7, 1025.

43. Ibid., vol. 8, 4.

44. *Elmira (N.Y.) Daily Advertiser,* October 20, 1864.

45. Toney, *Privations,* 106.

46. *Elmira (N.Y.) Daily Advertiser,* October 29, 1864; the threat of a flood quickly subsided at that time.

47. O.R., vol. 7, 1065.

48. *Elmira (N.Y.) Daily Advertiser,* November 16, 1864.

49. *O.R.,* vol. 7, 1104.

50. Ibid., 1065.

51. *Elmira (N.Y.) Daily Advertiser,* November 18, 1864.

52. *Sanitary Commission Records,* microfilm file F775-3, box 628, Butler Library, Columbia University.

53. Ibid.

54. *O.R.,* vol. 7, 1184–85.

55. Ibid., 1173.

56. Huffman, *Confederate Soldier,* 100.

57. Toney, *Privations,* 100–101.

58. Ewan, "Prison Life," 13.

59. Ausburn Towner, *A History;* Clay W. Holmes, *Elmira Prison Camp.* Both authors offer an enthusiastic defense of the administration of the prison camp.

60. *O.R.,* vol. 7, 1180.

61. Ibid., 1195; Thompson, *Organization,* 167–68.

62. *O.R.,* vol. 7, 1093.

63. Ibid.

64. Ibid.

65. Ibid., 1094.
66. Ibid., 1134.
67. Ibid., 1135–36.
68. Ibid., 1136.
69. Ibid., 1157.
70. Ibid., 1201.
71. National Archives, "General and Special Orders," December 6, 1864, vol. 3, 398–99.
72. Ibid., 405.
73. National Archives, "Medical Officers's Files," box 506.
74. *Portland (Maine) Daily Press,* January 24, 1876.

CHAPTER 7

1. Jones and Keuchel, eds., "Rebel's Diary," 2461.
2. *O.R.,* vol. 7, 1272.
3. National Archives, "Medical Officers' Files," box 556.
4. Ibid.
5. Ibid.
6. Ibid.
7. Ibid., box 555.
8. *O.R.,* vol. 8, 1000–1001.
9. Ibid., 999.
10. "Characteristics of American Soldiers," *Army and Navy Journal* 2, no. 17 (December 17, 1864): 265.
11. Ibid. 2, no. 20, "The Elmira Barracks" (January 20, 1865), 309.
12. Dunbar Rowland, ed., *Jefferson Davis, Constitutionalist: His Letters Papers and Speeches* (Jackson: Mississippi Department of Archives and History, 1923), vol. 6, 506; Edey was released from Elmira in February 1865.
13. The numerous official reports from Elmira on the status of clothing stated "indifferent clothing," "there is some destitution," "good," "insufficient," "insufficient for this climate," "comfortable," "good, most having plenty, except overcoats, and those are on hand," "good, some few exceptions where pants and shoes are needed," "very fair," "need pants and underclothing for those discharged from the smallpox hospital," "hospital clothing be allowed, which would afford opportunity for cleansing the woolen and underclothing of the patients." *O.R.,* vol. 7, 997, 1124, 1146, 1167, 1184, 1213, 1240; vol. 8, 3, 39, 181.
14. Ibid., vol. 7, 667.

15. Ibid.

16. Ibid., 573–74.

17. Ibid., 785.

18. "Treatment of Prisoners during the War," *Southern Historical Society Papers* 1, no. 4 (April 1876): 294.

19. Ibid., 295.

20. Ibid.

21. *O.R.,* vol. 7, 582.

22. Ibid., 583.

23. Boyd McDowell Paper, file 500-315, Chemung County Historical Society.

24. *O.R.,* vol. 7, 926; 929; a copy of Ould's letter to Mulford also went to General Hitchcock, 930.

25. Ibid., 988–89.

26. Ibid., 1117.

27. Ibid., 1217.

28. File 500-325, Chemung County Historical Society.

29. *O.R.,* vol. 7, 1207.

30. Ibid., vol. 8, 23–24.

31. Ibid., 24.

32. Ibid., 90.

33. Ibid., 106.

34. Ibid., 137.

35. Ibid., 994.

36. Ibid., 180.

37. *Elmira (N.Y.) Daily Advertiser,* February 9, 1865.

38. Ibid., February 20, 1865.

39. *O.R.,* vol. 8, 237.

40. Maj. Daniel S. Printup Letters, file 500-325, Chemung County Historical Society (hereafter cited as Chemung County Historical Society, "Printup Letters," file 500-325); there is no documented response from General Beall to Major Printup's letter in the files of the Chemung County Historical Society.

41. *O.R.,* vol. 6, 503–4.

42. Chemung County Historical Society, "Printup Letters," file 500–325.

43. *O.R.,* vol. 8, 748–50; General Beall's final figures for furnishing supplies to 8,143 prisoners of war at Elmira under the Ould–Grant agreement are: 1,948 blankets, 2,575 coats, 2,810 pairs of pants, 2,394 shirts, 2,830

drawers, 3,758 pairs of socks, 2,320 pairs of shoes, and 307 packages from the South.

44. On February 2, 1865, the *Elmira (N.Y.) Daily Advertiser* reported that two *New York Tribune* newspapermen who escaped in January from a Southern prisoner-of-war camp claimed that "the rebels are still starving our men, and murdering them by cold, when they might supply them with food and fuel." On January 12, 1865, the *Advertiser* claimed: "Our Southern foes have become adepts [*sic*] in causing slow starvation. . . . Hearty, robust and stalwart men have thus been subjected to the fiendish process . . . [and] drag themselves homeward to disclose the awful tale. And yet such is called civilized warfare, such is [*sic*] would disgrace barbarians and savages." This was, the newspaper concluded, "cruelty, exposure and barbarity such as the world never heard before."

45. "Retaliation," *Army and Navy Journal* 2, no. 23 (January 28, 1865): 358.

46. "Treatment of Prisoners," *Philadelphia Medical and Surgical Reporter* 12, no. 18 (February 11, 1865): 295.

47. John N. Opie, *A Rebel Cavalryman with Lee, Stuart, and Jackson* (Chicago: W. B. Conkey, 1899), 318.

48. Huffman, "Prisoner of War," 548.

49. Jones and Keuchel, eds. "Rebel's Diary," 2462.

50. *O.R.,* vol. 7, 1185.

51. *Elmira (N.Y.) Daily Advertiser,* January 19, 1865.

52. Ibid., February 11, 1865.

53. Ibid., February 21, 1865.

54. Ibid., February 23, 1865.

55. Ibid., January 30, 1865.

56. *O.R.,* vol. 8, 1000.

57. Holmes, *Elmira Prison Camp,* 321.

58. Toney, *Privations,* 111–12.

59. *O.R.,* vol. 8, 181.

60. Ibid., 215.

61. Toney, *Privations,* 100.

62. Ibid.

63. Ewan, "Prison Life," 16.

64. *O.R.,* vol. 8, 98.

65. National Archives, "Letters and Telegrams Received," box 43.

66. *O.R.,* vol. 8, 182.

67. *Elmira (N.Y.) Daily Advertiser,* February 14, 1865.

68. National Archives, "Letters and Telegrams Received," box 43.

69. *O.R.*, vol. 8, 1000–1001.

70. Ibid.

71. Huffman, *Confederate Soldier*, 104.

72. *O.R.*, vol. 8, 420.

73. *Elmira (N.Y.) Daily Advertiser*, April 10, 1865.

74. Jones and Keuchel, eds., "Rebel's Diary," 2463.

CHAPTER 8

1. *Elmira Star-Gazette*, July 15, 1952; Scot Jenkins, "Confederate Spy Visits Elmira," *Chemung Historical Journal* 42, no. 3 (March 1997): 4621 (hereafter cited as Jenkins, "Confederate Spy").

2. Bruce Catton, *The Civil War* (New York: American Heritage Publishing, a division of Forbes, 1985), 267.

3. Jenkins, "Confederate Spy," 4621; John F. Doyle, "Beating Murder Charges in Lincoln's Assassination," *Washington Times*, July 6, 1997, B3.

4. *Elmira (N.Y.) Daily Advertiser*, April 24, 1865.

5. Toney, *Privations*, 115.

6. Ibid.

7. *Elmira (N.Y.) Daily Advertiser*, April 26, 1865.

8. Ibid.

9. *O.R.*, vol. 8, 1001.

10. Ibid., 1002.

11. "Letters Sent to Commanding Officers of Barracks, Posts, and Organizations, October 1864–February 1866," RG 110, series 2342, Letter Book 1, 344, National Archives.

12. National Archives, "Letters Sent," box 43.

13. *Elmira (N.Y.) Daily Advertiser*, June 21, 1865.

14. National Archives, "Volunteer Service Branch," box 361.

15. *Elmira (N.Y.) Daily Advertiser*, June 20, 1865.

16. Huffman, "Prisoner of War," 548.

17. File 500–315, Chemung County Historical Society.

18. *O.R.*, vol. 8, 1002–3.

19. Jones and Keuchel, eds., "Rebel's Diary," 2459.

20. Toney, *Privations*, 120.

21. *O.R.*, vol. 8, 1003.

22. The Elmira death toll of 2,950 was confirmed in a February 2, 1998, interview with Ms. Therese Sammartino, staff assistant at the Technical

Support Service, Department of Veterans Affairs, National Cemetery Systems, Washington, D.C. Ms. Sammartino cited a department data book published in 1980 (hereafter cited as "Sammartino interview, February 2, 1998"). Also, see memo of Lt. Col. Stephen Moore, MC 130, folder 1, Chemung County Historical Society.

23. *O.R.,* vol. 8, 997–1003.

24. Ibid., 986–1004; the other major prison camps in the North and their respective death rates were: Alton (Illinois), 11.8 percent; Camp Chase (Columbus, Ohio), 8.7 percent; Camp Douglas (Chicago), 12.4 percent; Camp Morton (Indianapolis), 10 percent; Fort Delaware (Delaware), 7.6 percent; Johnson's Island (Pulaski, Ohio), 2.7 percent; Point Lookout (Maryland), 5.6 percent, and Rock Island (Illinois), 15.8 percent.

25. Henry Steele Commager, ed., *The Blue and Gray: The Story of the Civil War as Told by Participants,* vol. 2 (New York and Indianapolis: Bobbs-Merrill, 1950), 685.

26. *Elmira (N.Y.) Daily Advertiser,* July 11, 1865.

27. Ibid., July 14, 1865.

28. Ibid., July 20, 1865.

29. National Archives, "Letters Sent," box 43; the last message, dated February 9, 1866, from Elmira's post commander to the War Department stated: "I have the honor to transmit herewith duplicate invoices and receipts for the records of this Dft. Rendz. which are properly packed & numbered in accordance with accompanying invoices & ready for transportation."

30. Sammartino interview, February 2, 1998.

31. *Congressional Record,* 44th Cong., 1st sess., January 11, 1876, 346 (hereafter cited as *Congressional Record*). Blaine's remarks were originally recorded on January 10; Hill repeated them on January 11.

32. "Statement of a United States Medical Officer," *Southern Historical Society Papers* 1, no. 4 (April 1876), 296–98; there is no mention of the medical officer's name.

33. *Congressional Record,* January 11, 1876, 347–48.

34. Ibid., 348.

35. Ibid.

36. Ibid., January 12, 1876, 382.

37. Ibid., 385.

38. Ibid.

39. Ibid.

40. *Elmira (N.Y.) Daily Advertiser,* January 13, 1876.
41. *Congressional Record,* January 12, 1865, 385.
42. Ibid.
43. *Portland (Maine) Daily Eastern Argus,* January 12, 1876.
44. *New York Tribune,* January 12, 1876.
45. *Natchez (Miss.) Daily Democrat and Courier,* January 12, 1876.
46. *Nashville American,* January 12, 1876.
47. *New York Times,* January 13, 1876.
48. *Charleston (S.C.) News and Courier,* January 15, 1876.
49. *Atlanta Constitution,* January 14, 1876.
50. *New York World,* January 12, 1876.
51. *Rochester (N.Y.) Democrat and Chronicle,* January 13, 1876.
52. *Elmira (N.Y.) Daily Advertiser,* January 14, 1876.
53. *Portland (Maine) Daily Press,* January 24, 1876.
54. *New York Times,* January 16, 1876.
55. Eric F. Goldman, *Rendezvous with Destiny: A History of Modern American Reform* (New York: Vintage Books, Alfred A. Knopf, a division of Random House, 1956), 183.
56. *O.R.,* vol. 6, 314.
57. Ibid., vol. 8, 606–14.
58. Interview with Eric Reinert, curator at the Andersonville National Historic Site, October 26, 2000; Sammartino interview, February 2, 1998.
59. Sammartino interview, February 2, 1998.
60. Interview with the Honorable Daniel J. Donahoe, February 24, 1998; Judge Donahoe held title to the 2.9 acres of land until it was deeded in 1987 to the Technical Support Service, Department of Veterans Affairs, National Cemetery Systems.
61. WSKG, *Helmira.*
62. *Elmira (N.Y.) Star-Gazette,* September 17, 1995.

BIBLIOGRAPHY

PRIMARY SOURCES

Documents, Diaries, Manuscripts, Letters

Addison, Walter D. Reminiscences. Thomas Jefferson Green Papers. Southern Historical Collection. Wilson Library, University of North Carolina, Chapel Hill.

Benson, Berry Wood. Papers. Southern Historical Collection. Wilson Library, University of North Carolina, Chapel Hill.

Bruin, Anne. Papers. Southern Historical Collection. Wilson Library, University of North Carolina, Chapel Hill.

Civil War Correspondence—Regimental. 6th Regiment, Maine Volunteers. Maine State Archives.

Gray, Charles Carroll. Papers. Southern Historical Collection. Wilson Library, University of North Carolina, Chapel Hill.

Harvey, Joseph Jackson. Letters. Grace Harris Family Papers. Elmira, N.Y.

Jones, Thomas C. Letter. Chemung County Historical Society.

Kidder, John Swain. Letters. Harrie Washburn Family Papers. Sharon Springs, N.Y.

Lauden, W. R. Letter. Chemung County Historical Society.

Listing of Confederate Soldiers Buried in the Woodlawn National Cemetery, Elmira, New York. Washington, D.C.: Technical Support Service, Department of Veterans Affairs, National Cemetery Systems, 1980.

Moore, Lt. Col. Stephen. Report. Chemung County Historical Society.

Morgan, Edwin D. Papers. Manuscripts and Special Collections, New York State Library.

Mosher, Charles Condit. Journal. Seneca Falls (N.Y.) Historical Society.

National Archives. Appointment-Commission-Personal File of Brev. Brig. Gen. Seth Eastman. RG 94. Series 3827.

———. Appointment-Commission-Personal File of Brev. Brig. Gen. William Hoffman. RG 94. Series 4647.

———. Medical Officers' Files of Brev. Col. Charles McDougall. RG 94. Box 361.

———. Medical Officers' Files of Brev. Lieut. Col. Eugene F. Sanger. RG 94. Box 506.

———. Medical Officers' Files of Maj. Anthony E. Stocker. RG 94. Boxes 555, 556, 1146.

———. Office of the Adjutant General Volunteer Service, Papers of Brev. Brig. Gen. Benjamin F. Tracy. RG 94. Box 361.

———. Papers of Brev. Brig. Gen. William Hoffman. RG 249. Series 16.

The following thirteen documents are classified as "Elmira Draft Rendezvous, General Records":

National Archives. "Endorsements, January 1864–February 1866." RG 110. Series 2345.

———. "Endorsements Relating to the Prisoner-of-War Depot, October 1864–July 1865." RG 110. Series 2346.

———. "Endorsements Sent by the Post Commander, January–December 1865." RG 110. Series 2347.

———. "Endorsements Sent by the Acting Assistant Adjutant General, November 1865–February 1866." RG 110. Series 2348.

———. "General and Special Orders, July 1863–January 1865." RG 110. Series 2351.

———. "General Orders, September 1864–January 1866." RG 110. Series 2352.

———. "Letters Sent, August 1863–February 1866." RG 110. Series 2341.

———. "Letters Sent to Commanding Officers of Barracks, Posts, and Organizations, October 1864–February 1866." RG 110. Series 2342.

———. "Letters and Telegrams Received, 1863–1865." RG 110. Series 2343.

———. "Proceedings of the Post Council of Administration Established of Examine Accounts of the Post Fund, January 1864–February 1866." RG 110. Series 2357.

———. "Special Orders, January 1865–February 1866." RG 110. Series 2355.

————. "Special Orders of the Adjutant General's Office, Headquarters of the Districts of Western and Northern New York at Albany, N.Y., Office of the Acting Assistant Provost Marshal General for the Western Division and Headquarters of the Department of the East, 1863–1866." RG 110. Series 2353.

————. "Telegrams Sent, 1864-1865." RG 110. Series 2349.

New York State Adjutant General's Office. Papers, April 22, 1861–July 9, 1861. New York State Archives.

Phisterer, Frederick, comp. *New York and the War of the Rebellion, 1861 to 1865.* 5 Vols. Albany, N.Y.: J. B. Lyon, 1912.

Printup, Maj. Daniel. Letters. Chemung County Historical Society.

Rowland, Dunbar, ed. *Jefferson Davis, Constitutionalist: His Letters, Papers and Speeches.* Vol. 6. Jackson: Mississippi Department of Archives and History, 1923.

Sanger, Eugene F. Last will and testament, November 30, 1896. Office of Register of Probate, County of Penobscot, State of Maine.

————. Papers. Record of the Office of the Adjutant General, Regimental Correspondence. Maine State Archives.

U.S. Sanitary Commission Records. Astor, Lenox, and Tilden Foundations. Manuscript Division, New York Public Library; microfilm file, Butler Library, Columbia University.

U.S. War Department, ed. *The War of the Rebellion: A Compilation of the Official Records of the Union and Confederate Armies.* 128 Vols. Washington, D.C.: Government Printing Office, 1880–1901.

Books

Benson, Susan W., ed. *Berry Benson's Civil War Book: Memoirs of a Confederate Scout and Sharpshooter.* Athens, Ga.: University of Georgia Press, 1962.

Bernard, George S., ed. *War Talks of Confederate Veterans.* Petersburg, Va.: Fenn and Owen, 1892.

Billings, John D. *Hardtack and Coffee: or The Unwritten Story of Army Life.* Boston: G. M. Smith, 1887.

Brockett, L. P., and Mary E. Vaughan. *Woman's Work in the Civil War: A Record of Heroism, Patriotism and Patience.* Philadelphia: Zeigler, McCurdy, 1867.

Commager, Henry Steele, ed. *The Blue and the Gray: The Story of the Civil War as Told by Participants.* 2 Vols. New York and Indianapolis: Bobbs-Merrill, 1950.

Crowell, Joseph E. *The Young Volunteer: The Everyday Experiences of a Soldier Boy in the Civil War.* Paterson, N.J.: Joseph E. Crowell *The Call,* 1906.

History of the DeWitt Guard, Company A, 50th Regiment National Guard, State of New York. Ithaca, N.Y.: Andrus, McChain, 1866.

Huffman, James. *Ups and Downs of a Confederate Soldier.* New York: William E. Rudge's Sons, 1940.

Keiley, Anthony M. *In Vinculis; or, The Prisoner of War.* Petersburg, Va.: Vindex, 1966.

King, John R. *My Experiences in the Confederate Army and in Northern Prisons.* Clarksburg, W.Va.: United Daughters of the Confederacy, 1917.

Leon, Louis. *Diary of a Tarheel Confederate Prisoner.* Charlotte, N.C.: Stone Publishing, 1913.

Opie, John N. *A Rebel Cavalryman with Lee, Stuart, and Jackson.* Chicago: W. B. Conkey, 1899.

Post, Lydia Minturn, ed. *Soldiers' Letters from Camp, Battle-Field and Prison.* New York: Bunce and Huntington, 1865.

Toney, Marcus B. *The Privations of a Private.* Nashville and Dallas: M. E. Church, South, Smith, and Lamar, 1907.

Wilkeson, Frank. *Recollections of a Private Soldier in the Army of the Potomac.* New York and London: G. P. Putnam's Sons, 1887.

Articles and Periodicals

"Characteristics of American Soldiers." *Army and Navy Journal* 2, no. 17 (December 17, 1864).

Davis, T. C. Untitled account of Davis's experience as a prisoner in Elmira. *Confederate Veteran* 2, no. 2 (February 1899).

"Elmira Barracks, The." *Army and Navy Journal* 2, no. 20 (January 20, 1865).

Ewan, R. B. "Reminiscences of Prison Life at Elmira, N. Y." *National Tribune Repository* 1, no. 3 (January 1908).

Howard, James Marion. "A Short Sketch of My Early Life." Name of publication not listed. Albertville, Alabama, June 12, 1917.

Huffman, James. "Prisoner of War," *Atlantic* 163, no. 4 (April 1939).

Jones, James P., and Edward F. Keuchel, eds. "A Rebel's Diary of Elmira Prison Camp." *Chemung Historical Journal* 20, no. 3 (March 1975).

"Memorial Day at Camp Chase, Ohio." *Confederate Veteran* 24, no. 8 (August 1916).

"Retaliation." *Army and Navy Journal* 2, no. 23 (January 28, 1865).

"Southerner Tells of Buying Liberty From Elmira Prison." *Elmira Sunday Telegram*. July 18, 1926.

Stamp, J. B. "Ten Months Experience in Northern Prisons." *Alabama Historical Quarterly* (Alabama Department of Archives and History, Montgomery, Ala.) 28, no. 4 (winter 1956).

Taylor, G. T. "Prison Experience in Elmira, N.Y." *Confederate Veteran* 20, no. 7 (July 1912).

"Treatment of Prisoners." *Philadelphia Medical and Surgical Reporter* 12, no. 18 (February 11, 1865).

"Treatment of Prisoners during the War." *Southern Historical Society Papers* 1, no. 4 (April 1876).

"Treatment of Prisoners during the War between the States, The." *Southern Historical Society Papers* 1, no. 3 (March 1876).

"Two Witnesses on Prison Mortality at Elmira." *Southern Historical Society Papers* 11, no. 11 (November 1883).

Vaughan, Carol, ed. "Erin Day by Day in Civil War." *Chemung Historical Journal* 22, no. 1 (September 1976).

Wade, F. S. "Getting Out of Prison." *Confederate Veteran* 34, no. 10 (October 1926).

Ward, John Shirley. "Responsibility for the Death of Prisoners." *Confederate Veteran* 4, no. 1 (January 1896).

Newspapers

Albany (N.Y.) Atlas and Argus, 1861, 1864.

Albany (N.Y.) Daily Knickerbocker, 1861.

Albany (N.Y.) Evening Journal, 1861, 1864.

Atlanta Constitution, 1876.

Auburn (N.Y.) Daily Advertiser and Union, 1864.

Baltimore Gazette, 1876.

Baltimore Sun, 1864.

Bangor (Maine) Whig and Courier, 1876.

Binghamton (N.Y.) Weekly Standard, 1862, 1864.

Boston Evening Transcript, 1863, 1864.

Boston Journal, 1876.

Boston Post, 1876.

Buffalo Morning Express, 1861.

Charleston (S.C.) News and Courier, 1876.

Cincinnati Daily Gazette, 1863.

Congressional Record, 44th Cong., 1st sess., 1876.

Corning (N.Y.) Journal, 1864, 1865.

Daily (Washington D.C.) National Intelligencer, 1864.

Elmira (N.Y.) Daily Advertiser, 1855, 1861, 1864, 1865, 1876.

Elmira (N.Y.) Daily Gazette, 1864.

Elmira (N.Y.) Daily Press, 1861.

Elmira (N.Y.) Daily Republican, 1854, 1855.

Elmira (N.Y.) Gazette, 1849.

Elmira (N.Y.) Republican and General Advertiser, 1834.

Elmira (N.Y.) Saturday Evening Review, 1870.

Elmira (N.Y.) Weekly Advertiser and Chemung County Republican, 1861.

Elmira (N.Y.) Weekly Gazette, 1861, 1862, 1863, 1864.

Frank Leslie's Illustrated Newspaper, 1857.

Ithaca (N.Y.) Citizen and Democrat, 1864.

Jackson (Miss.) Daily Times, 1876.

Montpelier (Vt.) Green Mountain Freeman, 1864.

Nashville American, 1876.

Natchez (Miss.) Daily Democrat, 1876.

New Orleans Times, 1876.

New York Courier and Enquirer, 1861.

New York Evening Express, 1864.

New York Evening Post, 1864.

New York Herald, 1864, 1876.

New York Times, 1861, 1862, 1863, 1864, 1865, 1876.

New York Tribune, 1864, 1876.

New York World, 1861, 1876.

Owego (N.Y.) Times, 1864.

Portland (Maine) Advertiser, 1876.

Portland (Maine) Daily Eastern Argus, 1876.

Portland (Maine) Daily Press, 1876.

Richmond Dispatch, 1876.

Richmond Examiner, 1864.

Rochester (N.Y.) Daily Union and Advertiser, 1861, 1864.

Rochester (N.Y.) Democrat and Chronicle, 1876.

Rochester (N.Y.) Evening Express, 1864.

Savannah Morning News, 1876.
Southern Tier (Elmira) Leader, 1876.
Trumansburg (N.Y.) News, 1864.
Utica (N.Y.) Herald, 1865, 1876.
Vicksburg (Miss.) Herald, 1864.

SECONDARY SOURCES

Ph.D. Dissertations, Master's Theses, Letters, Papers

McDowell, Boyd. Paper. Chemung County Historical Society, n.d.

Ottman, Walter Henry. "A History of the City of Elmira, N.Y." Ph.D. diss., Olin Library, Cornell University, 1900.

Ramsdell, William S. "John W. Jones: An Elmira Hero." First Baptist Church (Elmira) Archives, 1997.

Schroeder, Louis E. "The Elmira Prison Camp: An Analysis of a Union-Controlled Prison Camp during the American Civil War." Master's thesis, Axinn Library, Hofstra University, 1976.

Simonds, Jeanine J. Letter. Chemung County Historical Society.

Snyder, Howard B. "The Wreck of the Prison Train." Chemung County Historical Society, n.d.

Steen, A. G. "Recollections of Elmira in Civil War Days." Chemung County Historical Society, n.d.

Thompson, William Young. "Organization, Supply, and Relief in the United States Sanitary Commission." Ph.D. diss., Davis Library, University of North Carolina, Chapel Hill, 1953.

Traweek, Mel. Letter. Chemung County Historical Society.

Turner, Welthea Hatheway. "The Elmira Prison Camp." Master's thesis, Elmira College, Chemung County Historical Society, n.d.

Television Documentary

"Helmira, 1864–1865: Andersonville of the North." WSKG (Binghamton, N.Y.) Public Television, May 13, 1993. Produced, written, and narrated by Bill Jaker.

Books

Adams, George Worthington. *Doctors in Blue: The Medical History of the Union Army in the Civil War.* New York: Henry Schuman, 1952.

Alexander, DeAlva Stanwood. *A Political History of the State of New York.* Vol. 2: *1833–1861;* Vol. 3: *1861–1882.* Port Washington, N.Y.: Ira J. Friedman, 1909.

Anbinder, Tyler. *Nativism and Slavery: The Northern Know Nothings and the Politics of the 1850s.* New York: Oxford University Press, 1992.

Barber, W. Charles. *Elmira College: The First Hundred Years.* New York, Toronto, and London: McGraw-Hill, 1955.

Barker, Alan. *The Civil War in America.* Garden City, N.Y.: Doubleday, a division of Random House, 1961.

Beitzell, Edwin W. *Point Lookout Prison Camp for Confederates.* Abell, Md.: Edwin W. Beitzell, 1983.

Billington, Ray Allen. *The Protestant Crusade, 1800–1860: A Study of the Origins of American Nativism.* Chicago: Quadrangle Books, 1964.

Brogan, D. W. *Abraham Lincoln.* New York: Schocken Books, 1963.

Brown, Dee. *Year of the Century: 1876.* New York: Charles Scribner's Sons, 1966.

Catton, Bruce. *The Civil War.* New York: American Heritage Publishing, a division of Forbes, 1985.

———. *A Stillness at Appomattox.* Garden City, N.Y.: Doubleday, 1954.

Cooling, Benjamin Franklin. *Benjamin Franklin Tracy: Father of the Modern American Fighting Navy.* Hamden, Conn.: Archon Books, Shoe String Press, 1973.

Cross, Whitney R. *The Burned-Over District: The Social and Intellectual History of Enthusiastic Religion in Western New York, 1800–1850.* New York: Harper Torchbooks, 1965.

Crowe, Charles, ed. *The Age of the Civil War and Reconstruction, 1830–1900: A Book of Interpretative Essays.* Homewood, Ill.: Dorsey Press, 1966.

Cullom, George W. *Biographical Register of Graduates of the U.S. Military Academy at West Point, N.Y.* Boston and New York: Houghton, Mifflin, 1891.

Current, Richard N. *Lincoln and the First Shot.* Philadelphia and New York: J. B. Lippincott, 1963.

———. *The Lincoln Nobody Knows.* New York: Hill and Wang, property of McGraw-Hill, 1964.

Dartmouth College and Associated Schools General Catalogue, 1769–1940. Hanover, N.H.: Dartmouth College Publications, 1940.

Davidson, Henry M., Henry B. Fruness, and Asab Isham. *Prisoners of War and Military Prisons.* Cincinnati: Lyman and Cushing, 1890.

Denney, Robert E. *Civil War Medicine: Care & Comfort of the Wounded.* New York: Sterling Publishing, 1995.

———. *Civil War Prisons & Escapes.* New York: Sterling Publishing, 1993.

Donald, David Herbert. *Lincoln.* New York: Simon & Schuster, 1995.

———. *Lincoln Reconsidered: Essays on the Civil War Era.* New York: Vintage Books, Alfred A. Knopf, a division of Random House, 1956.

Ellis, David M., James A. Frost, Harold C. Syrett, and Harry J. Carman. *A Short History of New York State.* Ithaca, N.Y.: Cornell University Press, 1962.

Fairchild, C. B. *History of the 27th Regiment, N.Y. Vols.* Binghamton: Carl & Matthews Printers, 1888.

Franklin, John Hope. *The Militant South, 1800–1861.* Boston: Beacon Press, 1956.

———. *Reconstruction: After the Civil War.* Chicago and London: University of Chicago Press, 1961.

Gabriel, Ralph Henry. *The Course of American Democratic Thought.* New York: Ronald Press, 1956.

General Catalogue of Bowdoin College and the Medical School of Maine: A Biographical Record of Alumni and Officers, 1794–1950. Portland, Maine: Anthoensen Press, 1950.

Glenn, Myra C. *Thomas K. Beecher: Minister to a Changing America.* Westport, Conn.: Greenwood Press, 1996.

Goldman, Eric F. *Rendezvous with Destiny: A History of Modern American Reform.* New York: Vintage Books, 1956.

Hager, Tina, and Cynthia Melendez, eds. *Elmira in the Civil War: Training Camp of the Blue, Prison Camp of the Gray.* Elmira: Chemung County Historical Society, 1991.

Hart, B. H. Liddell. *Sherman: Soldier, Realist, American.* New York: Dodd, Mead, 1929.

Hedrick, Ulysses Prentiss. *A History of Agriculture in the State of New York.* Albany: New York State Agricultural Society, 1933.

Heitman, Francis B., ed. *Historical Register and Dictionary of the United States Army, from Its Organization September 29, 1789, to March 2, 1903.* Vol. 1. Washington, D.C.: Government Printing Office, 1903.

Hendrick, Burton J. *Lincoln's War Cabinet.* Garden City, N.Y.: Doubleday, 1946.

Hesseltine, William B., ed. *Civil War Prisons.* Kent, Ohio: Kent University Press, 1962.

————. *Civil War Prisons: A Study in War Psychology.* New York: Frederick Unger Publishing, property of Continuum International Publishing Group, 1971.

History of Elmira, Horseheads, and the Chemung Valley. Elmira: A. B. Galatain, 1868.

History of Penobscot County Maine, with Illustrations and Biographical Sketches. Cleveland: Williams, Chase, 1882.

History of Tioga, Chemung, Tompkins, and Schuyler Counties, New York. Philadelphia: Everts and Ensign, 1879.

Holmes, Clay W. *The Elmira Prison Camp: A History of the Military Prison at Elmira, N. Y.* New York: G. P. Putnam's Sons, 1912.

Hyman, Harold M. *A More Perfect Union: The Impact of the Civil War and Reconstruction on the Constitution.* Boston: Houghton Mifflin, Sentry edition, 1975.

Klees, Emerson. *Underground Railroad Tales: With Routes through the Finger Lakes Region.* Rochester, N.Y.: Friends of the Finger Lakes Publishing, 1997.

Leckie, Robert. *None Died in Vain: The Saga of the American Civil War.* New York: HarperCollins, 1990.

Lerwill, Leonard L. *The Personnel Replacement System in the United States Army.* Vol. 1: *Colonial Period-World War I.* Office of the Chief of Military History: Department of the Army, 1952.

Linderman, Gerald F. *Embattled Courage: The Experience of Combat in the American Civil War.* New York: Free Press, 1987.

Marvel, William. *Andersonville: The Last Depot.* Chapel Hill: University of North Carolina Press, 1994.

McDermott, John Francis. *The Art of Seth Eastman.* Washington, D.C.: Smithsonian Institution, 1959–1960.

————. *Seth Eastman: Pictorial Historian of the Indian.* Norman, Okla.: University of Oklahoma Press, 1961.

————. *Seth Eastman's Mississippi: A Lost Portfolio Recovered.* Urbana: University of Illinois Press, 1973.

McKay, C. E. *Stories of Hospital and Camp.* Philadelphia: Claxton, Remsen, and Haffelfinger, 1876.

McPherson, James M. *Battle Cry of Freedom: The Civil War Era*. New York and Oxford: Oxford University Press, 1988.

Medical and Surgical History of the Civil War, The. Vol. 5. Wilmington, N.C.: Broadfoot Publishing, 1991. [Formerly entitled *The Medical and Surgical History of the War of the Rebellion (1861–65)*.]

Mitchell, Reid. *Civil War Soldiers*. New York: Viking Penguin, 1988.

Mott, Edward Harold. *Between the Ocean and the Lakes: The History of the Erie*. New York: John S. Collins, 1899.

Mulford, Uri. *Pioneer Days and Later Times in Corning and Vicinity, 1789–1920*. Corning, New York: Uri Mulford, publisher, 1979.

Murdock, Eugene Converse. *Patriotism Limited, 1862–1865: The Civil War Draft and Bounty System*. Kent, Ohio: Kent State University Press, 1967.

Muzzey, David Saville. *James G. Blaine: A Political Idol of Other Days*. Port Washington, N.Y.: Kennikat Press, 1934.

Nichols, Roy Franklin. *The Disruption of American Democracy*. New York Free Press, 1967.

Outline History of Tioga and Bradford Counties in Pennsylvania, Chemung, Steuben, Tioga, Tompkins, and Schuyler in New York, An. Elmira: Gazette, 1885.

Pearce, Haywood J. *Benjamin H. Hill: Secession and Reconstruction*. Chicago: University of Chicago Press, 1928.

Potter, David M. *The Impending Crisis, 1848–1861*. New York, Hagerstown, Md., San Francisco, and London: Harper Torchbooks, 1976.

———. *Lincoln and His Party in the Secession Crisis*. New Haven, Conn.: Yale University Press, 1962.

Pratt, Fletcher. *A Short History of the Civil War*. New York: Pocket Books, 1962.

———. *Stanton: Lincoln's Secretary of War*. New York: W. W. Norton, 1953.

Randall, J. G., and David Donald. *The Civil War and Reconstruction*. Boston: D. C. Heath, 1961.

Roland, Charles P. *The Confederacy*. Chicago: University of Chicago Press, 1960.

Rozwenc, Edwin C., ed. *The Causes of the American Civil War*. Boston: D. C. Heath, 1961.

Sandburg, Carl. *Abraham Lincoln: The Prairie Years and the War Years*. 3 Vols. New York: Dell Publishing, property of Harcourt, Brace, 1954.

Sketches of the Alumni of Dartmouth from First Graduation in 1771 to the Present Time, with a Brief History of the Institution. Cambridge, Mass.: Riverside Press, 1967.

Speer, Lonnie R. *Portals to Hell: Military Prisons of the Civil War.* Mechanicsburg, Pa.: Stackpole Books, 1997.

Stampp, Kenneth M. *America in 1857: A Nation on the Brink.* New York: Oxford University Press, 1992.

———. *The Era of Reconstruction, 1865–1877.* New York: Alfred A. Knopf, 1966.

Taylor, Eva. *A Short History of Elmira.* Elmira: Steele Memorial Library, 1937.

Thomas, Benjamin P., and Harold M. Hyman. *Stanton: The Life and Times of Lincoln's Secretary of War.* New York: Alfred A. Knopf, a division of Random House, 1962.

Thomas, Emory M. *The Confederate Nation: 1861–1865.* New York: Harper Colophon Books, 1979.

Towner, Ausburn. *A History of the Valley and County of Chemung from the Closing Years of the Eighteenth Century.* Syracuse, N.Y.: D. Mason, 1892.

Weigley, Russell F. *Quartermaster General of the Union Army: A Biography of M. C. Meigs.* New York: Columbia University Press, 1959.

Williams, Harrison. *Legends of Loudoun: An Account of the History and Homes of a Border County of Virginia's Northern Neck.* Richmond: Garrett and Massie, 1938.

Williams, T. Harry. *Lincoln and the Radicals.* Madison: University of Wisconsin Press, 1960.

Wilson, Amy H., and Peg Gallagher. *Chemung County: An Illustrated History.* Elmira: Chemung County Historical Society and Chemung County Chamber of Commerce, 1999.

Wilson, Rufus W. *Intimate Memories of Lincoln.* Elmira: Primavera Press, 1945.

Articles and Periodicals

Anderson, Robert. "The Elmira Prison Camp." *New York State Folklore Quarterly 27,* no. 2 (summer 1961).

Barber, W. Charles. "Elmira as Civil War Depot and Prison Camp." *Chemung Historical Journal* 6, no. 1 (September 1960).

Boltz, Martha. "Elmira: A Prison of Horror for Confederates." *Washington Times,* March 4, 2000.

Boyd, Joseph C. "Shohola Train Wreck: Civil War Disaster." *Chemung Historical Journal* 9, no. 4 (June 1964).

Burns, Joseph. "Horseheads: Canal Town to Industrial Center." *Chemung Historical Journal* 1, no. 1 (September 1955).

Bushnell, David I. "Seth Eastman: The Master Painter of the North American Indian." *Smithsonian Miscellaneous Collections* 87, no. 3 (April 11, 1932).

Byrne, Thomas E. "Black History: The Negro in Elmira." *Chemung Historical Journal* 14, no. 1 (September 1968).

———. "Elmira 1861–1865; Civil War Rendezvous." *Chemung Historical Journal* 9, no. 4 (June 1964).

———. "Elmira's Civil War Prison Camp: 1864–65." *Chemung Historical Journal* 10, no. 1 (September 1964).

———. "Tunnel Escape." *Elmira Sunday Telegram,* November 25, 1962.

Catton, Bruce. "Prison Camps of the Civil War." *American Heritage* (division of Forbes) 10, no. 5 (August 1959).

"Chemung First in Civil War." Undated newspaper article; newspaper source not listed. Chemung County Historical Society.

"Companion Eugene Francis Sanger." *Military Order of the Loyal Legion of the United States,* circular no. 8, series of 1897, no. 146.

"Companion Thomas Raynesford Lounsbury." *Military Order of the Loyal Legion of the United States,* circular no. 7, series of 1915, no. 1144.

"Confederate Dead at Elmira." *Confederate Veteran* 22, no. 4 (September 1914).

Connelly, Catharine S. "The Chemung Canal: 19th Century Freightway." *Chemung Historical Journal* 1, no. 4 (June 1956).

Cranmer, Neil D. "Chemung County's Part in the Civil War." *Chemung Historical Journal* 1, no. 1 (September 1955).

Douglas, Joseph A. "The Ironic Role of African Americans in the Elmira, New York, Civil War Prison Camp." *Afro-Americans in New York and History* 23, no. 1 (January 1999).

Doyle, John F. "Beating Murder Charges in Lincoln's Assassination." *Washington Times,* July 6, 1997.

"Elmira and Andersonville; Their 'Pathetic Bond.'" *Chemung Historical Journal* 7, no. 3 (March 1962).

"Famous 'Battle of Chemung' Fought on Water Street at Baldwin during Civil War, Several Soldiers Meeting Death." Newspaper source not listed, August 1923. Chemung County Historical Society.

"Forts of Seth Eastman, The." *Periodical* 7, no. 1 (spring 1976)

Gray, Michael P. "Uncovering a Ring Leader." *Chemung Historical Journal* 43, no. 4 (June 1998).

"Ground-Breaking for Canal 'Great Day' in 1830." *Chemung Historical Journal* 1, no. 4 (June 1956).

Henry, James O. "The United States Christian Commission in the Civil War." *Civil War History* 6, no. 4 (December 1960).

Hilbert, Alfred G. "Southside Barracks—A Guessing Game." *Chemung Historical Journal* 31, no. 1 (September 1985).

Hoar, Victor M. "Sketches of Elmira's 107th Infantry Regiment." *Chemung Historical Journal* 5, no. 3 (March 1960).

Horigan, Michael. "Elmira Prison Camp—A Second Opinion." *Chemung Historical Journal* 30, no. 3 (March 1985).

"How the 'Rebs' Escaped from Elmira." *Elmira Sunday Telegram,* July 22, 1951.

Imholte, John Quinn. "The Legality of Civil War Recruiting: U.S. Versus Gorman." *Civil War History* 9, no. 4 (December 1963).

Jackson, Jack. "The Great Locomotive Wreck." *Civil War Times Illustrated* 33, no. 6 (January/February 1995).

Jenkins, Scot. "Confederate Spy Visits Elmira." *Chemung Historical Journal* 42, no. 3 (March 1997).

Kieffer, J. Arthur. "The Battle of Chemung." *Chemung Historical Journal* 45, no. 4 (June 2000).

———. "The St. Patrick's Day Flood of 1865." *Chemung Historical Journal* 46, no. 2 (December 2000).

Levine, Steven N. "The Elmira Death Camp." *Upstate New Yorker* 3, no. 4 (September/October 1997).

Marsden, Malcolm. "Upstate New York and Leatherstocking's Legacy." *Torch* 70, no. 3 (spring 1997).

McNamara, Robert. "Elmira's Dachau for Confederate Prisoners," *Catholic Courier-Journal (Rochester, N.Y.),* October 8, 1964.

"Memorial Honors the Blue and the Grey." *Chemung Historical Journal* 31, no. 1 (September 1985).

Merrill, Arch. "Elmira Alibi Saved Hunted Southern Spy." *Elmira Star-Gazette,* July 15, 1952.

Moore, Robert H., II. "Break Out!" *Civil War Times Illustrated* 30, no. 5 (November/December 1991).

Morrell, Carl. "Elmira's Elusive Northside Civil War Barracks." *Chemung Historical Journal* 42, no. 1 (September 1996).

Powell, Morgan Allen. "Cotton for the Relief of Confederate Prisoners." *Civil War History* 9, no. 1 (March 1963).

Ramsdell, William S. "Woodlawn's Sexton." *Chemung Historical Journal* 43, no. 1 (September 1997).

Robertson, James I., Jr. "The Scourge of Elmira." In *Civil War Prisons,* ed. William B. Hesseltine. Kent, Ohio: Kent State University Press, 1962.

Scovel, Jim. "A Civil War Nightmare." *Newsday, Weekend,* part 2, October 5, 1984.

Smith, James L. "Civil War Resolutions of Erin Town Board." *Chemung Historical Journal* 7, no. 1 (September 1961).

Taylor, Eva C. "Holmes and His Sources for 'The Elmira Prison Camp.'" *Chemung Historical Journal* 1, no. 2 (December 1955).

———. "'Rail-Road Guide'—A Literary Gem." *Chemung Historical Journal* 20, no. 3 (March 1975).

Thompson, William Y. "The U.S. Sanitary Commission." *Civil War History* 2, no. 2 (June 1956).

Tomlinson, Lois R. "Highlights of the Canal Days." *Chemung Historical Journal* 1, no. 4 (June 1956).

"Underground Railroad: Route to Freedom." *Chemung Historical Journal* 6, no. 4 (June 1961).

Walls, Matthew S. "Northern Hell on Earth." *America's Civil War* 3, no. 6 (March 1991).

Way, Peter. "Evil Humors and Ardent Spirits: The Rough Culture of Canal Construction Laborers." *Journal of American History* 79, no. 4 (March 1993).

Wright, Abner C. "Underground Railroad Activities in Elmira." *Chemung Historical Journal* 14, no. 1 (September 1968).

Zeidenfelt, Alex. "The Embattled Surgeon, General William A. Hammond." *Civil War Times Illustrated* 17, no. 6 (October 1978).

Newspapers

Bangor (Maine) Daily Whig and Courier, 1897.

Corning (N.Y.) Leader, 1985, 1989, 1993.

Elmira (N.Y.) Evening Star, 1906.

Elmira (N.Y.) Star-Gazette, 1913, 1928, 1951, 1952, 1985, 1993, 1995.

Elmira (N.Y.) Sunday Telegram, 1951, 1962.

Elmira (N.Y.) Telegram, 1884, 1913.

Montgomery (Ala.) Advertiser, 1902.

Nashville Banner, 1914.

National (Washington, D.C.) Tribune, 1914.

New York Times, 1915.

New York Tribune, 1915.

Owego (N.Y.) Gazette, 1915.

Philadelphia Press, 1884.

Pike-Wayne (N.Y.) Eagle, 1961.

Richmond Times-Dispatch, 1914.

Wellsville (N.Y.) Daily Reporter, 1891.

Interviews

Byrne, Thomas E. June 25, 1988. At the time of this interview the late Mr. Byrne was Chemung County historian and editor of the *Chemung Historical Journal.*

Donahoe, Hon. Daniel J. February 24, 1998.

Farr, George. December 5, 1995. Mr. Farr is the historian for the Town of Elmira.

Grant, Mrs. Dorothy Lewis. February 27, 1998.

Hilbert, Alfred G. March 28, 1988. The late Mr. Hilbert served as staff historian at the Chemung County Historical Society for many years.

Hoff, Rev. Donald. March 5, 1998.

Lester, Rev. Robert. January 16, 1996.

Reinert, Eric. October 4, 2000. Mr. Reinert is the curator at the Andersonville National Historic Site.

Sammartino, Ms. Therese. February 2, 1998.

INDEX